MW00777736

LITERACY AND MOBILITY

Pushing forward research on emerging literacies and theoretical orientations, this book follows students from different tracks of high school English in a "failing" U.S. public school through their first two years in universities, colleges, and jobs. Analytical and methodological tools from new literacy and mobility studies are employed to investigate relations among patterns of movement and literacy practices across educational institutions, neighborhoods, cultures, and national borders. By following research participants' trajectories in and across scenes of literacy in school, college, home, online, in transit, and elsewhere, the work illustrates how students help constitute and connect one scene of literacy with others in their daily lives; how their mobile literacies produce, maintain, and disrupt social relations and identities with respect to race, gender, class, language, and nationality; and how they draw upon multiple literacies and linguistic resources to accommodate, resist, and transform dominant discourses.

Brice Nordquist is Assistant Professor, Writing and Rhetoric, Syracuse University, USA.

Expanding Literacies in Education

Jennifer Rowsell and Cynthia Lewis, Series Editors

Visit **www.routledge.com**/education for additional information on titles in Expanding Literacies in Education

LITERACY AND MOBILITY

Complexity, Uncertainty, and Agency at the Nexus of High School and College

Brice Nordquist

Routledge
Taylor & Francis Group

NEW YORK AND LONDON

First published 2017
by Routledge
711 Third Avenue, New York, NY 10017

and by Routledge
2 Park Square, Milton Park, Abingdon, Oxon, OX14 4RN

Routledge is an imprint of the Taylor & Francis Group, an informa business

© 2017 Taylor & Francis

The right of Brice Nordquist to be identified as author of this work
has been asserted by him in accordance with sections 77 and 78 of the
Copyright, Designs and Patents Act 1988.

All rights reserved. No part of this book may be reprinted or reproduced
or utilized in any form or by any electronic, mechanical, or other means,
now known or hereafter invented, including photocopying and recording,
or in any information storage or retrieval system, without permission in
writing from the publishers.

Trademark notice: Product or corporate names may be trademarks or
registered trademarks, and are used only for identification and explanation
without intent to infringe.

Library of Congress Cataloging in Publication Data
Names: Nordquist, Brice, author.
Title: Literacy and mobility : complexity, uncertainty, and agency at the
nexus of high school and college / by Brice Nordquist.
Description: New York : Routledge, [2017] |
Series: Expanding literacies in education ; 5 |
Includes bibliographical references and index.
Identifiers: LCCN 2016049446| ISBN 9781138189867 (hb) |
ISBN 9781138189874 (pb) | ISBN 9781315641409 (ebk)
Subjects: LCSH: Literacy—Social aspects—United States. |
English language—Rhetoric—Study and teaching—Social aspects
—United States. | Educational mobility—United States.
Classification: LCC LC151 .N67 2017 | DDC 428.0071/2--dc23
LC record available at https://lccn.loc.gov/2016049446

ISBN: 978-1-138-18986-7 (hbk)
ISBN: 978-1-138-18987-4 (pbk)
ISBN: 978-1-315-64140-9 (ebk)

Typeset in Bembo and Stone Sans by
Florence Production Ltd, Stoodleigh, Devon

CONTENTS

ACKNOWLEDGEMENTS

Anything of value in the following pages should be attributed, first, to the students and teachers whose generosity and expertise made this project possible. Participants shared their time, energy, desires, struggles, classrooms, and commutes. The depth of their understandings and complexity of their practices could fill volumes. Consequently, any shortcomings in the following representations should be attributed only to me.

Anything else of value likely came, directly or indirectly, from a long line of influence, instruction, and mentorship. Among the teachers and colleagues who contributed most significantly to this project, Bronwyn Williams, Bruce Horner, and Min-Zhan Lu deserve special recognition. In addition to providing constant support and feedback, Bronwyn opened up possibilities for moving the work forward and guided my pursuit of these. Likewise, Bruce and Min have sharpened my reading, writing, and thinking throughout the project and through every stage of my career. Extending this line of guidance and support, Samantha NeCamp has selflessly read, reread, and discussed ideas and drafts with remarkable candor and consideration. She has been my first and best reader. Tom Fox, Marilyn Cooper, and Gesa Kirsch have also done a great deal to help develop my thinking on theories and practices of mobility, complexity, and methodology.

The editors of Routledge's *Expanding Literacies in Education* series, Cynthia Lewis and Jennifer Rowsell, have been not only patient, supportive, and encouraging, but also tremendously insightful in their commentary on drafts of the manuscript and always kind and generous in their efforts to help navigate the publication process. Likewise, Naomi Silverman has been a model editor. She has provided space and pushed at all the right times, in all the right ways, always from a position of kindness and understanding. Without the expertise and guidance of Cynthia, Jennifer, and Naomi this book would not have been possible.

I would like to thank the College of Arts and Sciences and my colleagues in the Department of Writing Studies, Rhetoric, and Composition at Syracuse University for providing the material conditions, the time and space, for this work. Special thanks to Lois Agnew, Tony Scott, and Collin Brooke for their teaching and research mentorship and to students from two graduate seminars on relations among literacies and mobilities—Gerhard Arakelian, Romeo Garcia, C.C. Hendricks, Vani Kannan, Jason Markins, Vincent Portillo, and Jana Rosinski— for helping me think through ideas presented in this text. I would also like to thank the Jefferson County Public School District for granting me access to one of its schools and to students and teachers under its care.

Thank you to my parents, Jim and Regina, for pushing me to achieve my goals while enabling me to define them for myself. Your hard work, guidance, and support have undergirded my work at every stage. Thank you, Kate, for being as understanding and patient during the writing process as any three-year-old could possibly be. And finally, thank you, most of all, to Abby for encouraging and enabling me to do this work. Your emotional, intellectual, and material support drove this project.

INTRODUCTION

> That I never fully assimilated the bourgeois belief that rehearsal predicts the future
> is without a doubt a working-class legacy.
>
> (Brodkey 1994)

In many ways, the themes of this book echo refrains that filled the ranch-style rental houses, used sedans and minivans, poster-clad classrooms, family gatherings, and church meetings of my childhood and adolescence. In their efforts to discern and, in some ways, determine the futures of the children under their care, the parents, grandparents, aunts and uncles, family friends, teachers and ministers that filled these spaces posed versions of a familiar question: "What will you be when you grow up?" And from earliest childhood, I knew my part: "baseball player," "rock star," "writer." It didn't take long for me to sort out a hierarchy of attainable careers from reactions to these answers. And in efforts to avoid condescension, I stopped sharing my desire to play ball and, instead, began offering more reasonable options: doctor, lawyer, minister. If she was within earshot, my mother faithfully concluded the refrain: "So as long as you go to college. College is not optional."

The inevitability of this proclamation, for which I am now grateful, was anchored by the weight of my parents' own educational and occupational histories. In contrast to their experiences at school and work, a college degree offered a measure of freedom and control. It promised stability and comfort. Like many moving from working-class to service-sector positions, my parents considered these achievements unattainable for themselves but essential for their children.

My family came from people on the move, out of necessity and by force— migrant cotton workers, Swedish immigrants, displaced Cherokee. And we ourselves were a family on the move. Following my father's work, we moved at least once a year for the first seven years of my education. From kindergarten through the sixth grade, I attended six public schools in six different districts in four states. This itinerancy meant that my intellectual ability was measured by the unique district and state standards operating in each new educational environment. Upon joining a fourth-grade class in Lafayette, Indiana in the middle of the school year, I failed to spell a single word correctly on a test over the names of state counties: Tippecanoe, Kosciusko, Bartholomew, Vermillion. Each name the teacher recited pushed me further away from the geographical and curricular space I was obliged to occupy. And each of my failed attempts to render these names correctly set me further back on the developmental timeline operating in this new environment. Kindly, the teacher patted my shoulder and assured me that the test wouldn't hurt my grade; she only wanted to determine where to start with me. And so the invisible boundaries that demarcated this unfamiliar state served as a diagnostic, marking me not only as an outsider but also as a student developmentally behind my classmates and "at risk" of falling further behind. My struggle to catch up in classes that I did not begin and would not finish continued throughout grade school.

I was a student at risk in transit across "a nation at risk." Beginning my educational career three years after the publication of the Reagan Administration's infamous report, I came to an understanding of the purpose of education and of myself as a student during the rise of an era of standardization that has now reigned for over three decades.[1] To stem the "rising tide of mediocrity" that threatened, and apparently still threatens, "our very future as a Nation and a people," the state departments responsible for my education took up the report's charge of school reform for the maintenance of the country's "competitive edge . . . in world markets" (*A Nation at Risk*, National Commission on Excellence in Education 1983, pp. 9, 10). To ensure that my peers and I would sharpen this competitive edge through "gainful employment" in a "new information economy," we would be trained and measured in accordance with state standards of achievement and arranged on appropriate tracks of study (National Commission on Excellence in Education 1983, p. 11). In Texas my academic ability and future potential was measured by the Texas Assessment of Academic Skills or the TAAS; in Oklahoma the OMAAP, in Kansas the KSA, and in Indiana the ISTEP.[2] My inconsistent performances on these exams, due in large part to my inconsistent presence in any one school or state system, kept me securely situated in "regular" academic tracks and, for the most part, out of honors and advanced-level classes. I expected little from these classes, and they demanded little from me.

By the time I reached middle school and my family entered a period of financial and geographic stability, my identity as an average student was firmly established among family, friends, and teachers. Through middle and high school, I floated by with grades good enough to keep me out of trouble at home and on sports fields after school. In this way, I spent my K-12 career riding the tide of mediocrity that threatened the nation. I graduated with a grade point average and test scores just good enough to gain access to an essentially open-admissions state university in the North Texas city that, by then, had become my family's home.

Unsurprisingly, upon entering college, I had very few ideas about what to make of the opportunity or of myself as college student. Slow to come to terms with the demands of late capitalism, my family and I still operated under the assumption that a college degree would ensure future success. It didn't matter what I studied, so long as I graduated. At the same time, my family's class status and the itinerancy of my childhood instilled a conviction that the future was ultimately out of my control. As Linda Brodkey expresses in the epigraph to this introduction, an assurance of or, at least, an illusion of control over the future may be a luxury of the middle class, and, like Brodkey, I've never been able to fully embrace this assurance.[3]

I didn't gain a sense of control over my own academic work or educational trajectory until my junior year of college—a level I attained only because my parents were patient and insistent. Under the guidance of a few professors who challenged me to identify and investigate ideas important to me and to see my literacy practices as tools of meaning-making and self-construction, I gradually became more comfortable experimenting with language and literacy and different ways of knowing and understanding myself and the world. Perhaps for the first time in my life, I began to make connections between literacies and ways of thinking and living. Subjects became interesting because I began to approach them as discourses, as malleable and in process. Possibilities for meaning and, thus, possibilities for being could be made with and from them. In other words, I began to see myself as a contributor to the *becomings* of particular classes, conversations, identities, and lines of inquiry shaping them. More and more, I gravitated toward teachers and courses that invited such becomings and avoided those that didn't.

As I reflect on this time in my life, I don't feel I was being called to a particular occupation or life pursuit; I wasn't discovering my passion. Rather, I was learning to exercise autonomy and exert agency in and through my work. I was not inspired to invest in this work by great texts or professors, though these certainly helped. Nor was I inspired by what this work might accomplish for me in the future. I was motivated by the work itself, in the present, and by the agencies made available through this work. It is important to note that I didn't experience this stage of my education as epiphanic; I was not once and for all transformed into an agent. Rather, I was beginning to realize the agency that emerged from language and literacy practices. I was beginning to feel practice and structure as mutually constitutive and to intuit the ways in which my literacies both accommodated and transformed the institutional structures that enabled and constrained my work.

While still I don't read this as a period of dramatic conversion, I do consider it a time when my education became meaningful to me, in large part because of this increased sense of control. So as I think about how to encourage my own students or the students participating in my research to recognize the value and complexity of their literacy practices in and out of school and to consider what they might accomplish with these practices, this time in my life imposes itself as both a guide and a puzzle. That I am much more interested in encouraging students to see themselves as active shapers of identities and societies than I am in bestowing the skills they are sure to need for the future is certainly a consequence of my own experience. However, I don't claim to fully understand how this gradual process of educational investment began, nor could I inventory the host of influences that enabled it. Consequently, the question of how students begin to see themselves as agents, as makers of the places, literacies, and identities that constitute the educational systems in which they participate, is one I pursue throughout this book.

Location and Intervention

Of course, my social and historical situatedness and my own political interests have shaped my pursuit of this question and the others that drive this research. My perceptions and interpretations have been shaped by the experiences recounted above, along with many others. In "Beyond the personal: Theorizing a politics of location in composition research," Gesa Kirsch and Joy Ritchie (1995) employ feminist interventions to consider how a politics of location might inform and change traditional research practices. They suggest that it is not enough for the researchers to claim experience as a source of knowledge and locate themselves unproblematically in the text. They must rather reflexively examine their histories, positions, and desires and the social, economic, cultural, ethnic, gender and personal forces and ideological structures shaping them.

Considering my own histories, alignments, and affiliations, I am particularly attuned to the roles literacy plays in maintaining and demarcating inequalities among social classes. My own history of educational mobility has conditioned me to recognize and promote the values of students' complex and concurrent mobilities and has made me perhaps less inclined to attend to their drawbacks. In celebrating the opportunities these mobilities create, I frequently neglect the possibilities they prevent. I am also especially sensitive to the consequences of academic tracking and standardization and sympathetic to the struggles of first-generation college students. While not a deliberate decision, this concern likely influenced my choice to focus on the mobilities of two first-generation students and one would-be first-generation student in the following chapters.

Reflecting on my changing locations as a participant-observer throughout this project, I've attempted to draw out the multiple, often conflicting, and ultimately unknowable positions assumed by both myself and my participants and make apparent the asymmetries of power that have informed our interactions (Powell and Takayoshi 2003). I have also tried to make use of these positions to move the project, however cautiously, beyond concerns of interpretation to intervention—from reflecting on, to telling about, to changing. Kirsch and Ritchie (1995) assert that unlike the seemingly objective and strictly hermeneutic projects of traditional research, feminist research is characterized by its pursuit of change: "Feminist researchers not only set out to study and describe . . . lives and experiences, but actively seek to understand and change the conditions of . . . social and political realities" (p. 536).

Of course, a researcher must pursue interventionist objectives with care, as asymmetries of power can undermine and threaten relations with participants. Kirsch and Ritchie suggest that researchers avoid attempting to create a false sense of equity and instead make their unequal relations transparent and engage in collaborative practice to help reduce the distance between themselves and participants (p. 538). In this way, research as interventionist praxis works from an admittance that the social hierarchies inherent in material, economic, and political contexts remain intact but that their potentially oppressive operation is mitigated through an open negotiation with participants through reciprocal practice.

Thomas Newkirk (1996) suggests that when engaging in this process of researcher–participant negotiation, "university researchers who study the class-rooms of public school teachers and subordinates (students and teaching assistants, nontenured faculty) have a special obligation to recognize the vulnerability of those they study" (p. 5). In light of the vulnerability of the high school and college students and teachers who participate in this study, I have taken special care to introduce and carry out this research in a way that makes potential problems, issues, and critical depictions apparent. To accomplish this transparency, I have undertaken this project with pedagogical goals in mind. By creating opportunities for my participants to not only reflect on their own linguistic and literacy practices, but also to reflect upon and talk back to my interpretations of these practices and reflections, I feel that they and I have been shaped and reshaped through the ongoing process of negotiation that constitutes this critical ethnographic project.

Following these feminist research orientations, the following chapters offer and theorize findings of a three-year, multi-sited ethnography investigating the complexity of students' movements within and among secondary and tertiary educational institutions. This project investigates entanglements of literacies and mobilities constituting and connecting students' high school-to-college trajectories and thereby provides glimpses into the mutually constitutive relations among scenes of literacy across space-time. While the study follows eleven students from a "failing" public high school in Louisville, Kentucky moving from different tracks of high school English through their first years at research universities, colleges, and full-time jobs, this book focuses specifically on the mobilities of three students: Nadif, Katherine, and James. I draw upon a range of data types collected while participating in these students' patterns of movement in and across scenes of literacy, conducting interviews in single sites and on the move, and analyzing their print-based and digital texts to represent intersecting and diverging movements across scenes of literacy. I use this data to investigate the ways in which students draw upon multiple literacies and linguistic resources to accommodate, resist, and transform conventions of discourse, genre, and discipline. Intersections and divergences among Nadif's, Katherine's, and James's trajectories reveal how language and literacy practices are informed by ideologies, experiences, and habituated practices of and desires for mobility available in past, present, and future scenes of literacy.

For example, the daily paths of Nadif and James intersect on a bus that shuttles them from economically depressed neighborhoods in South Louisville to their high school in an affluent East Louisville neighborhood. When they arrive at school, Nadif, a first-generation Somali immigrant, joins Katherine, a Mexican American student, in advanced-level courses such as AP English. Meanwhile, James, an African American student, is assigned to "regular" courses, including a remedial English class. After school Nadif and James meet again at a city bus stop, where a northbound bus takes Nadif to his dual enrollment Pan-African Studies course at a research university, and a southbound bus takes James back to his neighborhood and part-time job as a grocery store clerk. Katherine drives her own car to work at the law firm of a family friend, where she takes dictations for legal documents and correspondence. After graduation, Nadif attends university on a full scholarship, Katherine's family pays for her enrollment at a community college, and James is forced to take on a second job after failing to secure funding for college.

Despite these diverging trajectories, my research reveals all three students as adept language users who blend a variety of languages, forms, and styles to multiple effects in their literacy practices. However, Nadif finds his own literate, linguistic, and discursive adaptations rewarding in ways that James and Katherine do not. In his movement from a refugee camp in Dadaab, Kenya to a preparatory school in Nairobi and from regular to advanced courses in U.S. high school and through college, Nadif comes to see his language and literacy practices as means of mobility. Contrastingly, authoritative sources of "standard English" often mark James's literate and linguistic innovations as deficiencies that prevent him from progressing from one predetermined level of education to the next. And Katherine's relentless attempts to conform to perceived standards and conventions of "college-level" writing belie the transformative aspects of her language practice. My reflections on the similarities and differences of these students' trajectories, along with the others followed over the course of this project, lead to considerations of the ways in which perceptions of language and literacy differences influence the material, representational, and embodied mobilities of student writers. In light of these observations, I assemble a theoretical framework for exploring relations between literacy and mobility and a methodology to show how these practices are shaped by and shape the demands, constraints, and possibilities for action in various scenes of literacy.

By working with students in and across scenes of literacy in high school, college, at work, home, in transit, and elsewhere this project complicates apparent boundaries between secondary and tertiary levels of education and in-school and out-of-school literacy practices; attends to conceptualizations of academic literacies from stakeholders "outside" the academy; provides insight into the complexity of students' movements within and between educational institutions; challenges notions of fixed locations and standards of language and literacy; and, thereby, works against the relentless future orientation of the U.S. educational–occupational system to recognize the value of students' literacy practices in the present. While this work is not without its shortcomings, I hope that, above all else, the depictions and interpretations presented here provide glimpses of the sophistication and innovation of students often overlooked, marginalized, excluded, and immobilized by our systems of education and society.

Notes

1   While standardized testing emerged alongside the Industrial Revolution, I follow Diane Ravitch (2010) and others in attributing the rise of the "standards movement" to *A Nation at Risk* (p. 22).
2   These accountability systems have since been modified—in some cases, several times—since the passage of No Child Left Behind in 2001.
3   I would also add that in an age of standardization and high-stakes testing, this sense of control may also be a luxury of enrollment in educational institutions with greater degrees of autonomy from state standards and assessments than those I attended or have researched.

References

Brodkey, L. (1994). Writing on the bias. *College English, 56*(5), 527.
Kirsch, G. E., & Ritchie, J. S. (1995). Beyond the personal: Theorizing a politics of location in composition research. *College Composition and Communication, 46*(1), 7–29.
National Commission on Excellence in Education. (1983). *A nation at risk: The imperative for education reform.* Washington, D.C.: United States Department of Education.
Newkirk, T. (1996). Seduction and betrayal. In P. Mortensen, & G. E. Kirsch (Eds.). *Ethics and representation in qualitative studies of literacy.* Urbana, IL: National Council of Teachers.
No Child Left Behind Act of 2001, P.L. 107-110, 20 U.S.C. § 6319 (2002).
Powell, K. M. and Takayoshi, P. (2003). Accepting roles created for us: The ethics of reciprocity. *College Composition and Communication, 54*, 394–421.
Ravitch, D. (2010). *The death and life of the great American school system: How testing and choice are undermining education.* New York: Basic Books.

1
LITERACY IN PLACE AND MOTION

Value increasingly arises not from what is but from what is not yet but can potentially become, that is from the pull of the future.

(Thrift 2008)

Even on the hoof, we remain in place. We are never anywhere, anywhen, but in place.

(Casey 1996)

An investment in education is an investment in the future. So goes the rallying cry of corporations, private foundations, government agencies, and other stake-holders within the U.S. education system. This conglomerate is currently investing unprecedented amounts of capital and labor in efforts to smooth out transitions between systems of education and a forever-future global economy. From *Every Student Succeeds* to the Gates Foundation's *Pathways for Student Success* and the *Common Core State Standards*, effectively managing the movement of students within and across institutions is presented as the key to education reform in the United States and around the world.

These reforms are premised on a familiar formula: educational–occupational mobility leads to economic progress and a more equitable society. As former U.S. Secretary of Education Arne Duncan (2014) exhorts:

Education is the civil rights issue of our time. . . . We must recommit, as a nation, to programs and policies that close opportunity gaps and help all students reach their potential. Only then will we be able to accelerate our nation's economic progress, increase upward mobility, and reduce social inequality for all Americans.

Duncan's programs and policies seek to push and direct flows of students through an increasingly streamlined school–work complex of institutions, investments, tradeoffs, standards, and alignments. As Jan Nespor (2004) asserts, "Schools are not just territories regulating kids' movements within their borders, but vehicles which physically and symbolically transport young people through and across social and material landscapes" (p. 311). In this way, we can think of schools as consisting of and contributing to intersecting and adaptive *mobility systems* that enable and manage predictable repetitions of movements of people, objects, texts, ideas, and information (Urry 2007). As assemblages of immobile structures and circulating entities, these systems create, distribute, and concentrate labor and capital (always unequally) and materialize place and scale. They enhance the potential mobility of some and diminish or halt the mobility of others (Sheller 2014). In this way, mobility systems are also always immobility systems with elements of viscosity, coagulation, and friction (Cresswell 2014).

In pursuit of educational, economic, and social progress, educational mobility systems bus students across cities and counties; usher them through hallways; admit and reject them from colleges; promote, suspend, and relocate teachers; manufacture and ship textbooks; circulate and collate assessments; (re)distribute and cut funds; divide up neighborhoods and cities; structure days, seasons, and years; and so on. The primary goal of these interconnected systems, as Duncan makes clear above, is the creation, distribution, and concentration of capital and labor. Students are sorted and transported along tracks of study designed to help them reach their productive and consumptive potentials so that the fruits of their labor can effectively feed back into national and global economies (Bowles and Gintis 1976, Bourdieu and Passeron 1977, Apple 1988).

To streamline this economic payoff, education is represented and enacted as series of stair-stepped, developmental trajectories. Within these closed mobility systems, there is no room for movements that intersect with, diverge from, or descend the staircase—mobilities that transport students to and from school, supply their worksheets and tests, vibrate in their pockets, interrupt their thoughts, shape their beliefs and perceptions. As if all the complexities of education could be plotted on a single line.

Attempts to chart journeys from one stage of development, grade level, institution, discourse community, and social class to another contribute to a preoccupation with destinations, their boundaries, and their attendant demands and a general neglect of the web of mobilities that constitute and connect these. To successfully move from one step to another, students must cultivate habits and accumulate the knowledge and skills demanded by self-evident future geographies—places, landscapes, natures, and bodies that motivate and govern action in the present.

Educational and political discourses render the future knowable and actionable by figuring space-time as a static grid used to individuate and measure students' movements among fixed and discrete locations. The demands of the job market

FIGURE 1.1 Screen Shot of Common Core State Standards Promotional Video

Source: D.C. Public Schools (2012). "Three Minute Video Explaining the Common Core State Standards." https://www.youtube.com/watch?v=5s0rRk9sER0.

must be met in college courses, which must meet the demands of more advanced courses, while the demands of college determine the objectives of high school, and so on down the line. Standards, outcomes, corresponding curricula and assessments, and discourses surrounding these disclose futures and condition and limit how they can be acted upon. They operate through a circularity that establishes relations between past, present, and future and self-authenticate these relations (Anderson 2010). But as geographer Andrew Baldwin (2012) asserts, such discourses "disregard the ways in which the future is very often *already present* in the present not as a discrete ontological time-space, but as an absent or virtual presence that constitutes the very meaning of the present" (p. 36). Or as feminist philosopher Karen Barad (2007) describes, "The past matters and so does the future, but the past is never left behind, never finished once and for all, and the future is not what will come to be in an unfolding of the present moment; rather the past and the future are enfolded participants in matter's iterative becoming" (p. 181).

And so by focusing on how to best prepare students for self-evident futures— the next grade level, the first year of college, an academic discipline, a job— policies, pedagogies, and assessments often disregard the ways in which imagined futures and embodied histories shape needs, desires, perceptions, practices, and places in the present. By confining conceptualizations of movement to places left behind and places of arrival, we often fail to consider the ways in which these places are connected and constituted by intertwined spatial and temporal mobilities. Fixations on progress toward, transition into, and transfer for the future often prevent us from recognizing education as a process of placemaking—of "matter's iterative becoming"—in the present (Barad 2007, p. 181).

In this way, the futurity of modern education obscures the material labor and achievements of teachers, students, and objects in the creation and transformation of places. By allowing preoccupations with geographies of the future to overshadow placemaking in the present, we run the risk of missing or devaluing the knowledge (re)produced in the interactions, struggles, and exchanges that make up our daily work together in and beyond the classroom. That is, we risk approaching knowledge as a corpus of representations and information that can be laterally and vertically integrated across contexts, systems of education, and courses of life (Ingold 2009, p. 354). But as Etienne Wenger (1998) asserts, "knowing is defined only in the context of specific practices" (p. 142). We come to know and demonstrate knowledge through effective participation in particular situations. And we learn how to participate through processes of apprenticeship, by sharing embodied and emplaced experiences with other people and things and thereby developing shared understandings of these experiences. In this way, "meaning or knowledge is discovered in the very process of imitating [. . .] movements" (Gieser 2008, p. 300).

While there are a number of factors contributing to the relentless future orientation of formal education and its models of vertically integrated knowledge, two modern conceits are central to the arguments of this book. The first proposes to isolate singular mobilities through depoliticized contexts, and the second assumes that such contexts preexist the movements that make them. In other words, the first conceit imagines a student's academic literacy development can be separated from their daily travel to and from school, their part-time job, their educational history and desires for the future. And the second figures locations of education—classrooms, school buildings, districts, grade levels, and so on—as predetermined and bounded containers of educational activity.

Kevin Leander, Nathan Phillips, and Katherine Taylor (2010) identify the "classroom-as-container" as a dominant discourse and "'imagined geography' of education, constituting when and where researchers and teachers should expect learning to 'take place'" (p. 329): "One might almost see the classroom as the epitome of immobility . . . representing not only conventions of material structure but also conventions of teaching practice, of schedule, of seating charts, and seatwork routines" (p. 332). According to anthropologist Tim Ingold's (2008, 2009) "logic of inversion," the intersecting pathways of people, materials, resources, ideas, and energies that constitute a classroom or any other place are converted into boundaries within which activity is contained. Following this logic, we tend to approach classrooms, schools, and colleges as places that exist rather than places that occur or become.

Alternatively, if we approach our courses as movements along overlapping and diverging paths, we might understand ourselves, students, and materials as co-creators of emergent rather than predetermined places. Formed through movement, places are events rather than things, topics rather than objects (Casey 1996, Massey 1994, Pennycook 2010). And courses are places-in-progress, continually produced out of their connections to other places over time— other classes, programs, institutions, neighborhoods, communities, techno- and mediascapes (Nespor 1997, Tusting 2000, Leander et al. 2010). In contrast to conceiving of classes and schools as closed mobility systems, approaching teaching and learning as placemaking involves attending to the "coming together of the previously unrelated," the constellation of processes constituting a place or course (Massey 2005, p. 141). By tracing associations and reflecting on temporal and spatial relations embedded in our interanimating practices, we might build knowledges of how places/courses are constituted. And these knowledges might help us recognize and mobilize our own agencies and the agencies of the people and things around us in the (re)creation and transformation of educational and civic systems.

This vision of collective creation and transformation shapes and is shaped by the research represented in this book. At the heart of this research are questions about the ways in which scenes of literacy (including those in classrooms) are constituted and connected by mobilities of people, objects, ideas, and information. What kinds of practices, relationships, and knowledges are possible when we approach our classrooms as "complexes of mobility"? (Lefebvre 1991). When our pedagogies account not just for circulations of texts, but also of people, practices, materials, ideas, and resources across classes and schools to other places-in-the-making? What does this process of mobilization do to the boundaries we construct or accept between courses, disciplines, institutions, and communities? As literacy researchers, what happens when a research site's appearance of solidity is destroyed—from individual texts to events, archives, programs, and institutions? How might foregrounding patterns, representations, and practices of movement reorient our attention to and alter our perceptions of literacy and language practice? What theories and methods can we adopt to more effectively attend to fleeting, distributed, multiple, complex, sensory, emotional, and kinesthetic dimensions of literacy and language?

To ground these questions and frame the practices represented throughout this book, this chapter provides theoretical touchpoints for considering relational and, thus, political dimensions of space-time and mutually constitutive relations among literacy practices, mobilities, and places.[1] The partial and subjective representations of practice I offer in these pages come from a three-year multi-sited, mobile ethnography investigating the complexity of students' movements within, between, and around high school and college. Like the vision of teaching and learning as placemaking presented above, this ethnographic project is a reflexive and experiential process through which my research participants and I coproduce knowledges about our literacies and mobilities, and about ourselves and systems.

Because knowledge is always situated in practice, to better understand how students and teachers know literacies and mobilities, I engage in and, inevitably, (re)shape their practices. These practices, which are wrapped up in processes of connecting and making places, are the products of the ethnographic project (Pink 2009). "The whole process of gathering and molding knowledge is part of that knowledge; knowledge construction *is* knowledge, *the process is the product*" (Blommaert 2009, p. 266). Accordingly, fieldwork, analysis, reflection, and representation are recursive rather than discrete stages in a linear process. This means that despite the book's order of presentation—a fairly conventional chapter arrangement from theory to practice and pedagogical application—the theoretical assemblage I trace out here is not foundational; it did not precede the research in my mind or on paper (at least not in any coherent way). These theoretical threads are woven in and out of the ethnographic project just like every other element—always back and forth, never before or after.[2]

My ethnographic orientation to literacies and mobilities engages not only metaphors, memories, projections, and interpretations of place and movement, which are already prevalent in literacy scholarship, but also traces entanglements of mobility patterns, representations, and practices by following students' and texts' physical movements in and through places (re)created and connected by these movements (Cresswell 2010). By participating in patterns of movement, I attempt to shed light on the distributed and fleeting ways in which people and objects make and maintain social and material realties (Law and Urry 2004, Büscher et al. 2011).

In both this chapter and the next, I present a range of theories and methods shaping this project. These are adapted largely from the transdisciplinary field of mobility studies, which I believe can help literacy researchers and teachers account for pluralities of moving bodies, objects, ideas, and texts that make up, connect, and separate literacy practices and scenes across space-time. I also believe attention to the complexity of movements within and among educational environments is crucial in light of increasing movements of people around the world; accelerating circulations of capital, ideas, images, messages, and services; and intensifying exertions of control over individual and collective mobilities imposed by neoliberal states and institutions (including K–16 education systems) fortified and streamlined to accommodate economic and competitive interests (Papastergiadis 2000, Suárez-Orozco 2005, Friedman 2009).

Dominant and Alternative Discourses of Literacy and Mobility

One challenge of discussing both literacy and mobility, taken together or separately, is that these terms have such deeply entrenched commonplace associations in conversations about education. Despite more than three decades of literacy studies documenting and theorizing literacies as multimodal, aesthetic, and material social practices (Heath 1983, Street 1995, Besnier 1995, Barton and Hamilton 1998, Baynham and Prinsloo 2009, Rowsell and Pahl 2015), popular and political discourses of education still subscribe to and propagate what Brian

Street (2001) labels "autonomous" models of literacy: "The exponents of an 'autonomous' model of literacy conceptualise literacy in technical terms, treating it as independent of social context, an autonomous variable whose consequences for society and cognition can be derived from its intrinsic character" (pp. 431–432). This dominant conception of literacy as a decontextualized and decontextualizing technology leading to cognitive and cultural advancement (Brandt and Clinton 2002) can be seen in recurring rhetorics of literacy crises, assessments of "basic skills" or "core competencies," grade-level equivalencies, advanced college credits, and so on. What's more, the notion that literacy can be acquired once and for all with proper resources and training enables the isolation of singular, unidirectional educational mobilities depicted above.

New Literacy Studies scholars work from a much more expansive—verging on all-encompassing—understanding of literacy. Paul Prior and Jodi Shipka (2003) offer a representatively comprehensive definition:

> Overall, we are arguing that literate activity consists not simply of some specialized cultural forms of cognition—however distributed, not simply of some at-hand toolkit—however heterogeneous. Rather, literate activity is about nothing less than ways of being in the world, forms of life. It is about histories (multiple, complexly interanimating trajectories and domains of activity), about the (re)formation of persons and social worlds, about affect and emotion, will and attention. It is about representational practices, complex, multifarious chains of transformations in and across representational states and media (cf. Hutchins, 1995). It is especially about the ways we not only come to inhabit made-worlds, but constantly make our worlds—the ways we select from, (re)structure, fiddle with, and transform the material and social worlds we inhabit.
>
> (pp. 181–182)

Prior and Shipka echo James Gee's (1990) notion of literacies as fluencies in various discourses—i.e., "ways of being in the world, or forms of life" (p. 142)—and his claim that situations or contexts are perpetually (re)created through practice in their assertion that literacies make and remake communities, subjectivities, and material environments (Leander and Sheehy 2004). Literacies draw on and draw together multiple temporalities; and not only histories, as Prior and Shipka assert, but also multiple presents and possible futures, as Baldwin and Barad describe above. They draw on and draw together multiple spatialities as well, "domains of activity," local–global. As Jennifer Rowsell and Kate Pahl (2015) write, "Literacy changes with practices, and transmutes across borders, languages and modes. Literacy is digital, immersive and networked" (p. 1). Literacies are also embodied—felt and sensed—and multi-mediated, and thus always involve physical, social, and cultural mobilities. Movement across space-time depends on literacy, just as literacy depends on spatial and temporal mobilities.[3]

Addressing the first half of this claim, sociolinguist Jan Blommaert (2010) argues that "people manage or fail to make sense across contexts; their linguistic and communicative resources are mobile or lack such semiotic mobility, and this is a problem not just of difference, but of inequality" (p. 3). Blommaert's assertion and its implications for physical and social mobilities is evidenced in an account from Daw, a Burmese refugee resettled in Louisville, Kentucky and the mother of Yo Shu, a high school senior also participating in this study. Yo Shu introduced me to his mother at a community literacy program conducted at a local Baptist church, where members of his family where learning English together.[4] When I asked Daw about her motivations for taking courses, I was surprised by the specificity of her response:

> I start to take English class after a bus driver yelled at me when I lost count of stops. I ask, "What stop it is?" And he says, "Can you read?" I left the bus quickly, not knowing where I was. I walk home afraid in darkness. I start taking English class the next week. I say, I will not be embarrassed again.

When the literacies Daw uses to ride the city bus—counting stops and following markers and signs—fail, the additional resources she draws on to reorient, such as asking the driver for help in English, are met with resistance. Not only does the driver not recognize counting stops as a valid or even conceivable literacy for bus riders, he responds to Daw's accented English and Southeast Asian, female body with a question intended to humiliate. She is compelled to proceed on foot because the driver is unwilling to negotiate across literate and bodily differences. Her language and literacy resources meet a roadblock and so her physical mobility is redirected and slowed.

The physical and literate (im)mobilities portrayed in Daw's account are bound up with social and cultural (im)mobilities, as the friction of this encounter serves as the most memorable motivation for her enrollment in English language and literacy classes. She hopes and is promised that these classes will lead to greater occupational and economic mobility, so she is willing to sacrifice valuable work and family time to take them. To move physically and socially in the world, city, and job market, Daw is told and believes she must expand her literate and linguistic repertoire.

The inextricability of language, literacy, and (im)mobility represented in accounts like Daw's has led some language and literacy scholars (Brandt and Clinton 2002, Blommaert 2010, Sebba 2010, Kell 2011, Canagarajah 2013, Leonard 2013, Rounsaville 2014) to call for a shift away from studies of languages and literacies in place to studies of languages and literacies in motion. Blommaert (2010) describes this shift as an "insertion of language in a spectrum of human action which is not defined purely in relation to temporal and spatial location, but in terms of temporal and spatial trajectories" (p. 21). He suggests that globalization forces scholars of language and literacy to unthink their place-based distinctions and biases and to reframe their work "in terms of trans-contextual networks, flows and movements" (p. 1).

Of course, Blommaert is right; a contemporary picture of global flows accelerating and complicating our lives in unprecedented ways intensifies our need to better understand relations between languages, literacies, and mobilities. Even so, presenting this need solely as a response to globalization risks figuring pasts and places as somehow immobile and a fully globalized future as somehow inevitable. As geographer Tim Cresswell (2010) asserts, "Any study of mobility runs the risk of suggesting that the (allegedly) immobile—notions such as boundaries and borders, place, territory, and landscape—is of the past and no longer relevant to the dynamic world of the 21st century" (p. 18). In dominant discourses of globalization, which are as powerful in education as they are in economics, a world of bounded places is replaced by a world of flows. In place of isolated localities, we get global connectivities. And students must be prepared to participate fully in this barrier-less future. But as I stated above, a failure to see place—and languages and literacies in place—as always already constituted by intersections of spatiotemporal mobilities leaves dominant educational discourses and mobility systems of singular, unidirectional trajectories unchallenged. The pursuit of participation in a future global imaginary overshadows mobilities constituting places in the present. Places may be perduring and consistent, but they are never inert.

And so while it may now be "widely conceded that human motion is definitive of social life [. . .] in our contemporary world," mobilities and disjunctures have always constituted, connected, and separated locations and systems of education (Appadurai 1996, p. 191). Likewise, movements of one kind or another have always been central to the projects of New Literacy Studies. Consider the cultural differences "carried to Roadville" by visitors from nearby Alberta and even the place names of Roadville and Trackton in Heath's *Ways with Words,* or the elderly Samoan women wearing Western T-shirts with "obscene captions" in Besnier's *Literacy, Emotion, and Authority.*

However, and for many good reasons, literacy scholars have tended to focus on causes and consequences of movement and have traditionally related everyday literacy practices to mobilities on larger scales. Literacy tends to be scaled down to local practice, text, and situation, and mobility tends to be scaled up to levels of society, culture, transnationality, transfer, and so on. This inverse scaling encourages a conflation of mobility and globality. As Alastair Pennycook (2012) warns, "All too often, the global is considered to be the context of movement and fluidity to be juxtaposed with the fixity of locality" (p. 118). We can trace local literacy practices through global trajectories or tease out the influences of global trajectories on local literacies. And these are valuable pursuits. But what happens to the linguistic and literate trajectories or mobilities that aren't recognized as global or globalizing? What happens to intimately small and mundane mobilities?—"those habitual movements through space that are often taken for granted or ignored" (Reynolds 2004, p. 45).

Daw's movement from a Burmese refugee camp in Thailand to Kentucky continues to shape her daily language and literacy practices. She traverses diverse linguistic and literate terrain through her communications with friends and family in Thailand, Burma, and around the world; her participation in refugee and immigrant communities in Louisville; and her daily interactions with city residents. The everyday literacies and languages she employs to navigate these environments can be traced outward through global mobilities, just as traces of these mobilities can be located in her daily literate and linguistic activities. Again, such acts of tracing are essential to our understandings of literacy. However, they can eclipse other mobilities also constituting and connecting languages, literacies, and places. As mobility scholars Mimi Sheller and John Urry (2006) assert, "Studies of human mobility at the global level must be brought together with more 'local' concerns about everyday transportation, material cultures, and spatial relations of mobility and immobility" (p. 212).

And so, aside from global, transnational mobilities, what other movements constitute the place-event of Daw's bus ride? There is, of course, the movement of the bus itself, the activities and gazes of fellow passengers, the immediate or distant histories of the bus driver predisposing him to a biting response, Daw's walk home in the dark, the fear she feels on certain city streets, her wait at the stop the next day for the same bus and the same driver, and so on, *ad infinitum*. Bound up with but not reducible to global trajectories, these micro-level, fleeting, material, embodied, and representational (im)mobilities have just as much influence on Daw's daily literacies as her participation in transnational flows, and her daily literacies have just as much influence on these mobilities. In other words, just as her movement from Thailand to the U.S. is bound up with literacies of bureaucratic paperwork, long-distance calling cards, emails, chats, and more, her daily movements through Louisville depend on literacies of reading bus routes and street signs, counting stops, appropriately gesturing, maintaining or avoiding eye-contact, maneuvering around fellow travelers, and so on. And these micro-bodily mobilities and literacies enable her to continue to move transnationally just as they enable her to stay put. To purchase a calling card, she must navigate through the city. To send remittances, she must learn the U.S. postal system. To stay in the United States, she must keep a job.

While many studies attend to material and embodied literacies, and some consider literacies in relation to transcontextual movements, few studies move back and forth across multiple and overlapping scales of space-time.[5] Even those that explicitly address mobility are often actually about literacies connecting or changing in relation to fixed places across space-time. The literacies and mobilities that constitute and connect these places and emerge in transit tend to go unobserved. In "Traveling literacies: multilingual writing on the move," Rebecca Lorimer Leonard (2013) offers a similar critique:

> [Literacy] research has typically focused on literacy in discrete points, as here or there, abroad or in-country (Canagarajah, 2011b; Cuban, 2009; Duffy, 2004; Guerra, 1998; Norton, 2000; Sarroub, 2005). Rarely do scholars consider the journey these literacies take with their writers. The actual movement or mobility of these literacy practices is treated implicitly, as the backdrop of literacy practices that have come from elsewhere—other places, cultures, languages—and appear in front of them.
>
> (2013, p. 16)

Leonard argues that because literacy research tends to focus on "the after-effects of movement, the paradox of mobility remains hidden" (p. 16). Following scholars of migration and mobility studies, she describes this paradox as the simultaneous fluidity of global activity and tightening of boundaries: "an ever-more-mobile world paradoxically causes an 'ideological hardening of social boundaries' (Jacquemet, 2005, p. 263)" (p. 14). To highlight the instability of literacy and language across these boundaries, the simultaneous mobilization and immobilization of linguistic and literate practices, Leonard approaches literacies as "in-process meaning-making activities," "*activities on the move, rather than happening in place*" (p. 17, emphasis added). In this way, she helps us consider how movement shapes and produces literacy practice by offering rich depictions of the ways in which "everyday multilingual writing" is affected by transnational migration (p. 19).

But in the same way that Blommaert's "sociolinguistics of mobility" posits "language-in-place" in opposition to "language-in-motion" (p. 5), Leonard's presentation of mobile literacies risks anesthetizing place.[6] Literacies are mobile *rather than* place-based practices. She writes, "while the defining characteristic of contemporary literacy studies is an attempt to understand how literacy is practiced in social situations and cultural contexts, this essay suggests that movement, itself, is a situation and a context" (p. 33). While I agree with Leonard's conclusion— literacies are always mobile, and movement is a social material event that can and should be studied more carefully by literacy scholars—I want to challenge the contrast on which it depends.

Social situations and cultural contexts cannot stand in opposition to mobility; they are constituted by mobilities. To contain and stabilize place, you have to immobilize and dematerialize it to some degree. As Nedra Reynolds (2004) asserts, rhetorics of mobility often "leave the materiality of place unexamined and reinforce the assumption that places, or their boundaries, are stable" (p. 40). But as I stated above, places do not exist in bounded containers; they occur or become in complexes of mobility. Even sedimented elements of place, temporary achievements of stability, are coordinated and maintained by countless mobilities (Pennycook 2010; Leander et al. 2010). In our studies of literacies and languages on the move, we must not forget to account for movements that materialize place.[7] The materiality of both literacy and place is located in movements of bodies and objects (Haas 1995).

From Enclosure to Emplacement, Transport to Wayfaring, Networks to Meshworks

Following critical and feminist geographers, literacy and language scholars have long challenged notions of bounded and static place by approaching places as products of interrelations embedded in material practice.[8] In such figurations places are spheres of "coexisting heterogeneity," of "contemporaneous plurality." They are also always in process, ongoing events initiated and sustained by convergences of diverse trajectories, the "simultaneity of stories-so-far" (Massey 2005, p. 9). To recognize these qualities of places, we must attend to the mobilities of people, objects, ideas, and information that circulate *within* as well as *among* them. So, while Leonard's proposal that movement is a situation and a context is true, the inverse is also true; situations and contexts are movements. And this is not a minor theoretical distinction. The tendency to dichotomize place and mobility, a symptom of the spatial conceits presented above and described by Ingold's logic of inversion, plays into the modular nature of modernity and thus into the narratives of progress, closed mobility systems, and hierarchical assemblages structuring modern education.

Addressing the centrality of containment in modern thought, Ingold (2009) explains how a logic of inversion transforms emplacement into enclosure, travel into transport, and ways of knowing into transmission (p. 30). By emplacement, he means something akin to Heidegger's dwelling; not the occupation of predetermined and fixed places, but rather the inhabitation of places in process. He proposes that places are produced, and thus we are emplaced, through movements: "There would be no places were it not for the comings and goings of human beings and other organisms to and from them, from and to places elsewhere" (Ingold 2008, p. 1808). These movements through, around, to, and between places create what Ingold describes as a *meshwork* in which the intersecting paths along which life is lived are knotted together at particular junctures to constitute places; the more paths or lifelines that intersect, the greater the density of the knot.

> A house, for example, is a place where the lines of its residents are tightly knotted together. But these lines are no more contained within the house than are threads contained within a knot. Rather, they trail beyond it, only to become caught up with other lines in other places, as are threads in other knots.
>
> (Ingold 2009, p. 33)[9]

In this way, our practices are not place-bound, but are rather place-binding (p. 33). Like Doreen Massey's description of spaces as convergences of diverse trajectories, Ingold's places are tied together by threads of movement. He uses the term *wayfaring* to describe the perambulatory movements constituting places.

Our entire lives unfold along these threads; "wayfaring is our most fundamental mode of being in the world" (p. 38). In accordance with Ingold's ontology, studying literacies and languages always involves following movements of people and things within and across places.[10] This highlights the fact that our conceptualizations of literacies as ways of being in the world (Gee 1990, Prior and Shipka 2003) require more robust theories and methodologies of mobility.

Ingold goes on to describe how enclosure reduces mobility to destination-based transportation. In contrast to wayfaring in which movements themselves constitute paths and places, transportation carries passengers from one pre-determined location to another. Through this inversion, movement becomes a series of trips between fixed points, as paths are transformed into dotted lines, divided into stages, and then rolled and packed into the confines of a destina-tion. "The lines linking these destinations, like those of an air or rail traffic map, are not traces of movement but point-to-point connectors" (Ingold 2009, pp. 36–37). Transportation is the *de facto* expectation of educational mobility systems described above. The network of connections becomes a grid used to individuate and measure students' movements between bounded locations. While all students (and all living organisms) form meshworks by co-creating places through their movements along intersecting and diverging paths, their mobilities are most often presented to and, thus, by them as a series of transitions between fixed stages and destinations (i.e., the Common Core staircase). This distinction between networks and meshworks is an important one for Ingold, as the lines of the latter are not connectors, but are rather the paths along which lives are lived: "it is in the binding together of lines, not in the connecting of points, that the mesh is constituted" (p. 38).

For Ingold, network epistemologies are developed in fixed locations. Systems of enclosure contain and transmit knowledges within particular sites. This harkens back to Leander et al.'s (2010) critique of the containerized classroom where learning is expected to "take place" (p. 329). The significance of this networked knowledge is not found in the story of its discovery, but rather in its integration with knowledges and skills acquired in past and future locations. According to this model, it is through processes of vertical integration that knowledge is developed. In the context of modern education, a vertically integrated classification system of learning objectives and outcomes corresponds to a laterally integrated curriculum connecting blocks of subject-based and classroom-contained knowledges and skills. Assessments of the efficacy of transmission and reception of these knowledges and skills are passed "upward" for analysis and fed into frameworks of progressively wider scope (Ingold 2009, p. 40).

But, then again, this is only the official view of what is supposed to happen in education. In reality, students and teachers, like everyone else, forge knowledge through practice, through movement. "Inhabitants, in short, know as they go, as they journey *through* the world *along* paths of travel. Far from being ancillary to the point-to-point collection of data to be passed up for subsequent processing into knowledge, movement is itself the inhabitant's way of knowing" (Ingold 2009, p. 41). Ingold uses the admittedly awkward neologism "alongly" to convey this sense of knowing *along* paths, rather than *across* locations or *up* hierarchical assemblages. Movement as wayfaring, as opposed to transport, yields alongly integrated ways of knowing. Knowledge is integrated in a meshwork of movements from place to place, not through fitting local particulars into global abstractions (p. 42).

The centrality of mobility to Ingold's ontology and epistemology of inhabitation, challenges literacy scholars and teachers to carefully attend to literacies and languages on the move, as Blommaert, Leonard, and others suggest. But to attach the need for this attention to processes of globalization or locate it in opposition to place-based or situated literacies limits the scope of our investigations of relations between literacies and mobilities. Again, to take up Prior and Shipka's call to approach literacies as ways of inhabiting and, thus, transforming material and social worlds in light of Ingold's claim that movement is our most fundamental mode of being in the world, we must adopt and adapt more expansive ways of understanding and studying relations between literacies and mobilities. For help with this task, I now turn to the field of mobility studies.

New Mobilities for New Literacies

More than a decade ago, Sheller and Urry (2006) introduced what they referred to, with a knowing wink, as a "new mobilities paradigm" emerging in the social sciences.

Their deliberately provocative claim of a paradigmatic shift challenged two extant and polarizing theoretical approaches to social science research: *sedentarism* and *deterritorialization*. It also sought to achieve a more holistic understanding of mobility by uniting fields of study formerly divided by disciplinary and subdisciplinary boundaries (Cresswell 2010, p. 18). Today, with contributions from diverse fields—sociology, anthropology, geography, communication, migration, gender, critical race, postcolonial, transportation studies, and more—work within this paradigm focuses on the interdependence of "embodied and material practices of movement, digital and communicative mobilities, the infrastructures and systems of governance that enable or disable movement, and the representations, ideologies, and meanings attached to both movement and stillness" (Sheller 2014, p. 789). In this way, a mobilities paradigm starts from a realist relational ontology (like Ingold's) and traces out practices and representations of mobility to show how ways of moving (ways of being) are always imbricated in multiple mobilities and fixities and conceptualizations of these. As geographer Peter Adey (2009) asserts, "Mobility is never singular but always plural. It is never one but necessarily many" (p. 18). This emphasis on interdependence among (im)mobilities across scales—from the bodily to the global—is the most convincing claim to the "newness" of the field (Cresswell 2010, p. 18). I also believe it is the aspect of the paradigm with the most potential for furthering the work of literacy studies.

Literacy studies explicitly engage mobilities in a number of sometimes overlapping, sometimes diverging areas of research. A short list of these includes spatial studies of literacy, studies of transition and transfer, circulation studies, translingual literacy, transnational literacy, studies of access and articulation (including disability studies), and digital literacies. Taken together these approaches provide robust accounts of relations between literacies and mobilities. However, they are seldom taken together. While these areas help us understand singular mobilities or interlocking mobilities within related spheres of activity, our robust and evolving understandings of literacy are seldom accompanied by multi-dimensional and multi-scalar conceptions of mobility.

As I suggest above, often missing from our focus on relations between local and global literacies are the entanglements of mobilities connecting and constituting places and scales. We can take the growing subfields of translingual literacy and transnational literacy as examples. Movement is central to both of these related but separate fields of study. Translingual literacy posits languages, language relations, language users, and contexts of language use as emergent and co-constitutive. In place of the stable, internally uniform, and discrete character of languages purported by monolingualism, translingualism postulates languages as fluctuating, internally diverse, and intermingling in character. As Min-Zhan Lu and Bruce Horner (2013) assert, "[Languages] are constantly in movement and rebirth through the labor of those recontextualizing them" (p. 599). Relatedly, studies of transnational literacies highlight the instability of literacy and language across space-time by attending to systems of social relations that move people and their literacies and languages across borders. As Lorimer Leonard, Kate Vieira and Morris Young (2015) assert, "the transnational inheres in an analysis of movement and of traces of that movement that animate even local sites of everyday literate practice" (p. viii). And so while translingual literacy attends to localized practices to show how these perpetually make and remake language systems, identities, and contexts, transnational literacy attends to the effects of global movements on local sites of everyday literacies by looking for traces of these movements in everyday life. The former analytic works like a microscope to show a seemingly stable and bounded cell interpenetrated with molecules and teeming with life, while the latter is like a seismograph that measures the force and duration of tremors after a quake.

Both of these analytics are invaluable, especially when trying to understand how people, objects, ideas, and information move or don't move through and around systems of education. Schools are diverse places—linguistically and nationally. However, their meaning-making trajectories—from local to global and global to local—tend to rely on discursive representations of mobility and seldom show, ethnographically, how movements of languages and literacies depend upon material and embodied mobilities. In other words, often missing is attention to the seemingly mundane movements and stoppages of bodies along with the systems that enable or disable their movements—movements of bodies across cities and counties, institutions and campuses, techno- and mediascapes, through hallways, on highways, and so on.

I suspect these absences are due, in part, to research methods that often stop at the collection of discursively (re)constructed mobilities; namely, textual analysis and interviews. While these methods are as effective (and as limited) as any others, when employed by themselves, they can present discourses of mobility— metaphors, memories, narratives, or texts—as the full story. But as Cresswell (2010) asserts, mobility always involves the entanglement of material movement, representations, and embodied experiences of movement. These entanglements have broadly traceable histories, so that at any one time there are pervading constellations of mobility (p. 18). To account for these constellations, we must attend to the interface between mobile physical bodies, represented mobilities, and the historical senses surrounding these. "To understand mobility without recourse to representation on the one hand or the material corporeality on the other is [. . .] to miss the point" (Cresswell 2006, p. 4). Ultimately, holistic under- standings of mobility require attention to all three aspects (p. 19).

For Cresswell, physical movement refers to mobilities of people, objects, and ideas that can be measured and mapped. For instance, I can map Daw's daily bus route and calculate the time it takes her to get from her neighborhood to work, or I can use a metric to measure her English reading level. But measurements don't address the meanings she and others attach to bus rides or reading tests, nor do they convey how she experiences these physically and emotionally. Representations of mobility also abound. Mobility has been figured as a threat, a privilege, a right, a condition of modernity, the goal of education, and so on. Daw's pursuit of English reading skills for the sake of social mobility is tied to the meanings she attaches to riding the bus, and these meanings are embedded in layers of individual and collective histories of marginalization on city buses. Finally, there is the embodied sense of mobile practice, which includes the habituation of the social (Bourdieu 1991). This involves the exhaustion and/or relief Daw might feel as she boards the bus at the end of the day, the concentration and embarrassment of counting stops, or the eagerness with which she approaches her literacy courses. "Mobility as practised brings together the internal world of will and habit (Merleau-Ponty 2002, Seamon 1979) and the external world of expectation and compulsion. In the end, it is at the level of the body that human mobility is produced, reproduced, and, occasionally, transformed" (Cresswell 2010, p. 20).

As I stated above, movement across space-time depends on literacy, just as literacy depends on spatial and temporal mobilities. While Blommaert, Leonard, and others help us understand the first half of this claim, Cresswell's arrangement helps us understand the second. All literacies involve physical, representational, and practiced aspects of mobility. All literacies and mobilities have physical realities, are culturally and socially encoded, and are experienced through practice. And all forms and aspects of literacy and mobility are political; that is, they shape and are shaped by relations of power (Cresswell 2010, p. 20). From transnational migration, to counting bus stops, to learning English, and raising children, if we are going to approach literacies as ways of being in the world (Gee 1990, Prior and Shipka 2003) we must attend to entanglements and politics of mobility.

Sheller and Urry (2006) begin to delineate a politics of mobility against the image of a traditionally sedentarist approach to social science research: "Sedentarism locates bounded and authentic places or regions or nations as the fundamental basis of human identity and experience and as the basic units of social research. It rests on forms of territorial nationalism and their associated technologies of mapping and visualisation" (pp. 208–209). Anthropologist Lissa Malkki (1992) asserts that this desire to divide up the world into bounded units produces a "sedentarist metaphysics" encouraging fixed and rooted ways of thinking about culture and identity as territorialized in property, place, region, and nation. Such ways of thinking result in severe consequences for mobile people—refugees, asylum seekers, immigrants, the homeless, itinerants, nomadic populations, and so on. Sedentarism treats the mobilities or displacements of such people, along with any movements outside controlled mobility systems, as threats to the normal order of society. The threat of unsanctioned mobility lies at the heart of James Scott's (1998) observation that the modern state and its institutions are engaged in a perennial struggle to discipline and control mobile people—perennial because their efforts are seldom successful.

We don't have to dig very deeply to uncover evidences of sedentarism in structures of modern education. As Foucault (1977) reminds us, schools are replete with "means of correct training" designed to discipline and control mobilities (p. 170). Strategies of containment, born from a sedentarist metaphysics, shape conceptions and experiences of schooling across scales, from federal policies to daily practices. Sedentarism informs rules and punishments for truancy and justifies in- and out-of-school suspensions. It influences the architectural designs of schools and the ways in which we arrange our classrooms. When we ban cell phones, administer hall passes, and regulate wardrobes, we are circumscribing mobilities. Our distinctions between schooled and vernacular literacies and standard and non-standard language varieties are inheritances of sedentarism. While some of these inheritances may be unshakeable in current systems of education, others are inexcusable. For instance, the widespread segregation of students within and across schools in the U.S. based on race, class, ability, and language is due, in large part, to the sedentaristic ways in which schools and cities are organized (Brooks et al. 2013; Walsemann and Bell 2010; Mickelson 2001).

Racism, exclusionary housing, suburbanization, restrictive zoning, and transportation inequity have historically and continue to segregate residents of Louisville, where this study takes place. As in many U.S. cities, racial, cultural, and economic barriers are materialized in Louisville's roadways. Ninth Street, which runs through the heart of downtown, splits the city's West and East Ends and separates black and white populations.[11] In an attempt to dissolve racial, economic, and cultural barriers, Louisville's Jefferson County Public School System (JCPS) is one of two districts in the nation to continue a system-wide desegregation program after federal oversight of integration in the district ended in the late 1990s.[12] While JCPS's program buses students often great distances in pursuit of diverse learning environments, many middle-class families elect to send their children to private preparatory schools or are able to secure spots in highly competitive, economically advantaged magnet schools.[13] This is how students from impoverished minority communities, like those participating in this study, end up in under-resourced "urban" schools in affluent, predominantly white neighborhoods. Even when schools are able to achieve some degree of socioeconomic and racial diversity, poor and minority students are, by and large, still segregated from their middle-class peers through mechanisms of enclosure and networked mobility systems; i.e., academic tracking, in-school suspension, English language learning, and special education programs.[14]

Mobility scholars discuss the differential capacities and opportunities for mobility among people—in this case, students with diverse abilities and intersectional raced, gendered, classed, and ethnic subjectivities—through concepts of *motility* and *mobile capital*. Sociologists Vincent Kaufmann and Bertrand Montulet (2008) define motility as "the manner in which an individual or group appropriates the field of possibilities relative to movement and uses them" (p. 45). An individual may have a high degree of physical motility while seldom exercising it; such as an able-bodied academic, like myself, with a car and a travel fund, who spends most of his time working behind a computer from home or in an office. Others—refugees like Daw, Yo Shu, Nadif, and students bused across Louisville—may experience significant physical displacement but have low motility in terms of capacities and choices for movement, especially if their movements are involuntary or circumscribed by the types of barriers and closed systems described above (Soja 2010, Sheller 2014). This uneven distribution of capacities in relation to physical, social, and political affordances for mobility can be conceptualized in terms of mobile capital (Kaufmann, Bergman and Joye 2004). Uneven distributions of mobile capital are crucial to processes of globalization, urbanization, and also education. The mobilities of some people, objects, ideas, and information depend upon immobilities, delays, exclusions, or displacements of others.

Anthropologist Anna Lowenhaupt Tsing (2005) uses the term "friction" to describe the "awkward, unequal, unstable, and creative qualities of inter-connection across differences" that enable and disable movement (p. 4). "Friction is not just about slowing things down. Friction is required to keep global power in motion" (p. 6). Mobility scholars have taken up the concepts of friction, motility, and mobile capital—along with concepts of mooring, turbulence, dwelling, and placemaking (Cresswell 2010, 2014; Ahmed 2003; Tolia-Kelly 2010)—to complicate notions of a deterritorialized or liquid global condition (Deleuze and Guattari 1987; Castells 1996; Bauman 2000; Hardt and Negri 2000). As Sheller (2014) asserts, "For mobilities researchers today it is not a question of privileging flows, speed, or a cosmopolitan or nomadic subjectivity, but rather of tracking the power of discourses, practices, and infrastructures of mobility in creating the effects (and affects) of both movement and stasis" (p. 794). In other words, mobilities research is concerned, by and large, with the politics of mobility, with the ways in which mobilities produce and are produced by social relations (Cresswell 2010, p. 21).

While this concern does frequently extend to political projects and power relations shaping economic, cultural, and environmental aspects of globalization, "the new mobilities paradigm also differs from theories of globalization in its analytical relation to the multi-scalar, non-human, non-representational, material, and affective dimensions of mobile life" (Sheller 2014, p. 794). As Tsing (2005) reminds us, friction accompanies mobilities of people, objects, texts, and capital across scales; indeed, there is no mobility without friction. She explains,

> A wheel turns because of its encounter with the surface of the road; spinning in the air it goes nowhere. Rubbing two sticks together produces heat and light; one stick alone is just a stick. As a metaphorical image, friction reminds us that heterogeneous and unequal encounters can lead to new arrangements of culture and power.
>
> (p. 5)

If literacies and languages depend on spatial and temporal mobilities, as I claim above, then friction is an essential component of the emergence and transformation of literacies and languages through practice, which makes it an essential component of agency. As Tsing (2005) asserts, "Speaking of friction is a reminder of the importance of interaction in defining movement, cultural form, and agency" (p. 6). These relations between friction, mobility, and agency bring us back to the notion of teaching and learning as placemaking presented above.

Pennycook (2010) asserts that the tendency to enclose or objectify places results from a failure to understand structure as the effect of sedimented repetition and argues that repetition of practice is a "form of renewal that creates the illusion of systematicity" (p. 47). In this way, the apparently preexistent and self-evident nature of a place and its practices is illusory because "repeating the same thing in any movement through time relocalizes that repetition as something different" (p. 41). He suggests that a "focus on movement takes us away from space being only about location, and instead draws attention to a relationship between time and space, to emergence, to a subject in process—performed rather preformed— to becoming" (p. 140).

When Yo Shu recites his teacher's interpretation of Morrison's *The Bluest Eye* in his English class, "corrects" an essay draft in accordance with the guidelines of standard written English presented in his *Little Brown Handbook*, completes a reading comprehension worksheet, and then sits quietly in his assigned seat, he is not merely accommodating the demands of a static classroom environment, he is bringing a history of participation in multiple and concurrent contexts and cultures to bear in each of these situations and is thereby (re)creating the place of the class with others through mobile practice. As cognitive scientists Humberto Maturana and Francisco Varela (1992) might suggest, Yo Shu is not participating in "*the* world but *a* world which [he] bring[s] forth with others" (p. 245).

But focusing on movements alone seldom enables us to see through illusions of fixity. Illusions are maintained because, like Yo Shu's, most mobilities and the social and material relations they (re)produce proceed exactly as expected. As Bruno Latour (1999) might suggest, locations of education are typically "black boxed," the relations constituting them remaining invisible until some disturbance provokes our attention. Latour uses the now dated example of an overhead projector to explain. During a presentation, no one notices the projector until it stops working. When technical support arrives on the scene to take it apart, the function of its individual components and their relations to each other are made visible. In the same way, we tend to take mobilities for granted until something breaks down. Until we are forced to contend with friction, we tend to overlook performance. And so to recognize the *becoming of place* and the work of teaching and learning as placemaking, we must attend to the interdependence of movement and friction, to the frictions that enable and inflect the forms and aspects of mobility that constitute and connect scenes of literacy across scales. We must attend not only to the literate and linguistic mobilities represented in Yo Shu's texts and speech and the frictions they encounter when they run up against perceptions and expectations of language standards, but also to his material and embodied mobilities across the classroom to ask for help on an assignment and the frictions that provoke and redirect these.

It is the friction involved in our uneven and unstable movements within and across "heterogeneous encounters" that brings matters of agency to the fore. Defining agency in terms of translingual literacy, Lu and Horner (2013) assert that agency emerges from the need and ability of individuals to "map and order, remap and reorder conditions and relations surrounding their practices, as they address the potential discrepancies between the official and practical, rather than focusing merely on what the dominant has defined as the exigent, feasible, appropriate, and stable 'context'" (p. 591). Here, the idea of agency is not confined to acts of resistance against institutional norms and demands. Rather, agency is enacted in processes of placemaking in which individuals play off of frictions or "discrepancies" to rearrange social and material relations. Agency emerges from relations between mobility and friction in processes of placemaking. To recognize this agency, individuals must have a sense of the field of possible trajectories and their own abilities to move alongside, against, or around the paths of others and seemingly stable structures. In other words, they must have a sense of their own motilities. It is the agencies enacted in students' physical, representational, and embodied mobilities and the literacies contributing to and emerging from these that I seek to better understand through the research represented in this book.

But Cresswell's call for attention to material, representational, and embodied mobilities raises significant questions (and, for me, doubts) about methodology. In an early appeal for methodological innovation in mobilities research, Law and Urry (2004) argue that traditional research methods in and around the social sciences deal poorly with

> the fleeting—that which is here today and gone tomorrow, only to reappear again the day after tomorrow. They deal poorly with the distributed—that is to be found here and there but not in between—or that which slips and slides between one place and another. They deal poorly with the multiple— that which takes different shapes in different places. They deal poorly with the non-causal, the chaotic, the complex.
>
> (pp. 403–404)

Likewise, in literacy research explicitly engaging issues of mobility, a recurring methodological question has been how to pin down a mobile phenomenon long enough to study it. One potential answer is that you try not to. Or, if that is an impossible task (which I suspect it often is), you, at least, also observe the phenomenon in motion. An alternative question could be: What can we learn about relations between literacy and mobility by following the material, representational, and embodied movements of people and things?

The next chapter pursues this question by considering how methodological innovations of mobility scholars might inform research in literacy studies. In this chapter, I argue that attention to interrelated literacies and mobilities requires the adoption of methods that can capture, perform, and sometimes intervene in fleeting, distributed, multiple, and complex processes of movement and also account for their sensory, affective, and material dimensions (Büscher et al. 2011). I also discuss the affordances and limitations of the mobile methods I employ to attend to students' trajectories in and across scenes of literacy in high school, college, at work, home, online, in transit, and elsewhere. Needless to say, I fall well short of Law and Urry's charge.

Notes

1 Following critical and feminist geographers (Thrift 1977, Pred 1981, Massey 1994), I use the term *space-time* or *time-space* to signal both the general context for movement and the inevitable product of movement. Space and time are mutually constitutive: space becomes dynamic and fluid through the passage of time, just as productions and experiences of time are contingent upon spatial variation. Consequently, all practices, activities, and events have both spatial and temporal attributes. Moreover, practice doesn't merely occur in space and time; space and time are essential elements of practice and are produced through practice. Following anthropologist Tim Ingold, I prefer the

term "place" to "space," as the latter tends to spiral into abstractions. Although, I do take both terms to signal meaningful, lived, and everyday social and material environments (Massey 2005).

2 As anthropologist Johannes Fabian (2014) asserts, "production of ethnography is not a unidirectional process, it works (starting at the moment when we take notes or make texts based on recordings) from both ends, research and writing" (p. 204).

3 The latter half of this claim is true in the sense that repetitions of ideas, words, phrases, events always involve relocations (movement) in space and time (Pennycook 2010).

4 All names of research participants are pseudonyms.

5 Of course there are exceptions, for instance: Nespor 1997, Prior 1998, Leander et al. 2010, Leander and Boldt 2013, Kell 2013.

6 Mike Baynham and Mastin Prinsloo (2009) make a similar move in their description of the field as a progression from first- to second- to third-generation literacy studies in which "the focus has shifted from the local to the translocal" (p. 2).

7 There is a corollary between this conception of place and the ideology of language presented by proponents of translingual literacy (Lu and Horner 2013, Canagarajah 2013). In place of the stable, internally uniform, atemporal, and discrete character of languages purported by monolingualism, translingualism postulates languages as fluctuating, internally diverse, and intermingling in character.

8 Scollon (2001), Scollon and Scollon (2004), Reynolds (2004) Nespor (1994, 1997), Leander and Rowe (2006), and Sheehy (2009) to name a few.

9 Nespor (2004) describes schools and classrooms in much the same way: "Classrooms and schools are only partially bounded intersections, crossroads (Rosaldo, 1989), or meeting places (Massey, 1999), constituted by the articulations of the processes flowing through them" (pp. 310-311).

10 Following anthropologist George Marcus's (1998) description of multi-sited ethnography, I discuss methods for following people and things in the next chapter.

11 "Hispanic/Latino," primarily Mexican-American, residents make up 5 percent of the city's population and are clustered in Sound End neighborhoods. Poverty rates for individuals who are "black/African American" and/or "Hispanic/Latino" are more than twice the rate of white individuals in Louisville (Metropolitan Housing Coalition 2015, p. 15).

12 In 2007 the U.S. Supreme Court struck down Louisville's voluntary school integration program for using race as a factor in school assignments. Louisville's integration plan now uses socioeconomic status as a measure to achieve diversity (Lewin 2007). This plan is discussed in more detail in Chapter 4.

13 As Alana Semuels (2015) reports, "The Archdiocese of Louisville has 35 elementary schools serving 13,755 students, and the percentage of Catholic students enrolled in those schools is the third highest in the country, 7.3 percent, compared to a national average of 2.3 percent."

14 As the U.S. Education Department's most recent Civil Rights Data Collection survey reports, fewer than 3 percent of English language learners are in gifted programs, and similar disparities exist for black and Hispanic students. Black and Hispanic students make up 38 percent of those enrolled at schools offering AP courses, but less than a third of them take such courses. Similar disparities are found in advanced math and science courses (Kamenetz 2016).

References

Adey, P. (2009). *Mobility*. New York: Routledge.

Ahmed, S. (Ed.). (2003). *Uprootings/regroundings: Questions of home and migration*. New York: Berg.

Anderson, B. (2010). Preemption, precaution, preparedness: Anticipatory action and future geographies. *Progress in Human Geography, 34*(6), 777–798.

Appadurai, A. (1996). *Modernity at large: Cultural dimensions of globalization.* Minneapolis: University of Minnesota Press.

Apple, M. W. (1988). *Teachers and texts: A political economy of class and gender relations in education.* New York: Routledge.

Baldwin, A. (2012). Whiteness and futurity: Towards a research agenda. *Progress in Human Geography, 36*(2), 172–187.

Barad, K. M. (2007). *Meeting the universe halfway: Quantum physics and the entanglement of matter and meaning.* Durham, NC: Duke University Press.

Barton, D., & Hamilton, M. (1998). *Local literacies: Reading and writing in one community.* New York: Routledge.

Bauman, Z. (2000). *Liquid modernity.* Cambridge, MA: Polity Press.

Baynham, M., & Prinsloo, M. (Eds.). (2009). *The future of literacy studies.* New York: Palgrave Macmillan.

Besnier, N. (1995). *Literacy, emotion, and authority: Reading and writing on a Polynesian atoll.* New York: Cambridge University Press.

Bill and Melinda Gates Foundation. (n.d.). Pathways for student success. Retrieved from http://postsecondary.gatesfoundation.org/areas-of-focus/pathways-for-student-success/. Accessed October 2013.

Blommaert, J. (2009). Ethnography and democracy: Hymes's political theory of language. *Text & Talk: An Interdisciplinary Journal of Language, Discourse and Communication Studies, 29*(3), 257–276.

Blommaert, J. (2010). *The sociolinguistics of globalization.* New York: Cambridge University Press.

Bourdieu, P., & Passeron, J. C. (1977). *Reproduction in education, society and culture.* London: Sage.

Bourdieu, P. (1991). *Language and symbolic power.* Cambridge, MA: Harvard University Press.

Bowles, S., & Gintis, H. (1976). *Schooling in capitalist America: Educational reform and the contradictions of economic life.* New York: Basic Books.

Brandt, D., & Clinton, K. (2002). Limits of the local: Expanding perspectives on literacy as a social practice. *Journal of Literacy Research, 34*(3), 337–356.

Brooks, J., Arnold, N. W., & Brooks, M. (2013). Educational leadership and racism: A narrative inquiry into second-generation segregation. *Teachers College Record, 115*(11), 1–27.

Büscher, M., Urry, J., & Witchger, K. (Eds.). (2011). *Mobile methods.* New York: Routledge.

Canagarajah, A. S. (2013). *Translingual practice: Global Englishes and cosmopolitan relations.* New York: Routledge.

Casey, E. (1996). How to get from space to place in a fairly short stretch of time: Phenomenological prolegomena. In S. Feld, & K. H. Basso (Eds.). *Senses of place.* Santa Fe, NM: School of American Research Press, 13–52.

Castells, M. (1996). *The rise of the network society.* Malden, MA: Blackwell.

Cresswell, T. (2006). *On the move: Mobility in the modern Western world.* New York: Routledge.

Cresswell, T. (2010). Towards a politics of mobility. *Environment and Planning D: Society and Space, 28*(1), 17–31.

Cresswell, T. (2014). Friction. In P. Adey, D. Bissell, K. Hannam, P. Merriman, & M. Sheller (Eds.). *The Routledge handbook of mobilities* (pp. 107–115). New York: Routledge.

Daw. Personal interview. 9 September 2012.

Deleuze, G., & Guattari, F. (1987). *A thousand plateaus: Capitalism and schizophrenia.* (B. Massumi, Trans.). Minneapolis: University of Minnesota Press.

Duncan, A. (2014). Statement by U.S. Secretary of Education Arne Duncan on the 50th Anniversary of the Civil Rights Act of 1964. U.S. Department of Education. Retrieved August 16, 2016, from www.ed.gov/news/press-releases/statement-us-secretary-education-arne-duncan-50th-anniversary-civil-rights-act-1964

Every Student Succeeds Act of 2015, P.L. Pub.L. 114-95. U.S.C. § 1177 (2015).

Fabian, J. (2014). Ethnography and intersubjectivity: Loose ends. *HAU: Journal of Ethnographic Theory*, 4(1), 199–209.

Foucault, M. (1977). *Discipline and punish: The birth of the prison.* New York: Vintage Books.

Friedman, S. S. (2009). The "new migration": Clashes, connections, and diasporic women's writing. *Contemporary Women's Writing*, 3(1), 6–27.

Gee, J. P. (1990). *Social linguistics and literacies: Ideology in discourses.* London: Falmer Press.

Gieser, T. (2008). Embodiment, emotion and empathy: A phenomenological approach to apprenticeship learning. *Anthropological Theory*, 8(3), 299–318.

Haas, C. (1995). *Writing technology: Studies on the materiality of literacy.* New York: Routledge.

Hardt, M., & Negri, A. (2000). *Empire.* Cambridge, MA: Harvard University Press.

Heath, S. B. (1983). *Ways with words: Language, life, and work in communities and classrooms.* New York: Cambridge University Press.

Ingold, T. (2008). Bindings against boundaries: Entanglements of life in an open world. *Environment and Planning A*, 40(8), 1796–1810.

Ingold, T. (2009). Against space: Place, movement, knowledge. In P. W. Kirby. *Boundless worlds: An anthropological approach to movement.* Oxford: Berghahn Books, 29–43.

Kamenetz, A. (2016). The civil rights problem in U.S. schools: 10 new numbers. National Public Radio. Retrieved August 21, 2016, from www.npr.org/sections/ed/2016/06/07/480957031/the-civil-rights-problem-in-u-s-schools-10-new-numbers

Kaufmann, V., Bergman, M. M., & Joye, D. (2004). Motility: Mobility as capital. *International Journal of Urban and Regional Research*, 28(4), 745–756.

Kaufmann, V., & Montulet, B. (2008). Between social and spatial mobilities: The issue of social fluidity. In W. Canzler, V. Kaufmann, & S. Kesselring (Eds.). *Tracing mobilities: Towards a cosmopolitan perspective* (pp. 37–56). Farnham and Burlington, VT: Ashgate.

Kell, C. (2011). Inequalities and crossings: Literacy and the spaces-in-between. *International Journal of Educational Development*, 31(6), 606–613.

Kell, C. (2013). Ariadne's thread: Literacy, scale, and meaning-making across space and time. *Working Papers in Urban Language and Literacies*, 118, 1–24.

Latour, B. (1999). *Pandora's hope: Essays on the reality of science studies.* Cambridge, MA: Harvard University Press.

Law, J., & Urry, J. (2004). Enacting the social. *Economy and Society*, 33(3), 390–410.

Leander, K. M., & Sheehy, M. (Eds.). (2004). *Spatializing literacy research and practice.* New York: Peter Lang.

Leander, K. M., & Rowe, D. W. (2006). Mapping literacy spaces in motion: A rhizomatic analysis of a classroom literacy performance. *Reading Research Quarterly*, 41, 428–460.

Leander, K. M., Phillips, N. C., & Taylor, K. H. (2010). The changing social spaces of learning: Mapping new mobilities. *Review of Research in Education*, 34(1), 329–394.

Leander, K. M., & Boldt, G. (2013). Rereading "A pedagogy of multiliteracies": Bodies, texts, and emergence. *Journal of Literacy Research*, 45(1), 22–46.

Lefebvre, H. (1991). *The production of space.* Cambridge, MA: Blackwell.

Leonard, R. L. (2013). Traveling literacies: Multilingual writing on the move. *Research in the Teaching of English, 48*(1), 13–39.

Leonard, R. L., Vieira, K., & Young, M. (2015). Special editors' introduction to Issue 3.3. *Literacy in Composition Studies, 3*(3), vi–xi.

Lewin, T. (2007). Across the U.S.: A new look at school integration efforts. *New York Times.* Retrieved from www.nytimes.com/2007/06/29/washington/29schools.html. Accessed June 2016.

Lu, M.-Z., & Horner, B. (2013). Translingual literacy, language difference, and matters of agency. *College English, 75*(6), 582–607.

Malkki, L. (1992). National geographic: The rooting of peoples and the territorialization of national identity among scholars and refugees. *Cultural Anthropology, 7*(1), 24–44.

Marcus, G. E. (1998). *Ethnography through thick and thin.* Princeton, NJ: Princeton University Press.

Massey, D. B. (1994). *Space, place, and gender.* Minneapolis: University of Minnesota Press.

Massey, D. B. (2005). *For space.* London: Sage.

Maturana, H. R., & Varela, F. J. (1992). *The Tree of Knowledge: The Biological Roots of Human Understanding.* Boston, MA: Shambhala.

Merleau-Ponty, M. (2002). *Phenomenology of perception.* New York: Routledge.

Metropolitan Housing Coalition. (2015). *State of Metropolitan Housing Report: 2015 A Year of Change.* 1–42. Retrieved from www.metropolitanhousing.org/wpcontent/uploads/member_docs/2015%20State%20of%20Metropolitan%20Housing%20Report.pdf. Accessed June 2016.

Mickelson, R. A. (2001). Subverting Swann: First- and second-generation segregation in the Charlotte-Mecklenburg schools. *American Educational Research Journal, 38*(2), 215–252.

National Governors Association Center for Best Practices, & Council of Chief State School Officers. (n.d.). *Common core state standards.* Common Core Standards Initiative. Retrieved from www.corestandards.org/. Accessed September 2011.

Nespor, J. (1994). *Knowledge in motion: Space, time and curriculum in undergraduate physics and management.* London: Routledge.

Nespor, J. (1997). *Tangled up in school: Politics, space, bodies, and signs in the educational process.* New York: Routledge.

Nespor, J. (2004). Educational scale-making. *Pedagogy, Culture and Society, 12*(3), 309–326.

Papastergiadis, N. (2000). *The turbulence of migration: Globalization, deterritorialization, and hybridity.* Malden, MA: Polity Press.

Pennycook, A. (2010). *Language as a local practice.* New York: Routledge.

Pennycook, A. (2012). *Language and mobility: Unexpected places.* Bristol: Multilingual Matters.

Pink, S. (2009). *Doing sensory ethnography.* Thousand Oaks, CA: Sage.

Pred, A. (1981). Social reproduction and the time-geography of everyday life. *Geografiska Annaler, 63*(1), 5–22.

Prior, P. A. (1998). *Writing/disciplinarity: A sociohistoric account of literate activity in the academy.* Mahwah, NJ: Lawrence Erlbaum Associates.

Prior, P. A., & Shipka, J. (2003). Chronotopic lamination: Tracing the contours of literate activity. In C. Bazerman, & D. Russell (Eds.). *Writing selves, writing societies: Research from activity perspectives.* Fort Collins, CO: WAC Clearinghouse, 180–238.

Reynolds, N. (2004). *Geographies of writing: Inhabiting places and encountering difference.* Carbondale: Southern Illinois University Press.

Rounsaville, A. (2014). Situating transnational genre knowledge: A genre trajectory analysis of one student's personal and academic writing. *Written Communication, 31*(3), 332–364.

Rowsell, J., & Pahl, K. (Eds.). (2015). *The Routledge handbook of literacy studies.* New York: Routledge.

Scollon, R. (2001). *Mediated discourse: The nexus of practice.* New York: Routledge.

Scollon, R., & Scollon, S. W. (2004). *Nexus analysis: Discourse and the emerging internet.* New York: Routledge.

Scott, J. C. (1998). *Seeing like a state: How certain schemes to improve the human condition have failed.* New Haven, CT: Yale University Press.

Seamon, D. (1979). *A geography of the lifeworld: Movement, rest, and encounter.* New York: St. Martin's Press.

Sebba, M. (2010). Discourses in transit. In A. Jaworski, & C. Thurlow (Eds.). *Semiotic landscapes: Language, image, space* (pp. 59–76). New York: Continuum International.

Semuels, A. (2015). The city that believed in desegregation. *The Atlantic.* Retrieved from www.theatlantic.com/business/archive/2015/03/the-city-that-believed-in-desegregation/388532/. Accessed July 2016.

Sheehy, M. (2009). *Place stories: Time, space and literacy in two classrooms.* New York: Hampton Press.

Sheller, M., & Urry, J. (2006). The new mobilities paradigm. *Environment and Planning A, 38*(2), 207–226.

Sheller, M. (2014). The new mobilities paradigm for a live sociology. *Current Sociology, 62*(6), 789–811.

Soja, E. W. (2010). *Seeking spatial justice.* Minneapolis: University of Minnesota Press.

Street, B. (1995). *Social literacies: Critical approaches to literacy in development, ethnography, and education.* New York: Longman.

Street, B. (2001). The new literacy studies. In E. Cushman, E. R. Kintgen, B. M. Kroll, & M. Rose (Eds.). *Literacy: A critical sourcebook* (pp. 430–432). Boston, MA: Bedford/St. Martin's.

Suárez-Orozco, M. (2005). Right moves? Immigration, globalization, utopia, and dystopia. In M. Suárez-Orozco, C. Suárez-Orozco, & D. Qin-Hilliard (Eds.). *The new immigration: An interdisciplinary reader* (pp. 3–20). New York: Routledge.

Thrift, N. (1977). *Introduction to time geography.* Norwich, UK: Geo Abstracts, University of East Anglia.

Thrift, N. (2008). *Non-representational theory: Space, politics, affect.* New York: Routledge.

Tolia-Kelly, D. P. (2010). *Landscape, race and memory: Material ecologies of citizenship.* Burlington, VT: Ashgate.

Tsing, A. L. (2005). *Friction: An ethnography of global connection.* Princeton, NJ: Princeton University Press.

Tusting, K. (2000). The new literacy studies and time. In D. Barton, M. Hamilton, & R. Ivanič (Eds.). *Situated literacies: Reading and writing in context* (pp. 35–54). New York: Routledge.

Urry, J. (2007). *Mobilities.* Cambridge, MA: Polity Press.

Walsemann, K. M., & Bell, B. A. (2010). Integrated schools, segregated curriculum: Effects of within-school segregation on adolescent health behaviors and educational aspirations. *American Journal of Public Health, 100*(9), 1687–1695.

Wenger, E. (1998). *Communities of practice: Learning, meaning, and identity.* New York: Cambridge University Press.

2

METHODOLOGY FOR MOBILE LITERACY

The key to understanding education isn't to be found in what happens in classrooms or schools but in the relations that bind them to networks of practice extending beyond.

(Nespor 1997)

I find myself surrounded by patchiness, that is, a mosaic of open-ended assemblages of entangled ways of life, with each further opening into a mosaic of temporal rhythms and spatial arcs.

(Tsing 2015)

When I was boy, the interplay of mobility, friction, and agency felt like rubber tires gripping and pushing the asphalt beneath my single-speed metallic blue bicycle. On quiet afternoons, I'd ride down our street across a major thoroughfare dividing voting zones and school boundaries and into a neighborhood of sprawling houses and lawns. I'd travel slowly up and down wide and winding streets, close to the curb, seldom encountering a resident, save through the gaps of their privacy fences. In this neighborhood, streetscapes hosted the traffic of service workers and visitors, while backyards and private drives were shielded by cedar screens erected to protect properties and their residents from wandering bodies, eyes, and imaginations. But as any traveler can attest, wooden fences vanish before the eyes of the passers-by moving at just the right clip.

According to environmental historian John Stilgoe (1998), "usually about eleven miles an hour does the trick. At that speed the explorer can see through the fence almost as though the fence had disappeared" (p. 110). Stilgoe's vanishing fence phenomenon is an example of what neuroscientists call visual completion, a process in which perception goes beyond the retinal image to fill in implicit properties of a scene. V. S. Ramachandran and Diane Rogers-Ramachandran (2010) explain, "When an object is partially hidden, the brain deftly reconstructs it as a visual whole" (para. 1). And so when viewing a dog behind a fence, we perceive a single dog partially hidden by opaque slats rather than separate dog slices. The retinal image comprises only fragments, but the brain's visual system—tied to memory, imagination, expectation, and desire—joins them together, reconstructing the object.

While this process of "filling in" works well in the presence of an animate object (dog, human, water sprinkler, etc.), when we stand motionless in front of a fenced and seemingly static scene, we don't automatically fill in the picture behind it; we tend to focus on planks rather than gaps. Until we begin moving, that is. When traveling at Stilgoe's magical speed, our attention is drawn to a succession of gaps and our visual imagination transforms slices of information into a coherent whole. As neuropsychologists Phillip Kellman and Thomas Shipley (1992) suggest, when occlusion meets motion, "the human visual system integrates spatially fragmentary information over time to achieve perception of objects and spatial layouts" (p. 193). In other words, movement alongside the fence activates a succession of visual data streaming through narrow gaps, and we automatically interpolate forms and boundaries from these slices of information. Movement causes the barrier to disappear by reorienting our attention, imagination, and perception to what lies between and beyond the planks. In this way, my bicycle and the marriage of mobility and perception it enabled granted me access to scenes of middle-class leisure and simultaneously reaffirmed my place on the other side of the fences. Immobilities always accompany mobilities, and friction is a precondition of agency.

In this chapter I want to consider how such marriages of mobility and perception can help us see and think differently about literacy practices and methods of observation and engagement in literacy studies. How might foregrounding and participating in patterns, representations, and practices of movement—Cresswell's (2010) entanglements of mobility—reorient our attention to and alter our perceptions of literacy and language practice? What can we learn about relations among the social, spatial, and cultural mobilities and everyday and academic literacies by following the movements of people, objects, ideas, and information? What method/ologies can we adopt and adapt to more effectively attend to fleeting, distributed, multiple, complex, sensory, emotional, and kinesthetic dimensions of literacy and language (Law and Urry 2004, Büscher et al. 2011)?

To contextualize these questions, I offer a brief consideration of ways in which student mobilities tend to be researched, represented, and analyzed in studies of academic literacy. While literacy scholars engage issues of mobility across areas of inquiry, from transfer studies to mobile computing, my focus here is on how mobility tends to be framed and observed in research on student transitions within and between educational institutions. I then present details of my own study of students' literacies and mobilities through high school and college in light of research frames and methods adapted from multi-sited ethnography and mobility studies. I reflect on affordances and limitations of my engagements with these method/ologies and consider what literacy research might gain from the mobilities paradigm introduced in the previous chapter, a paradigm that seeks to fold theories of (im)mobility into the empirical to better understand movements and stoppages of people, objects, ideas, and information across scales (Sheller and Urry 2006, Büscher et al. 2011, Sheller 2014).

In these ways, the chapter seeks to forward conversations of spatiality and mobility in literacy studies by engaging not only discursive representations of these concepts, but also by offering frames and methods for attending to and participating in material and embodied movements within and through complex systems. Central to this engagement is a consideration of the tensions that inhere in the relationship between the fixity of representation and the flux of mobile practice, a tension that presents questions of how to make practices legible without immobilizing them in a transparent text. Massey (1994) addresses the limitations of representing a transitory world by asserting that texts, whose properties "necessarily fix," appear to deaden a life in flow (p. 15). To work against this deadening, while acknowledging that it cannot ultimately be avoided, I pursue open-ended representations of entangled mobilities and literacies "in a mosaic of temporal rhythms and spatial arcs" (Tsing 2015, p. 20). Considering the limits of my own and my research participants' time, space, and perspectives, the mosaic is necessarily incomplete; we are only able to trace trajectories for brief durations and short distances through limited frames. Nevertheless, I believe the stories offered in this book, the themes they share, and the methods employed to listen to and (re)tell them can serve as productive points of departure for researching and teaching relations among literacies and mobilities.

From Transitions to Mobilities, Communities to Assemblages

In the previous chapter, I drew on mobility studies to challenge two conceits of modern education: the first figuring movement as isolated from contexts of power and the second figuring contexts as preexisting the movements that simultaneously constitute and are constituted by them. Underlying these presentations is a need to situate languages, literacies, and individuals in their institutional and developmental places. In contrast, an understanding of literacies and mobilities as practices with entangled material, representational, and embodied dimensions necessitates a spatiotemporal approach to place, which sees space and time as essential elements of practice, produced through practice (Pennycook 2010). This approach enables us to move beyond presentations of places as fixed and discrete locations to consider the ways in which they are actually *occurrences* or *events*, constituted by mobilities of people, objects, ideas, and information within and across overlapping scales of space-time. By attending to mobile and literate practices as acts of making places and subjectivities, we can shift the focus of student movements in and among educational environments from merely joining and conforming to (re)making assemblages and realizing agencies.

However, approaching literacy teaching and learning as placemaking can undercut hard-fought institutional standings and disciplinary boundaries. Any sustained deviation from modern education's forward march of progress places individuals, programs, departments, and disciplines in precarious and sometimes untenable institutional positions. *Education for the future* is easier and often more essential to explain and justify to politicians, trustees, administrators, funders, colleagues, parents, students, and to ourselves than *education for the present*. Without promises of progress and development—the "frames [that] sort out those parts of the present that might lead to the future" (Tsing 2015, p. 20)—we are left with the unsettling, frightening, but also generative realities of precarity and indeterminancy. But as Tsing suggests, "precarity *is* the condition of our time":

> Precarity is the condition of being vulnerable to others. Unpredictable encounters transform us; we are not in control, even of ourselves. Unable to rely on a stable structure of community, we are thrown into shifting assemblages, which remake us as well as our others. We can't rely on the status quo; everything is in flux, including our ability to survive.
>
> (p. 20)

Tsing asks what we might notice about ourselves and environments when we are no longer stuck within imaginative frameworks of progress: "As progress tales lose traction, . . . it becomes possible to look differently" (p. 22). But more often than not, institutional expectations and demands succeed in discouraging serious attempts to look and think otherwise about practices and structures. Institutions work to preserve the status quo. And so it's difficult to imagine how we might begin to explain and justify institutionalized education outside narratives of unified progress-time. How can we keep futures open or, at least, bend arcs of progress in multiple directions for our students and ourselves? How can we help students and teachers come to see themselves as co-creators of these arcs? What do we stand to gain from thinking through precarity rather than or in addition to progress? What do we stand to lose? To move effectively through frictions of precarity and progress, I propose we teach and research mobilities rather than transitions and think through assemblages rather than communities.

As a sedentarist conceptualization of movement, transitioning depends on discrete locations, fixed stages of development, and stable communities. Transitions are Ingold's (2009) point-to-point connectors linking predetermined destinations. Studies and programs of academic literacy often rely on linear concepts of transition and representations of transitioning students for the formation of disciplinary and programmatic identities. To maintain institutional positions at thresholds between assumed pasts and anticipated futures—from one grade level to another, from high school to college, and from general education to disciplinary expertise—and thereby accommodate the material and economic demands of an increasingly integrated school–work system, teachers and scholars of academic literacies often reconstruct students' educational histories and forecast their academic and occupational futures to trace trajectories from fixed points of departure to fixed points of arrival. Like locations on a map, these points represent clustered communities of self-evident social relations, ideologies, values, genres, and practices.

Following the shift from autonomous to ideological models of literacy initiated by Street, Heath, and others, many scholars and teachers of academic literacies shifted their theoretical and pedagogical commitments in the 1980s and 1990s from coding and correcting reading and writing processes to developing understandings of literacies as social practices. As an alternative to the developmental, upward-and-onward narrative of growth offered by autonomous models linking literacy to cognitive development, "socially minded" literacy teacher-researchers proposed narratives of mobility that positioned student-informants as "outsider[s], standing outside a bounded area that defines the community of discourse" (Williams 1989, p. 250). According to Joseph Williams (1989), this narrative exchanges notions of higher and lower thinking for divisions between "insider thinking (socialized/expert thinking) and outsider thinking (not yet socialized/novice thinking)." This exchange requires a reconsideration of students' movements into new educational communities as processes of joining. Acknowledging mobility as movement within contexts of power, Williams asserts that "the movement from outside the circle to inside is not natural, inevitable, developmental." And so "the student who appears to be unable to join the community may in fact not be unintelligent, intellectually immature, etc., but rather a novice, unsocialized in ways that make him appear unintelligent, intellectually immature, etc." (p. 250).

Drawing on a range of community-based approaches to observing and theorizing social and cultural practice—from speech communities (Hymes 1974) to literacy events (Heath 1983), discourse communities (Gee 1990), and communities of practice (Lave and Wenger 1991)—models of academic socialization like those described by Williams tend to figure college as a specific domain of reality constituted by values and activities that maintain a pre-established and self-evident social order. To join this order, students must first acknowledge their locations on the margins of a bounded community and reevaluate their ties to previous communities. As students gradually learn to leave familiar literacies behind, they move through stages of socialization, learning the ways of being, knowing, and doing that lead to legitimate membership in an academic community. While notions of bounded and unified "communities of practice" have been roundly critiqued across disciplines for their tendencies to contain culture in the local (Harris 1989, Brandt and Clinton 2002, Kell 2009, 2011, Leander et al. 2010, Blommaert 2010), narratives of academic socialization continue to dominate descriptions of student transitions into and through systems of education.

In one of many examples, Nancy Sommers and Laura Saltz (2004) seek to better understand the role writing plays in students' transitions into college through data collected in their expansive and influential *Harvard Study of Undergraduate Writing*. From a review of "600 pounds of student writing, 520 hours of transcribed interviews, and countless megabytes of survey data" (p. 126), Sommers and Saltz conclude that first-year students must embrace roles as novices—"adopting an open attitude to instruction and feedback, a willingness to experiment, . . . and a faith that, with practice and guidance, the new expectations of college can be met"—before they can begin the process of "writing *into* expertise" (p. 134). They write, "If there is one great dividing line in our study between categories of freshmen writers, the line falls between students who continue throughout the year not to see a 'greater purpose in writing than completing an assignment' and freshmen [sic] who believe they can 'get and give' when they write" (p. 140). The former students cannot escape "high school idea[s] of academic success," while the latter accept the transactional nature of "college-level" writing; that is, they see writing as something that can be produced, distributed, exchanged, and consumed for purposes other than assessment.

While I read the introductory phrase of this quotation as an acknowledgement of an oversimplified presentation of student expectations, perceptions, and performances, an unacknowledged, and perhaps more damaging, reduction exists in Sommers and Saltz's dichotomization of the pseudo-transactional literacies of students' educational histories and academic literacies "that matter" in college (p. 139). This dichotomy not only reduces the complexity of literacies associated with high school, but also precludes or ignores the possibility that students are remembering, participating in, and conceptualizing scenes of literacy outside contexts of formal education or that such activities might influence their approaches to academic literacies in the first year of college.[1] In other words, to depict a process of academic socialization, Sommers and Saltz isolate and abstract a single mobility—student transitions from high school to college—and thereby eschew the complexity of mobilities within and across multiple sites of activity. This simplification reifies spaces of high school and college and reduces incoming students' histories of participation in various scenes of literacy to insufficient ways of doing, being, and knowing.

In this study, Sommers and Saltz are participating in an enduring pattern of reification that precedes and extends beyond them.[2] And like the objectives of most participants in this trend, theirs are worthy of pursuit. However, what a mobilities paradigm calls into question about such presentations is not the validity of their ends, but rather the methods employed and narratives constructed to chart progress toward them. In other words, like Sommers and Saltz, I want my students to "see what they can 'get' and 'give' through their writing"—I want them to "see a larger purpose for writing other than completing an assignment"—but I question the ways in which space-time and subjectivities are figured in representations of student movements in relation to these ends (p. 146). By charting movements between absolute places left behind and places of arrival, such representations neglect the complexity of entangled material, representational, and embodied mobilities connecting and constituting meshworks of secondary and tertiary education. Rather than the places themselves existing in states of internal complexity, flux, and consequent friction, the only frictions in this figuration reside *between* places and frames of time; the meritocratic and mechanical nature of high school is in tension with the exploratory and generative nature of college. Consequently, incoming students are positioned between two worlds (rather than among many): "The first year of college offers students the double perspective of the threshold, a liminal state from which they might leap forward—or linger at the door" (Sommers and Saltz 2004, p. 125). And so students have two options: they can move forward or not at all.

Before I let this critique silently position my own teaching and research outside the influence of such sedentaristic assumptions, I should pause to remember the plank in my eye. While my research has been motivated, in large part, by a desire to challenge dismissals or devaluations of students' literacy histories and linguistic repertoires, like those evidenced in the Harvard study, the research represented in this book was originally planned and proposed within a framework shaped by many of the assumptions critiqued above. Below is a passage that appears in both my original research proposal to the University of Louisville's Institutional Review Board (my home institution at the time of the study) and a proposal to the Jefferson County Public School Systems's division of Accountablity, Research, and Planning:

> The purpose of this study is to examine students' attempts to reconcile disjunctions between preconceptions, experiences and projections of academic literacies in the transition from secondary to tertiary education. I plan to study the ways in which students draw from available linguistic and literate resources and presentations of "college and career readiness" circulating in their high school and college literacy classrooms to read and write themselves into college.

Like many studies of students' educational transitions, this study began with a proposal to attend to makings of connections across preexisting communities; it was not attuned to the literacies and mobilities making and remaking the "communities" themselves. In Ingold's terms, I was interested in understanding students' ways of knowing *across* locations rather than *along* paths constituting these locations (see Chapter 1). As long as beginning and ending points are already established and actors already determined, such sedentaristic methodologies can reveal a great deal about general trends and trajectories. However, when places and actors are not so stable and possibilities for action not so predictable, these methodologies have a difficult time keeping up with mobilities constituting and connecting scenes of literacy across space-time.

This original proposal reveals my presumption that it would be possible to study students' transitions from high school to college without also attending to past, present, and future mobilities within and across scenes of literacy in and out of school. It elides micro-level material and embodied mobilities by privileging representational mobilities and macro "transitions" between predetermined destinations of high school and college. College is figured as a fixed location that students must "read and write themselves *into*" rather than a constellation of places they co-produce through practice.

And rather than challenging projections of self-evident futures—standards, measures, and feelings of "college and career readiness"—I propose to help students verify their authenticity. Here is a passage from an email I sent to the principal of the high school where I began my research requesting approval for the study:

> As a college writing teacher and assistant administrator, . . . I'd like to provide students with a direct connection to the University's composition program while helping them with their current work in any way that I can . . . I hope that this study will benefit students who choose to participate by helping them reflect on their literacy experiences in high school and by challenging them to consider how they might apply these experiences in the future.

In this message, I present myself as a representative from students' not-so-distant academic futures and leverage my position at a familiar institutional threshold— the University's first-year composition requirement—to gain access to the high school and its students and teachers. While pitching a study to institutional gatekeepers is often very different than working it out for yourself with participants, I did believe at the time that I could reciprocate my participants' efforts by providing a window into their educational futures. This self-presentation rests on at least two false assumptions: First, that I could, in good faith, predict the literacy demands and opportunities of students' educational futures; and second, that the students participating in this study might benefit from even more *reminders of the future*.[3]

But as my research shifted from projection to participation, I found myself confronted with and integrated into shifting assemblages, unable to rely upon stable structures of community (Tsing 2015, p. 20). Or rather, the precarity of my participants' lives, of my own life, of the structures and practices of K-16 education, of my roles in the project, and of the research itself taught me that the bounded and stable communities of high school and college I proposed to observe were not at all bounded and stable. They were rather effects of ongoing re-assemblages. As Latour (2005) suggests, "Social aggregates are not the object of an *ostensive* definition—like mugs and cats and chairs that can be pointed at by the index finger—but only of a *performative* definition" (p. 34). Groups are not settled and static but are rather sustained through group-making efforts:

"If you stop making and remaking groups, you stop having groups" (Latour 2005, p. 35).

Attending to shifting assemblages, to the intertwined material practices that (re)make groups and places, requires an ethnographic orientation, and ethnographic knowledge production depends upon shifting assemblages. While I may have understood the first half of this claim at the outset of the study (ethnography as a methodology of and for complexity), I did not fully understand the second: that like any other movement, the move toward ethnographic knowledge relies upon frictions among and within shifting assemblages of people, objects, and ideas. As anthropologist Johannes Fabian (2001) asserts, "The ethnographic knowledge process is not initiated simply by turning our gaze on objects that are given . . . The process is initiated only once it encounters resistance in the form of incomprehension, denial, rejection, or why not, simply Otherness" (p. 25). The remaining sections of this chapter introduce the ethnographic knowledge process represented in and extending beyond the pages of this book by describing its shifting conditions and forms, the mobilities and frictions driving it, and method/ologies that have helped to document and make some sense of it all.

Noticing Mobilities

To attend to the complexity of associations made and remade within and across places, a literacy ethnographer must develop an epistemological and ontological sense of places and subjectivities in perpetual movement. As evidenced above, I did not enter into the study with this sense. The sedentarism of my original research plan reflects what appeared to be, from the outset, stable educational environments hosting predictable patterns of movement. Bells sounded and students arrived to classes on time (for the most part). They filed into rows of desks and took out textbooks, notepads, and pens. They silenced and slipped phones into their pockets and removed earbuds before teachers started in with daily lessons (for the most part). They listened, worked, responded to questions, offered insights, teased and sometimes ignored each other and their teachers. Bells sounded again and they packed up and were ushered down hallways and into other classrooms where they repeated similar routines.

I observed and participated in these routines for approximately two years at a public high school in Louisville, Kentucky, which I'll call Hughes. I visited the school two or three days a week to work with students and teachers in three separate senior-level English courses.[4] Hughes's "literacy lead" assigned me to these courses, paired me with three teachers, including herself, and placed me as a tutor-researcher in an Advanced Placement Literature and Composition course, a Dual Enrollment Composition course, and a regular English course. I began the study at Hughes for a number of reasons: (1) The school is known for the diversity of its student body. While Hughes is located in an affluent, predominantly white neighborhood in East Louisville, the Jefferson County Public School

System (JCPS) buses large numbers of students from economically depressed, predominantly minority neighborhoods to the school, contributing to a population in which 64 percent are students of color and 74 percent qualify as "economically disadvantaged." Hughes also has a large contingent of English language learners. During the 2011/12 school year, over 6 percent of the total student population was labeled "limited English proficiency" and enrolled in the school's English as a Second Language Program (Jefferson County Public Schools n.d., *2012–2013 Data Books*). (2) Prior to the study, I worked with two English teachers training to teach the first course of the University of Louisville's composition sequence for dual enrollment credit at Hughes. As Assistant Director of Composition, I met with these and other teachers in a small cohort to discuss ideas emanating from a graduate course they were taking on writing pedagogy. My relationships with these teachers challenged many of my preconceptions about academic literacies in secondary schools and provided insight into the complexity of teaching "college writing" in high school. (3) Finally, Hughes was only three miles from my residence when the study began, a proximity especially important considering that my primary means of transportation at the time was a single-passenger motor scooter that I drove in all manner of weather.

I spent about four months at Hughes as an in-class tutor before developing research questions and goals. During this time, I observed classroom practices; listened to students' and teachers' concerns about past, present, and future literacy demands; participated in class discussions when invited; and talked with students about literacy practices in and out of school. I read essay drafts and assignment prompts and provided feedback. I attended faculty and school board meetings, school assemblies, and sporting events. I learned what I could from students, teachers, staff, and material surrounds about the practices that constituted scenes of literacy at Hughes and about the institutional, social, cultural, and historical influences shaping these practices.

Because I was not looking for or thinking in terms of mobility beyond macro-level transitions and because the movements and frictions of people, objects, ideas, and information I observed and participated in were predictable, if not entirely expected, during my first several months at the school, I approached classrooms and the school itself as containers of activity (Leander et al. 2010). While I considered and documented how these containers shaped activities, I was not immediately attentive to the ways in which they were (re)shaped and maintained through practice. My fieldnotes from the project's initial stages are filled with depictions of static contexts shaping students' academic literacies. I sketched the following classroom layout of regular English in my second week at Hughes. The image is accompanied by a corresponding fieldnote transcribed for legibility.

REG ENG, 10/12/10: Noticing self-segregation of students within the class. Groups clustered by race, gender, language. Male less integrated than female. The arrangement of desks may add to this; it's difficult for students

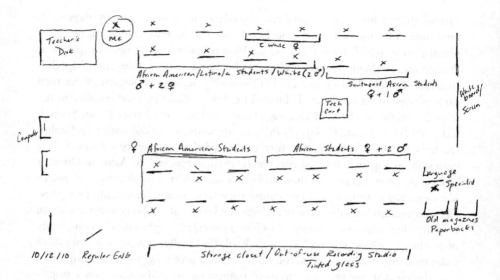

FIGURE 2.1 Image of Fieldnote, Classroom Map

to see each other or talk across the room. Teacher moves up and down the center aisle, directing instructions to specific groups of students. Changes tone and register for each group. Whiteboard/screen has not been used, not a focal point. Many students would have trouble seeing the board/ screen from their seats; I do not have a clear line of sight. I need to find a way to reposition myself in the room, tricky because this would mean joining a group and taking or adding a seat.

Both the drawing and the reflection are essentially static. The only representations of movement are of the teacher moving up and down the center aisle and of me imagining how I might secure a better vantage point. In these notes, the actors with the most potential for movement, or motility, are the ones with the most authority. Students, on the other hand, are stuck in blocks of racial, gender, national, and linguistic affiliation. While relations between student groupings and the spatial layout of the room are significant, my representations freeze the students and the space by ignoring changes over time.

Of course, as I made these observations, students were moving with each other, objects, and ideas within and beyond the classroom, and so was I. But I was not attuned to these mobilities and their attendant frictions nor to the assemblages and agencies they enabled. I was not attentive to the class's *becoming of place*, only to the becoming of connections between places. By this I mean that my focus on discursive representations of macro movements between places of high school and college overshadowed micro (im)mobilities constituting the classroom scenes in which I participated. Without a disruption to the seeming stability of such scenes and to the project itself, my fieldwork would have likely stopped at description and thus failed to engage ethnographic knowledge production.

Ethnography is reduced to fieldwork when it is approached as a complex of methods for collecting data and contextualizing practice. Blommaert (2009) suggests that "Even in anthropology, ethnography is often seen as a synonym for description" (p. 260). Following Fabian, he asserts that "Static interpretations of context . . . are anathema and to the extent that they occur in ethnographic writing they should be seen as either a rhetorical reduction strategy or, worse, as a falsification of the ethnographic endeavor" (p. 266). This is because ethnographic knowledge is always grounded in relationships between researchers and participants. As Fabian states above, ethnographic knowledge depends upon resistance, collisions among researchers' and participants' perspectives and needs and their desires and struggles for recognition. The ethnographer cannot observe and describe literacies and mobilities from a distance; they must feel them, provoke and follow them, misunderstand to move closer to understanding. Their ignorance is a critical point of departure. This movement toward understanding through friction (contact and negotiation) enables the coproduction of ethnographic knowledge.

By positioning myself as an expert on students' future academic literacies and attending to their present practices against the backdrop of these futures, I was, perhaps, also positioning myself outside the scenes of literacy I observed. While I would have denied the position of distant and objective observer at any point in the project, this is how most students—accustomed to a culture of educational surveillance—must have initially perceived me. And reciprocity in research means, in part, that you don't get to settle the matter of your own roles (Powell and Takayoshi 2003). As long as students had no need or desire to understand what I was doing in their classrooms and as long as I approached their places and practices as given, there would be little opportunity for the contact and negotiation across differences essential to ethnographic knowledge production.[5] Fortunately for the project and unfortunately for students and teachers, these stabilities and distances were short lived.[6] Like a busted pipe that forces attention to flows of water constantly coursing to and through a building, a major institutional upheaval soon disrupted all of our routines, assemblages, and perceptions.

When I began research at Hughes, the school was awaiting the results of an audit conducted the year before by the Kentucky Department of Education because its reading and math proficiency scores on core content standardized tests were among the lowest in the state. Very little was said about this audit in my first four months at the school. For most teachers and students, the process was remembered, distantly, as one of many bureaucratic hoops extending behind and before them. But early in the spring term, the state released the results of its assessment, and they were worse than anyone at the school anticipated. So much worse that JCPS's superintendent invoked Kentucky House Bill 176 to declare "a state of emergency" at Hughes. Among other things, this initiated the replacement of the school's principal and the relocation of many members of the faculty and staff.[7] While I discuss the details and consequences of this ruling at more length in the next chapter, here I want to emphasize the ways in which this measure of insufficient progress for students, teachers, and administrators highlighted the precarity of assemblages constituting the school and connecting it to "networks of practice extending beyond" (Nespor 1997). As Tsing (2015) suggests, thinking through precarity opened up possibilities for seeing literacy practices differently, as tracing and charting paths knotted together at particular junctures, places of multiplicity and heterogeneity in and out of school (Ingold 2009, Massey 2005).

This perceptual shift and gradual reconceptualization (ongoing through this process of writing) was due, in large part, to the relentless future orientation of educational reform initiatives critiqued in the previous chapter. The forceful and systematic imposition of future geographies on the minds, practices, and material spaces of students and teachers was a major component of the school's post-audit reform. Beginning in the spring term after the audit and growing in intensity through the following academic year, *rhetorics of readiness* proliferated as state officials pushed school administrators to increase efforts to promote and implement newly devised Common Core State Standards. For school officials, the precarity of the present demanded a more clearly delineated future. The standards provide the discourse of this singular future, a plan for progress towards it, and the means to measure this progress.

As doubts and fears surrounding concerns of "college and career readiness" spread from administrative offices to classrooms, hallways, local media outlets, and dining room tables, more and more students called on me to share my knowledge of the post-secondary scenes of literacy they were apparently unprepared to join. The more students asked me to map the geographies of their futures, the more I was confronted with my inability to do so. Despite my own experiences as a college writing instructor, I could not anticipate the scenes of literacy they would encounter in their own versions of college or compare the demands of these scenes to standards of readiness promoted by the Common Core. For me, the certainty and specificity of the future conjured by the standards highlighted the impossibility of making such predictions. And so a collision of messages and measures of readiness, student apprehensions about their futures beyond high school, and my inability to detail these futures generated questions about representations and realities of the future and the mobilities they demanded and denied. How were students projecting themselves and how were they being projected into future scenes of literacy? How were their literacies and mobilities in the present shaped by and shaping these projections?

The pursuit of these questions required a methodological shift from intensive investigations of single sites to an ethnographic approach attentive to circulations within and across multiple places in progress. If pathways connecting secondary and post-secondary scenes of literacy did not preexist the mobilities of people, objects, ideas, and information constituting them, I would need a mode of ethnography designed to trace these paths through associations among sites of high school and college. As Leander et al. (2010) assert, "In empirical work leading to theory building, a more fully relational perspective on mobility and learning will only come into being to the extent that specific relations are followed, traced, and analyzed" (p. 335). I've found frames and methods for such empirical work in the research imaginaries of multi-sited ethnography and mobility studies.

Multi-sited, Mobile Ethnography

Growing out of a world-system framework (Wolf 1982, Wallerstein 1991) and anthropology's *Writing Culture* project of the mid-1980s (Clifford and Marcus 1986), multi-sited ethnography engages cultural dispersions and disjunctures of globalization and late capitalism by moving "out from the single sites and local situations of conventional ethnographic research designs to examine the circulation of cultural meanings, objects, and identities in diffuse time-space" (Marcus 1998, p. 79). By tracing cultural formations within and across specific locations, ethnographers working in this tradition map relationships among sites of research. While these maps suggest aspects of larger systems, the goal of the research is not holistic representation. As anthropologist George Marcus (1998) asserts, "There is no global in the local-global contrast now so frequently evoked. The global is an emergent dimension of arguing about the connection among sites in a multi-sited ethnography" (p. 83). By tracing circulations that build and maintain these connections, the ethnographer seeks to better understand the lifeworlds of participants and aspects of a system constituted through their intertwined mobilities.

As suggested above, the upheaval at Hughes in many ways compelled my own multi-sited approach by highlighting the fragility and disposability of alignments and programs previously trusted to transport students from high school to college. The abrupt removal of standards, curricula, and people and the imposition of others forced my participants and me to confront the indeterminacy of schooling in both the present and the future.[8] Once oriented to indeterminacy and precarity, our work together began to turn up too many concurrent and competing trajectories across scenes of literacy and institutions to ignore or explain with stair-stepped models of unified progress-time. It became impossible to separate movements from high school to college from movements across classrooms; personal and institutional histories; nations, states, and cities; media- and technoscapes; languages and identities. Through the lens of precarity, my participants and I began to see these entangled mobilities as constantly forming and reforming emergent systems of education.

Nespor (2004) emphasizes the importance of scale-making to the emergence of such systems. Following human geographers, he describes educational scales as spatial and temporal orders generated as students (and teachers) "move—not just physically, but in the form of representations such as grades, test scores, reports, and evaluations—detach themselves (or are separated) from certain locations, circulate (or are circulated) through others, and finally assemble (or are accumulated) at certain sites" (pp. 309–310). In this sense, scales are not static frames of reference moving up or out from micro to macro, local to global. Rather, like places, they are historically negotiated, sometimes extended and sometimes condensed by patterns of movement across space-time.

Expanding and politicizing Ingold's conceptualization of pathways discussed in the previous chapter, Nespor's notion of scaling emphasizes the simultaneity of lifepaths along with their differences in expanse, durability, and temporality. When a student is bused to one school rather than another, tracked into remedial or advanced courses, labeled "gifted," "at risk," or "limited English proficiency," they are moving and being moved across multiple, overlapping scales. And when they work across tracks, languages, subject positions, histories of participation, and digital networks, they are extending, layering, and re-making scales. Whether transgressive or compliant, forced or chosen, their material, representational, and embodied (im)mobilities make and remake educational scales. And their identities are assumed, prescribed, and developed in accordance with and across these scales. "Educational scales are thus 'envelopes of spacetime' (Massey 1999, p. 22) into which certain identities (but not others) can be folded." This makes scale both an object and a means of power (Nespor 2004, p. 310).

Nespor identifies five aspects of educational scale-making. First, scales are made through the production and circulation of artifacts—textbooks, student essays, teaching materials, curricula, standards, test scores, grade point averages, and so on (p. 310). Second, they are products of the spatial arcs and temporal rhythms shaping and shaped by students' movements to, through, and around schools. Neighborhood boundaries, daily commutes, course schedules, seating charts, academic calendars, and school facilities scale education in particular ways. Third, scales are defined by distributions of people and objects across space-time. We are always entangled with other people and objects across multiple and concurrent environments through our *historical bodies* (discussed in more detail below). By bringing bodies into contact with each other, schooling grants access, however limited, to a multitude of times and places. Fourth, educational scale is defined, in part, by the ways in which official representations of education foreground some student and teacher practices and identities and erase or suppress others. This measure of scaling was especially pronounced at Hughes as reform efforts included a rebranding campaign that fronted forward-looking, future-oriented initiatives and students and suppressed or punished transgressions that brought school-based places and practices into contact with places and practices outside of school.[9] Fifth, and finally, Nespor asserts that educational scales are created when students and teachers "calibrate" or make sense of school-based events, experiences, and identities in light of events, experiences, and identities elsewhere. This process of calibration is always ongoing as the "meanings of teaching and learning . . . are shaped by events and spacetimes outside the classroom; and changes in these alter the conditions and possibilities of schooling" (Nespor 2004, p. 313). As cities, neighborhoods, systems of transportation, households, work schedules, and social networks change, so do the natures of teaching and learning.

I find Nespor's breakdown of educational scale-making useful for materializing a multi-sited ethnography because it concretizes the simultaneity of scales constituting and extending educational systems and thereby provides a framework for considering ways students move and are moved across concurrent scales. From seats in classrooms to seats on school buses, when moving across grade levels and institutions or digital networks, students are always participating in multiple overlapping and diverging scales. The only way to trace these scales, their interconnections, and the systems they articulate is to follow the patterns of movement that make and maintain them.

Marcus offers a number of techniques for following the movements of people, things, and ideas, but not all of them require researchers to move with participants or objects of study. In fact, while multi-sited ethnography is a valuable methodology for imagining and mapping relations across sites of research, it can tend to focus on destinations rather than on the mobilities connecting and constituting them. In this way a multi-sited ethnography is not always a mobile ethnography. As Ingold and Jo Lee Vergunst (2008) assert, "Even multi-sited fieldwork (Marcus 1998) focuses on the sites themselves, as though life were lived at a scatter of fixed locales rather than along the highways and byways upon which they lie" (p. 3). As I asserted in the previous chapter, to account for entanglements of material, representational, and embodied mobilities, literacy ethnographers must work at the interface between mobile physical bodies and representations of mobility. Such work not only requires participating in patterns of movement while conducting research, but also attending to embodied experiences of movement and accounting for knowledges coproduced on the move.

The current study takes up this work through a method Marcus (1998) identifies as the most obvious and conventional approach to multi-sited ethnography: "following the people." His description of the procedure is unsurprising: "to follow and stay with the movements of a particular group of initial subjects" (p. 90). While I take up this method for reasons Marcus proposes—to trace connections among scenes of literacy in high school, college, and everyday life—I also move with research participants to better understand relations between their everyday literacies and embodied mobilities. Developing this understanding with students requires attention to the ways in which literacies and (im)mobilities within and across places are conditioned by historical bodies.

Ron and Suzie Scollon (2004) describe the historical body as an individual's "life experiences, their goals or purposes, and their unconscious ways of behaving and thinking" (p. 46). Concordant in many ways with Pierre Bourdieu's (1991) notion of *habitus*, the concept of the historical body situates memories, experiences, skills, and capacities more precisely in the individual body and thus accords with the theory of embodied knowledge presented in the previous chapter. As Blommaert and April Huang (2009) assert: "Participants in social action bring their real bodies into play, but their bodies are semiotically enskilled: their movements and positions are central to the production of meaning, and are organized around normative patterns of conduct" (p. 275). For example, the students participating in this study have long been accustomed to systems of education, the layouts of school buildings and classrooms, interactions with classmates and teachers, and the discourses that justify and organize their work. This familiarity enables them to adequately navigate educational spaces; they know where and when to go, what kinds of activities to engage in when they get there, and how to perform these activities. Their historical bodies have been formed in ways that make them recognizable as students and in ways that habituate and routinize most of their practices (Blommaert and Huang 2009, p. 274). Moreover, students bring their historical bodies into play, as we have seen, in dynamic and emergent places. The patterns of mobility that constitute these places contribute to an accumulated history of normative expectations, and accommodating and/or resisting such histories is part of the process that builds a historical body. In this way, historical bodies and places are mutually constitutive: We become enskilled through our participation in social and material places, and the histories of participation we bring to these places contribute to the practices that constitute them.

The Scollons's notion of the historical body offers a powerful frame for observing and analyzing cultural knowledges embedded in micro-bodily movements. The concept draws our attention to associations made in the movement of a head to a desk or a hand into the air. It helps us consider the cultural knowledges presencing in a student's route through a school or city and in their stoppages through an assignment. Reflecting on our own historical bodies can help us better understand why we tune into or out of certain conversations or gravitate toward some student-participants rather than others. To attend to convergences of literacies and mobilities, it is not enough to consider traces of mobility in texts or in discursive representations of movement; rather, mobile literacy ethnography requires attention to the ways in which historical bodies influence more-than-representational doings of mobility.

To materialize and systematize our attention to entangled literacies and mobilities, my participants and I employed a number of mobile methods over the course of this project. I met all participants in the English classes where I served as a tutor-researcher. Students were selected from each course according to their expressed interest in the study, their age (eighteen years or older for purposes of consent), and their college or career plans after graduation. I did not turn away any student interested in participating. This openness resulted in a group of participants with significant differences across lines of race, gender, class, language, ability, and nationality.

While the accounts presented in the following chapters draw upon research conducted with three high school English teachers and eleven students, the core of the study was developed in collaboration with three students from Hughes's class of 2012, who continued with the project in the years following their high school graduations.[10] In addition to continuing participant-observation in the English classes introduced above, conducting interviews, and collecting student and teacher texts from these classes, I began to attend more closely to the practices of these three participants. To better understand how these students connected literacies and identities across places and scales, I traced their patterns of movement in classes, traveled with them to school and work in cars and on buses, walked with them through hallways and across campuses, and navigated digital environments alongside them. The methods described below emerged from my movements with these students.

Mapping Multi-scalar Mobilities

The task of tracing relationships formed by traversals within and across far-flung scales presents considerable challenges for this study and for multi-sited ethnography in general; the greatest of these being the very complexity it works to understand and represent. Considering the irreducible complexity of associations assembled through students' mobile practices, I've grappled with how to avoid the futility of the cartographers in Jorge Luis Borges's "Del rigor en la ciencia," who strike a "Map of the Empire whose size was that of the Empire." The decision to work closely with a small group of students opened up possibilities for methods of tracing material mobilities that could avoid producing maps too cumbersome to be useful.

While methods of "time-space mapping" (Kwan 2002, Reynolds 2004, Kenyon 2006, Ivanič et al. 2009) would be insufficient for attending to representational and embodied mobilities or relations of power shaping these, they would prove useful for tracing material patterns of movement within, around, and between institutions. By producing time-space maps and using them as elicitation materials in interviews, my participants and I discovered ways in which mobile literacies extended through histories of participation and scenes in and out of school. Mapping also helped us develop understandings of how patterns of movement through the city and school shaped perceptions and experiences of academic literacies in the present (at the time of the study) and projections of possible futures. We used methods of mapping in two ways: to track patterns of movement in classrooms and to chart daily travels to, from, and through schools.

I began experimenting with time-space mapping as a method of classroom observation soon after Hughes's restructuring process began. In contrast to the static sketch of the regular English class presented above, time-space maps track circulations of bodies and texts around classrooms; patterns of interactions between students, teachers, and objects; and the timing of these interactions. The sketch presented below in Figure 2.2 traces the bodily and textual movements of one research participant, Katherine, over the course of a single period of Advanced Placement Literature and Composition.

Students in this class are arranged in a circle to encourage open discussion, and the teacher (represented as a circle herself) assumes a position alongside the students. I've drawn a box around the "X" marking Katherine, and I've represented myself with a triangle. After a brief full-class discussion of a previously introduced essay assignment (a comparative analysis of Oscar Wilde's *The Picture of Dorian Gray* and Albert Lewin's 1945 film adaptation of the novel), the period is devoted to drafting and workshopping student essays. The dotted lines in the sketch designate the trajectories of Katherine's essay draft, hand-delivered in sections to peer reviewers (and myself) in exchange for portions of their essays. The solid lines designate her continual movements across the room to confer with the teacher and to consult a stack of writing guides and reference books. Each line is marked with the temporal window in which these exchanges occurred.

Like every map (even Borges's), this one misses most of the practices constituting the scene. Katherine's micro-bodily movements are not represented, nor are the representations of mobility—assumptions, expectations, perceptions, and desires—conditioning her practice. The map does not show her embodied experiences of movement—the anxiety and support she feels as she moves toward the teacher, the frustration and boredom of thumbing through an MLA style guide, the pleasure and vulnerability of exchanging texts and ideas with class-mates, or the restlessness of sitting still. As participant-observer, I tried to capture

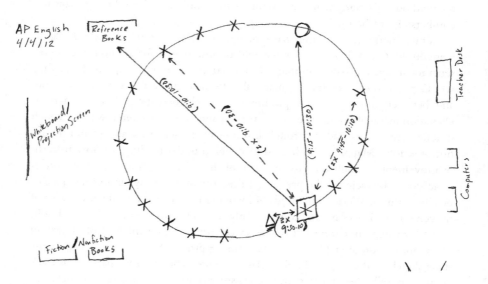

FIGURE 2.2 Image of Fieldnote, Time-Space Mapping

what I could of these entangled mobilities in fieldnotes, follow-up interviews, photographs, and in the collection of artifacts, but, of course, these methods also fall well short of a "full picture."

Despite their shortcomings, time-space maps did turn up significant patterns of mobility over time. Like the maps of transport planners, sketches of classroom activity highlighted the importance of quotidian routines, participants' allocations of time, and access to and usage of materials. Aggregating the content of these maps also revealed sometimes unlikely student relationships formed through ongoing collaborations across time and space. Tracing the threads of these collaborations became a central concern of the project, demonstrated most clearly in Chapter 4.

In addition to mapping participants' material movements within classes, I asked them to keep a time-space log of movements (at least, those they were comfortable sharing) through the school and city. These logs consisted of five rows designating school days and two columns, one to record locations and another to record times. Participants kept these logs, with mixed results, over the course of two weeks— one week devoted to movements through the school and one to movements through the city. During follow-up interviews, participants and I geo-referenced locations on existing school and city maps and traced movements between locations over time. While this method of time-space mapping was overly demanding for students whose daily lives were already filled with paper forms and activity reports, the maps did reveal material patterns of movement through and spatial uses of the school and city that were surprising for students and myself.[11] For instance, we were startled by the distance and variable timing of daily commutes to school. While participants felt the toll of these commutes in their bodies and frequently expressed frustration over inadequate transportation, mapping them out gave us all a greater sense of the difficulty and significance of traveling to, from, and through the school and the impact of these mobilities on educational practices and opportunities. As Nespor (2004) suggests, methods of mapping helped us consider how structures of schooling are not only defined by scales of standardized curricula, testing regimes, school division policies, or even school-specific pedagogical programs, but also by itineraries within and across classrooms, schools, and neighborhoods that stretch educational structures out in time and space (p. 323). In this way, methods of time-space mapping helped me identify and temporarily join itineraries or patterns of movement that seemed particularly consequential to students' experiences and practices of academic literacy.

Moving with People and Texts

While they suggested paths to follow throughout the project, methods of time-space mapping didn't precede my participation in students' patterns of movement. In fact, I was introduced to the affordances of mobile interviewing and observing entirely by accident. While research in education and the social sciences has for some time been trending in the direction of more dynamic and place-sensitive interviewing and observation techniques (Elwood and Martin 2000, Kusenbach 2003, Lee and Ingold 2006, Leander and Rowe 2006, Pink 2009, Evans and Jones 2011, Leander and Boldt 2013), research in the humanities has remained largely text-based and sedentary. As an inheritor of this tradition, the possibility of "shadowing" students' movements had not occurred to me.

Fortunately, my research participants did not share my disciplinary blinders. After trying in vain for weeks to arrange meetings with students in the safe interview space of the school library, one participant finally admitted that he was likely never going to have time to sit for an interview during or after school. Between class and work schedules, extracurricular activities, and family obligations, he seldom had time to himself. As a consolation, he invited me to join him on the city bus. Out of desperation, I accepted. As we began to ride the bus together on a regular basis, we recognized the value of mobile interviewing and participant-observation for describing and understanding entanglements of mobility and literacy. And I began implementing these methods in research with other students.

In her of study of urban mobility in Santiago de Chile, Paola Jirón (2011) describes her movements with research participants in terms of shadowing: "Shadowing involves accompanying the participants individually on their daily routines, observing the way the participants organise and experience their journeys, sharing and collaboratively reflecting on their experience on the move" (p. 42). Jirón demonstrates how accompanying travelers helped her better under-stand the effects of daily commutes on historical bodies, how "the complexity of changing transport modes, of climbing on and off buses, of body pressing against body, getting lost, feeling scared or disoriented, being fondled, robbed or amused" leaves traces on bodies and mental and emotional lives (p. 42). In this way, she presents shadowing as a method for investigating relations between embodied and representational mobilities. Shadowing provides her glimpses into the ways people experience and navigate social and cultural landscapes as well as material environments.

Like Jirón, I've found shadowing to be a valuable method for attending to the entangled literacies and mobilities that propel students not only through their daily commutes to and from school, but also between classes, down hallways, across campuses and digital networks. From discussion board posts drafted on mobile phones while riding the bus and text messages sent to employers from school hallways, to college applications completed with parents and siblings at kitchen tables, shadowing participants revealed multiple and diverse ways in which literacies intertwine with material, representational, and embodied mobilities across space and time. In this way, methods of shadowing married mobility and per-ception in ways that enabled my participants and me to see and think differently about literacy practices.

Moreover, shadowing proved to be an invaluable method for tracing "text trajectories" across space-time. As Catherine Kell (2013) asserts, "mobility is not necessarily only connected with people moving, but with the semiotic resources they have to project their meanings across contexts, in which case it is the texts they create and project that are mobile" (p. 9). Through written texts and other modes and tools of communication—speech, visuals, gestures, computers, pencils, etc.—people project meaning-making within and across places. Kell proposes that by following these trajectories ethnographically across at least some of their sequences, we might better understand multi-scalar dimensions of literacy practice (pp. 20–21). By following trajectories of students and their texts across classrooms, school buses, inboxes, smartphones, teacher's desks, and portfolios, I attempt to show how the meanings they project are translated across places and audiences according to the values and expectations of different educational scales. This process of shadowing also reveals ways in which multiple text trajectories—academic essays, text messages, facebook threads, and so on—intersect and interact to create meshworks of meaning-making extending across space-time.

I shadowed participants in three ways over the course of the project. First, I followed each of the three students in my smaller group of participants for a single day from their homes to school, between classes, to work or extracurricular activities, and back home. During these shadowing sessions I conducted informal interviews with students about their experiences of daily travel to, from, and through school and work and about the literacy practices that accompanied, occasioned, and shaped this travel. In semi-private and quiet settings (e.g. buses, cars, and study halls), I recorded these conversations. In more public settings (classrooms, lunchrooms, hallways, workplaces, etc.), I observed, kept fieldnotes, and participated in conversations and activities when invited. Second, I joined one participant, Nadif, on a city bus ride from Hughes to the university once a week for several months. Over the course of these shared rides, Nadif and I developed what Theresa Lillis (2001) calls a "long conversation." Individual sessions covered a range of discussion topics from histories of participation to current assignments and plans for the future. I recorded these discussions and composed "talkback sheets" from the transcripts (Lillis 2001, p. 147). These sheets reflected my attempts to bring Nadif's concerns and interests to the center of subsequent discussions and thereby *lengthen* our conversation. Finally, I followed two participants from their bus stops on the south side of Louisville to Hughes on three occasions over the course of a single week. During these 30- to 45-minute rides, I quietly observed and took notes, which I used to prompt discussion in follow-up interviews. These shared bus rides produced much of the ethnographic knowledge presented in Chapter 4.

A Final Note on Ethnographic Knowledge

Frictions enabling movement toward ethnographic knowledge are especially pronounced in multi-sited, mobile ethnography, as shared movements within and across places and times involve a perpetual transformation of subjectivities and relations of power. Participation in these shifting assemblages required me to continuously reexamine my own positions and desires and the social, cultural, and personal forces and ideological structures (re)shaping them. Over the course of the study, my roles as tutor, researcher, instructor, advisor, advocate, friend, institutional outsider, and institutional agent diverge and overlap in accordance with the changing subjectivities of the students I follow. In some moments and stages of the research process, students conceive of me as an authority of academic literacy, and in others participants approach me as a student, ignorant of their literacy experiences in and out of school. As you can imagine, my own movement between poles of authority and ignorance provokes a range of participant responses. From positions of generosity to dependency, frustration, dismissal and resentment, my and my participants' subjectivities and attendant practices and emotions constitute a complex meshwork of power relations in perpetual flux. The following chapters reveal ways in which my participants, myself, and our understandings are shaped and reshaped through an ongoing process of negotiation.

In the next chapter, I flesh out the mobility narratives of the three participants discussed above. I begin with the narrative of Nadif, a high school senior and first-generation Somali immigrant. Nadif's story of movement from the world's largest refugee camp in Dadaab, Kenya to a "failing" public high school in the United States and eventually through his first year at a metropolitan research university helps to flesh out an understanding of literacy as mobile practice. I then employ this framework to read the mobility narratives of two of Nadif's high school classmates: James, an African American student seeking full-time employment after his access to higher education is blocked by a number of institutional and economic barriers; and Katherine, a second-generation Mexican American honors student who struggles to reconcile the disjunctions between her preconceptions, experiences, and projections of academic literacies and career aspirations as she moves from high school through her first year at community college. The stories of these students' intersecting and diverging trajectories reveal ways in which institutionalized constructs of college and career are reproduced and transformed in their language and literacy practices.

Notes

1 In addition to reducing the complexity of literacy practices associated with K-12 education, this representation perpetuates the false assumption that most students enter college immediately after high school. In reality, only 5 percent of students enrolled in American higher education attend college within a year of graduating from high school. According to Clay Shirky, "the bulk of students today are in their mid-20s or older, enrolled at a community or commuter school, and working towards a degree they will take too long to complete. One in three won't complete, ever. Of the rest, two in three will leave in debt" (Friedersdorf 2016).

2 See Bartholomae 1986, Beaufort 1999, 2007, Carroll 2002, Curtis and Herrington 2000, 2003, Haswell 1991, Patterson and Duer 2006.

3 I discuss the proliferation of these "reminders of the future" in more detail in subsequent chapters.

4 I began working as a tutor in these three classes in October 2010. After receiving IRB approval, the official study began in February of 2011. In addition to keeping up with the trajectories of graduating seniors, I returned to Hughes for the 2011/12 academic year and worked with graduating seniors through the 2012/13 academic year.

5 In hindsight, I recognize that what students initially needed more than predictions of their futures was attention to and validation of their work in the present. While they were open to sharing and receiving feedback on their present writing in the early stages of the project, they were not as interested in possible relations between academic literacies in high school and college.

6 Another friction propelling the ethnographic process is that struggles and hardships of participants are often translated into lines of inquiry by the ethnographer. While working together on and around these struggles/inquiries can be mutually beneficial, such acts of translation inevitably lead to misunderstandings, disappointments, and conflicts. To ignore or deny these conflicts is to ignore or deny the power dynamics and hierarchical relationships shaping communications among researchers and participants.

7 I assume that I would have not been granted access to the school had this ruling been made a few months earlier.

8 Sadly, the teachers I worked with were much more accustomed to this indeterminacy.

9 The account of erasure and discipline surrounding the "Urban Survival Guide" presented in Chapter 3 is a case in point.

10 Details of these student's lives are introduced through the intersecting and diverging mobility narratives that fill the following chapters. A table providing demographic information for participants not introduced in the following chapters is included in Appendix A.

11 I have since experimented using GPS technology to trace movements through space and time, also with mixed results. For more on mapping through locative media see Gordon and de Souza e Silva (2011).

References

Bartholomae, D. (1986). Inventing the university. *Journal of Basic Writing*, 5(1), 4–23.

Beaufort, A. (1999). *Writing in the real world: Making the transition from school to work*. New York: Teachers College Press.

Beaufort, A. (2007). *College writing and beyond: A new framework for university writing instruction*. Logan: Utah State University Press.

Blommaert, J. (2009). Ethnography and democracy: Hymes's political theory of language. *Text and Talk: An Interdisciplinary Journal of Language, Discourse and Communication Studies*, 29(3), 257–276.

Blommaert, J., & Huang, A. (2009). Historical bodies and historical space. *Journal of Applied Linguistics*, 6(3), 267–282.

Blommaert, J. (2010). *The sociolinguistics of globalization*. New York: Cambridge University Press.

Bourdieu, P. (1991). *Language and symbolic power*. Cambridge, MA: Harvard University Press.

Brandt, D., & Clinton, K. (2002). Limits of the local: Expanding perspectives on literacy as a social practice. *Journal of Literacy Research*, 34(3), 337–356.

Büscher, M., Urry, J., & Witchger, K. (Eds.). (2011). *Mobile methods*. New York: Routledge.

Carroll, L. A. (2002). *Rehearsing new roles: How college students develop as writers*. Carbondale: Southern Illinois University Press.

Clifford, J., & Marcus, G. E. (Eds.). (1986). *Writing culture: The poetics and politics of ethnography.* Berkeley: University of California Press.

Cresswell, T. (2010). Towards a politics of mobility. *Environment and Planning D: Society and Space, 28*(1), 17–31.

Curtis, M., & Herrington, A. (2000). *Persons in process: Four stories of writing and personal development in college.* Urbana, IL: NCTE.

Curtis, M., & Herrington, A. (2003). Writing development in the college years: By whose definition? *College Composition and Communication, 55*(1), 69–90.

Elwood, S. A., & Martin, D. G. (2000). "Placing" interviews: Location and scales of power in qualitative research. *The Professional Geographer, 52*(4), 649–657.

Evans, J., & Jones, P. (2011). The walking interview: Methodology, mobility and place. *Applied Geography, 31*(2), 849–858. http://doi.org/10.1016/j.apgeog.2010.09.005.

Fabian, J. (2001). *Anthropology with an attitude: Critical essays.* Stanford, CA: Stanford University Press.

Friedersdorf, C. (2016). The typical college student is not who you think it is. *The Atlantic.* Retrieved from www.theatlantic.com/education/archive/2016/07/the-typical-college-student-is-not-who-you-think-it-is/489824/?utm_source=atlfb. Accessed July 2016.

Gee, J. P. (1990). *Social linguistics and literacies: Ideology in discourses.* London: Falmer Press.

Gordon, E., & Silva, A. de S. e. (2011). *Net locality: Why location matters in a networked world.* Malden, MA: Wiley-Blackwell.

Harris, J. (1989). The idea of community in the study of writing. *College Composition and Communication, 40*(1), 11–22.

Haswell, R. H. (1991). *Gaining ground in college writing: Tales of development and interpretation.* Dallas, TX: Southern Methodist University Press.

Heath, S. B. (1983). *Ways with words: Language, life, and work in communities and classrooms.* New York: Cambridge University Press.

Hymes, D. H. (1974). *Foundations in sociolinguistics: An ethnographic approach.* Philadephia: University of Pennsylvania Press.

Hymes, D. (Ed.). (2010). *Foundations in sociolinguistics: An ethnographic approach.* London: Routledge.

Ingold, T., & Vergunst, J. L. (Eds.). (2008). *Ways of walking: Ethnography and practice on foot.* New York: Routledge.

Ingold, T. (2009). Against space: Place, movement, knowledge. In P. W. Kirby. *Boundless worlds: An anthropological approach to movement.* Oxford: Berghahn Books, 29–43.

Ivanič, R., Edwards, R., Barton, D., Martin-Jones, M., Fowler, Z., Hughes, B., . . . Smith, J. (2009). *Improving learning in college: Rethinking literacies across the curriculum.* London: Routledge.

Jefferson County Public Schools. (n.d.) *2012–2013 Data Books.* Division Data Management, Planning and Program Evaluation. Retrieved August 31, 2016, from http://assessment. jefferson.kyschools.us/DataBooks1213/High_Data_Book.html.

Jirón, P. (2011). On becoming the shadow. In M. Büscher, J. Urry, & K. Witchger (Eds.). *Mobile methods* (pp. 36–53). New York: Routledge.

Kell, C. (2009). Literacy practices, text/s and meaning making across time and space. In M. Prinsloo & M. Baynham. *The future of literacy studies* (pp. 75–99). New York: Palgrave.

Kell, C. (2011). Inequalities and crossings: Literacy and the spaces-in-between. *International Journal of Educational Development, 31*(6), 606–613.

Kell, C. (2013). Ariadne's thread: Literacy, scale, and meaning-making across space and time. *Working Papers in Urban Language and Literacies, 118*, 1–24.

Kellman, P. J., & Shipley, T. F. (1992). Perceiving objects across gaps in space and time. *Current Directions in Psychological Science, 1*(6), 193–199.

Kenyon, S. (2006). Reshaping patterns of mobility and social exclusion? The impact of virtual mobility upon accessibility, mobility and social exclusion. In M. Sheller, & J. Urry (Eds.). *Mobile technologies of the city* (pp. 102–120). London: Routledge.

Kusenbach, M. (2003). Street phenomenology: The go-along as ethnographic research tool. *Ethnography, 4*(3), 455–485.

Kwan, M. P. (2002). Feminist visualization: Re-envisioning GIS as a method in feminist geographic research. *Annals of the Association of American Geographers, 92*(4), 645–661.

Latour, B. (2005). *Reassembling the social: An introduction to actor-network theory.* Oxford: Oxford University Press.

Lave, J., & Wenger, E. (1991). *Situated learning: Legitimate peripheral participation.* New York: Cambridge University Press.

Law, J., & Urry, J. (2004). Enacting the social. *Economy and Society, 33*(3), 390–410.

Leander, K. M., & Rowe, D. W. (2006). Mapping literacy spaces in motion: A rhizomatic analysis of a classroom literacy performance. *Reading Research Quarterly, 41*, 428–460.

Leander, K. M., Phillips, N. C., & Taylor, K. H. (2010). The changing social spaces of learning: Mapping new mobilities. *Review of Research in Education, 34*(1), 329–394.

Leander, K. M., & Boldt, G. (2013). Rereading "A pedagogy of multiliteracies": Bodies, texts, and emergence. *Journal of Literacy Research, 45*(1), 22–46.

Lee, J., & Ingold, T. (2006). Fieldwork on foot: Perceiving, routing, socializing. In S. Coleman, & P. Collins (Eds.). *Locating the field: Space, place and context in anthropology* (pp. 67–86). Palo Alto, CA: Ebrary.

Lillis, T. M. (2001). *Student writing: Access, regulation, desire.* New York: Routledge.

Marcus, G. E. (1998). *Ethnography through thick and thin.* Princeton, NJ: Princeton University Press.

Massey, D. B. (1994). *Space, place, and gender.* Minneapolis: University of Minnesota Press.

Massey, D. B. (1999). *Power-geometries and the politics of space-time.* Heidelberg: Department of Geography, University of Heidelberg.

Massey, D. B. (2005). *For space.* London: Sage.

National Governors Association Center for Best Practices, & Council of Chief State School Officers. (n.d.). *Common core state standards.* Common Core Standards Initiative. Retrieved from www.corestandards.org/. Accessed September 2011.

Nespor, J. (1997). *Tangled up in school: Politics, space, bodies, and signs in the educational process.* New York: Routledge.

Nespor, J. (2004). Educational scale-making. *Pedagogy, Culture and Society, 12*(3), 309–326.

Patterson, J. P., & Duer, D. (2006). High school teaching and college expectations in writing and reading. *English Journal, High School Edition, 95*(3), 81–87.

Pennycook, A. (2010). *Language as a local practice.* New York: Routledge.

Pink, S. (2009). *Doing sensory ethnography.* Thousand Oaks, CA: Sage.

Powell, K. M., & Takayoshi, P. (2003). Accepting roles created for us: The ethics of reciprocity. *College Composition and Communication, 54*(3), 394–422.

Ramachandran, V. S., & Rogers-Ramachandran, D. (2010). Reading between the lines: How we see hidden objects. *Scientific American.* Retrieved from www.scientificamerican.com/article/reading-between-the-lines/. Accessed October 2015.

Reynolds, N. (2004). *Geographies of writing: Inhabiting places and encountering difference.* Carbondale: Southern Illinois University Press.

Scollon, R., & Scollon, S. W. (2004). *Nexus analysis: Discourse and the emerging internet.* New York: Routledge.

Sheller, M., & Urry, J. (2006). The new mobilities paradigm. *Environment and Planning A, 38*(2), 207–226.

Sheller, M. (2014). The new mobilities paradigm for a live sociology. *Current Sociology, 62*(6), 789–811.

Sommers, N., & Saltz, L. (2004). The novice as expert: Writing the freshman year. *College Composition and Communication, 56*(1), 124–149.

Stilgoe, J. R. (1998). *Outside lies magic: Regaining history and awareness in everyday places.* New York: Walker and Co.

Tsing, A. L. (2015). *The mushroom at the end of the world: On the possibility of life in capitalist ruins.* Princeton, NJ: Princeton University Press.

Wallerstein, I. M. (1991). *Geopolitics and geoculture: Essays on the changing world-system.* New York: Cambridge University Press.

Williams, J. M. (1989). Two ways of thinking about growth: The problem of finding the right metaphor. In P. Maimon, B. F. Nodine, & F. W. O'Connor. *Thinking, reasoning, and writing* (pp. 245–255).New York: Longman.

Wolf, E. R. (1982). *Europe and the people without history.* Berkeley: University of California Press.

3

SCHOOL SYSTEMS OF (IM)MOBILITY

> If we want America to lead in the 21st century, nothing is more important than giving everyone the best education possible—from the day they start preschool to the day they start their career.
>
> (Barack Obama 2013)

While there is very little agreement among stakeholders concerning the causes of and solutions to problems with the U.S. education system, there is widespread agreement that the system is broken. Asserting that public education is well beyond repair in his opening remarks at the 2005 National Summit on High Schools, Bill Gates states:

> America's high schools are obsolete. By obsolete, I don't just mean that our high schools are broken, flawed, and under-funded—though a case could be made for every one of those points. By obsolete, I mean that our high schools—even when they're working exactly as designed—cannot teach our kids what they need to know today. Training the workforce of tomorrow with the high schools of today is like trying to teach kids about today's computers on a 50-year-old mainframe. It's the wrong tool for the wrong times.

To keep pace with the ever-accelerating *economy of tomorrow*, Gates insists we must smooth transitions and speed up processing times between stages and locations of education. Toward this end, the primary focus of the Gates Foundation's "Educational Pathways" project (2014) is "Improv[ing] transitions between preschool and elementary school, middle school and high school, and high school and college" (gatesfoundation).[1] President Obama agrees that streamlining and, when possible, collapsing stages of education is a key step to making sure every student has exposure to some form of post-secondary education.[2] Speaking about his "plan to make college more affordable," Obama (2013) asserts that if "a higher education is still the best ticket to upward mobility in America—and it is—then we've got to make sure it's within reach. We've got to make sure that we are improving economic mobility, not making it worse" (p. 6). For Obama, Gates, and other reformers, the key to closing achievement gaps, increasing economic opportunity, and ensuring and thriving democracy is shaping K–16 education into a more efficient and coherent *mobility system.*

In this chapter, I continue to investigate the complexity of students' material, representational, and embodied mobilities within and across scenes of literacy by considering the ways in which the bounded units of accountable space-time that sequence educational activities are arranged in *mobility systems* enabling and managing predictable repetitions of movement. I begin with an analysis of educational alignment initiatives to demonstrate how such systems are comprised of processes and materials that circulate people, objects, ideas, and information at various scales and speeds via a host of routeways (Urry 2007, p. 52). I then demonstrate the ways in which the most influential alignment initiative in the U.S., the Common Core State Standards, is implemented to exert control over the movements of students in and beyond high school. Finally, I show how following students' entangled literacies and mobilities can reveal frictions and agencies across routes despite this exertion of control. In other words, I point to evidences of *wayfaring* within and against systems designed for effective and efficient transport (Ingold 2009).

Choices within and among routeways represent the potential for movement or *motility*, which Vincent Kaufmann (2002) defines as "the way in which an individual appropriates what is possible in the domain of mobility and puts this potential to use for his or her activities" (p. 37). As discussed in Chapter 1, high motility provides opportunities for circulation, enhancing mobile-capital for some and diminishing it for others (Urry 2007, p. 52). While social scientists tend to look to fields of transportation and communication—bus routes, footpaths, networked computers, etc.—when considering the operations of mobility systems, conceiving of standardized education as a network of intersecting and adaptive mobility systems emphasizes the ways in which the institutional and individual needs and desires that drive these systems are located in processes and sustained by promises of mobility.

Pathways to Prosperity

The organization of schools as mobility systems is, perhaps, most evident in the increasingly widespread construction of pathways and pipelines, like Gates' above, aligning learning outcomes and assessments on primary, secondary, and tertiary levels of education with anticipated job opportunities and demands. The Lumina

Foundation's *A Path to Alignment* report lays out the neoliberal agenda of such initiatives:

> In today's global age—an era in which a well-educated citizenry is absolutely vital to economic success and social progress—a truly aligned education system has become all but indispensable. Without such a system, it will be next to impossible for us to forge the necessary human capital—the talent—that can power our economy and ensure a thriving democracy.
>
> (Conley and Gaston 2013, p. 2)

According to this appeal, a conflation of economic, social, and national progress depends upon the design of systems that can efficiently transport individuals "from the day they start preschool to the day they start their career" and thereby effectively transform them into human capital or, to borrow from Heidegger (1977), "standing-reserve." Students are convinced to undergo this transformation with a promise that as long as they are willing to be modeled by the needs of capital, they will be granted a secure place in the economic hierarchy. But such promises are not tenable in an era of late capitalism.

While educational credentials have become more and more relevant to one's life choices, we are long past the point when a college education can be presented as a reliable vehicle for social mobility (Blacker 2013, p. 243). As Samir Amin (2011) explains, "We speak highly of continuing education, which the rapidity of the transformation of productive systems imposes from now on. But this training is not designed to favour social mobility towards the top, with a few unusual exceptions." Amin goes on to assert that, at its best, continuing education staves off obsolescence (and unemployment); for today's workers, "additional knowledge and perhaps new knowledge is necessary to simply retain their place in the hierarchy" (p. 557).

Despite this reality, or more likely because of it, the quest for a unified educational system that can fulfill promises of prosperity has accelerated in the reign of neoliberalism. As the Lumina Foundation report makes clear, the objective of perpetual educational reform is the fabrication of knowledge workers and the enhancement of their productivity. Figure 3.1 demonstrates this streamlining and commodification of education in the form of a "Career Pathways" project sponsored by the U.S. Department of Education. To address concerns that "the education and skill levels of American youth and adults are not keeping pace with today's global economy" and to help achieve the Obama Administration's goal for the U.S. to have the "highest proportion of college graduates in the world by 2020," the Department of Education is investing heavily in articulation and alignment initiatives and working to support state and local efforts in their implementations (U.S. Department of Education 2015, p. 5). According to the *Jobs for the Future* report in which it is published, Figure 3.1 shows how "articulated pathways can make it far easier for youth and adults to advance through progressive levels of the education and training system *as quickly as possible*"; how such programs align with post-secondary education; how "progressive modules of education and training can align with *stackable credentials* and employment opportunities"; how "*on- and off-ramps* allow participants to *move easily* between the labor market and further education and training"; and how dual-enrollment and co-enrollment "can *accelerate* credential attainment" (U.S. Department of Education 2015, pp. 11–12).

In a system created in the image of an anticipated market and thus built for speed and versatility, knowledge and skills are contained and administered in "artificial boxes of time" that "bear no relationship to a task" (Heath and McLaughlin 1994, pp. 483-484). And thus education is valued solely by its potential payoff in the future. An individual who reaches the farthest target—graduating with a B.A. or B.S.—is supposedly prepared for life and work in *geographies of the future*.

For Bourdieu and Passeron (1977), in such depictions, "to be a student is to prepare oneself by study for an occupational future. [. . .] the action of studying is a means to an end which is external to it [. . .] present action takes on its full meaning only in terms of a future which the present prepares for it by preparing its own negation" (pp. 56–57). This negation of the value of educational work in the present also has the effect of temporally and spatially encapsulating the activities of schooling from other meaningful activities. Because linear progress in closed mobility systems is presented as the primary indicator of future

The Postsecondary Alignment of Programs of Study and Adult Career Pathways

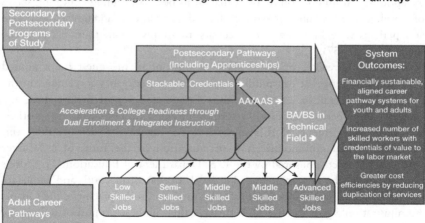

FIGURE 3.1 Postsecondary Alignment Chart, U.S. Department of Education

Source: United States Department of Education, Office of Career, Technical, and Adult Education. (2015). Advancing Career and Technical Education (CTE) in State and Local Career Pathways Project: *Jobs for the Future*. Washington, D.C.

achievement, the only literacies and mobilities of real value are the ones that supposedly measure potential for upward economic-social-cultural mobility. But as I've asserted elsewhere, this reduction of literacy education to exchange value disregards the complexity of associations assembled through mobile practice within and across scenes of literacy. Even the most future-oriented systems are shaped by *wayfaring* and *historical bodies*; that is, by perambulatory movements constituting places and by embodied memories, experiences, skills, and capacities (Ingold 2009, Scollon and Scollon 2004).

Of particular interest to me are the ways in which students' motilities are enhanced and diminished through interactions with(in) and exchanges across scenes of literacy and scales of education. For instance, like other participants in this project, Katherine, who I introduced in the previous chapter and will discuss at length in this one, participated in a number of co- and extracurricular literacy activities during her senior year of high school that influenced her perceptions of possibilities for moving through mobility systems of formal education. When I first met Katherine, she was teaching sign language to deaf children and their parents once a week at a local hearing and language academy and working at the law firm of a family friend, where she translated Spanish dictations into legal documents and correspondences in English. Over the course of our work together, Katherine and I became interested in the ways her practices in these seemingly separate scenes of literacy shaped her perceptions of linguistic and literate possibilities in high school and college and, in turn, her motility in these systems. While she readily associated her work in the law firm with her academic literacy practices and saw this work as contributing to her successful movement through high school, she actively attempted to disassociate her work with deaf students from her performances of academic identity in high school classes. As I explore later in this chapter, Katherine's own connections between workplace and academic literacies seemed to enhance her linear movement through the highly regulated mobility system of high school. However, her reluctance to connect language and literacy practices at the hearing and language academy with her academic literacies may have served to block choices for alternative trajectories, which, perhaps, also diminished her motility in these systems.

In an effort to trace such connections and demonstrate the complexity of students' movements within and among locations of high school, college, and work, the remainder of this chapter draws upon a range of data types—mobile observations and interviews, time-space maps, images and student texts—to represent three students' intersecting and diverging mobility narratives. Although they are necessarily limited, my hope is that the perspectives offered in these narratives demonstrate ways in which threads connecting scenes of literacy are constituted by entangled material, representational, and embodied mobilities. While they reveal ways in which educational and occupational mobility-systems endeavor for control and containment by enabling and imposing predictable repetitions of movement, these narratives also show how agency emerges through mobile literacies informed by past patterns of thought and action (historical bodies) and multiple possible futures.

Buying (and Selling) a Stairway to Heaven

Recognizing the complexity of student mobilities from high school to college and career works, in many ways, against the predominant assumptions and political projects of literacy scholarship and administration. Without the assumption of a self-evident and static paradigm for reading and writing in high school, it becomes difficult to define and facilitate transitions or "paradigm shifts" into college (Sommers and Saltz 2004, p. 140). And as I suggested in the previous chapter, our ongoing projects of institutional recognition and disciplinary differentiation continue to rely upon conceptualizations of transition from fixed points of departure to fixed points of arrival.

As previously discussed, my own tacit acceptance of singular trajectories connecting or, more accurately, separating high school and college almost prevented me from seeing and exploring the emergence and transformation of the scenes of literacy in which I participated. At the start of my research, this dynamism was especially difficult to perceive in high school because the linguistic and literate innovation of students and teachers was often obfuscated by the seemingly comprehensive control of national, state, district, and institutional literacy policy.

The reform efforts implemented as a result of the Kentucky Department of Education's (KDE) audit of Hughes (discussed in the previous chapter) enveloped the school in a web of surveillance as state officials collected test data, conducted classroom observations and interviewed faculty, staff, students, and parents. This "uninterrupted play of calculated gazes" worked from top to bottom—from state representatives to administrators, teachers and students—but also from bottom to top and laterally, as students were encouraged to indict their teachers, and teachers were encouraged to indict each other (Foucault 1977, p. 176). In the end, auditors identified five deficiencies in the school: poor classroom behavior; lack of academic rigor; unclear expectations for students, teachers, and administrators; misuse of resources; and insufficient guidance counseling.

These "findings" resulted in the replacement of the school's principal and the restaffing of its teachers. Teachers were required to reapply for their positions and, ultimately, 30 percent of them were relocated as a result of the audit. The teachers who remained were subjected to increasingly restrictive policy and oversight governing their teaching methods and objectives. While unions and contracts prevented the overt governance of classroom practices, newly appointed administrators wasted no time in exerting disciplinary power through "humble modalities" and "minor procedures"—unannounced observations, lesson plan templates, daily achievement reports, increased examinations—to measure and (re)train staff and students (Foucault 1977, p. 170).

Hughes' newly appointed principal, who started in the late spring of my first year at the school, was a member of a taskforce assembled and trained by the district to tighten administrative control in and, thereby, "turn around" low-performing schools. Along with other newly appointed administrators, she was trained to "understand, predict, monitor, halt, and transform corporate failure" (Kentucky Department of Education 2010, p. 1). Despite convincing evidence suggesting that "failing" schools are seldom successfully restructured by any of the remedies prescribed by No Child Left Behind (Ravitch 2010), JCPS officials implemented a "turnaround management" program to equip administrators of low-performing schools with strategies to increase reading and math proficiency rates on standardized tests, ensure students' readiness for college and career, and reduce dropout rates. Borrowing this program from two schools of business—Detroit-Mercy Graduate School of Business and the University of Virginia Darden School of Business—JCPS focused administrative efforts on "inspiring staff obsession with targets and goals," "tracking and communicating Performance Measures and Growth Metrics," providing "relentless supervision and support," and requiring "persistent debriefing" to ensure "collective efficacy" (Kentucky Department of Education 2010, p. 2).

In anticipation of Kentucky Senate Bill 1, requiring the implementation of a new assessment and accountability system by the following school year (2011/12), Hughes's principal was tasked with inspiring staff and student obsession with and tracking progress toward the targets and goals of the new Kentucky Core Academic Standards (KCAS). Identical to the National Governors Association and Council of Chief State School Officers' Common Core State Standards (CCS), the thrust of the Kentucky Core English Language Arts standards is the achievement of "college and career readiness" for all students. To ensure this achievement, standards are "designed to be grade specific in a cumulative progression" (Wheat 2011, p. 3).[3] In this highly regulated mobility system, students are ushered up a "grade-by-grade staircase" rising in complexity from beginning to college and career readiness levels and comprised of the "skills and understandings all students must demonstrate by the end of each grade" (Kentucky Department of Education 2013).

Michael, a senior in AP English, described his understanding and experience of this curricular staircase like this:

> I kind of think the way it's set up is like in the first two years [grades nine and ten] any writing you do is kind of the whole informal thing, sort of just getting out all of that need to write from personal experience. And then, once you hit your junior year, it's like you should have that all out of your system. Let's start writing the way you're going to have to write for the rest of your life.

Julie, another high school senior, describes the reflective and exploratory journaling sessions that began each of her dual enrollment English classes as mechanisms of purgation: "I write what I want to write so that when we're finished journaling I can do what I have to write for the future." And Kim explains how she "actually write[s] a lot—for my friends, online, for myself" but doesn't "see how any of that relates to writing for school or getting ready for college. Real writing is for grades, a degree, you know, a job. You know, writing that matters in the *real world*."

The rhetoric of readiness driving the new curriculum and internalized by these students was also circulated in an extensive school-wide rebranding campaign associated with the cultural reform efforts of the turnaround program. One way to "inspire obsession with targets" is to surround students and teachers with visual representations of these targets at every turn. Reform efforts began with a rebranding campaign that involved canvassing the school with *reminders of the future*.

Figure 3.2 shows the effects of this campaign on Hughes's main hall. As students move through this corridor, day in and day out, their projected futures literally hang over their heads. Banners of local colleges and universities serve as signposts orienting students toward promises of the future intended to inspire their work in the present. The central location of the clock in this image serves as a reminder that progress toward this future is measured in bounded units of time. Every ring of the bell maintains a temporal organization in which time unfolds irreversibly toward the next step on the staircase.

FIGURE 3.2 Photo of Hughes' Main Hallway

I read this image as a representation of the way neoliberal education seeks to control students' mobilities under the guise of inspiration. Students who are effectively inspired to defer gratification for their work, to privilege the promised exchange value of their education over its use value in the present, are much easier to control and transport from one stair step to the next than students who question the nature of the work and challenge mediations apparently linking the present to the future. As I argue later in this chapter, I believe students who are inclined to question the value of their present educational activities are better prepared to meet the challenges of their inevitably unpredictable futures.

In addition to hanging banners, turnaround efforts involved tightening control of representations of students, teachers, and their work by converting spaces previously used for public announcement and personal expression (bulletin boards, classroom doors, whiteboards, television screens) into displays for the promotion of a "culture of high expectations"—another key component of the turnaround program. Like the banners, most of the displays on classroom walls and doors and in hallways were (re)designed to promote and celebrate unified progress. For instance, for an eight-foot bulletin board display in the main hall, graduating seniors were photographed in front of a backdrop reading "Bobcats Have Options."[4] Students in the photos held up college acceptance letters under a banner reading "Wild for College."

Of course, I agree these achievements are well worth celebrating. However, the display endorses the post-secondary school "options" of 44 graduating seniors while excluding the options of the 144 other students who graduated alongside them. To maintain a promise of prosperity, diversions from sanctioned pathways are excluded from public display. When such diversions are presented to the public, they are typically formulated as statistics to bolster the need for more reform.

For instance, to demonstrate this need and generate monetary and political support for reform, the High School Center at the American Institute for Research opens its "College and Career Readiness Fact Sheet" with an apparently startling statistic: "Ninety-three percent of middle school students report that their goal is to attend college. However, only 44% enroll in college, and only 26% graduate with a college diploma within six years of enrolling" (Fact Sheet 2014, p. 1). As the Lumina Foundation might suggest, with numbers like these, the U.S. economy, along with its democratic system, are likely to collapse at any moment. And so supporters of reform work to prevent this collapse by building a culture of high expectations that names students who stay on track and numbers those who don't. Of course, elected officials and educational administrators are not the only ones building and maintaining this culture. Researchers of literacy and education, like myself, often rely on statistics like those presented in the "College and Career Readiness Fact Sheet" to secure funding for research from foundations like Lumina and Gates. Even when conceived as an effort to redirect institutional resources to those who need it most, research supported by neoliberal sponsors involves participating in and perpetuating the project of education as always, only for the future.

As evidenced in Michael's, Julie's, and Kim's comments above, this relentless future orientation often prevents students (and teachers) from recognizing the value and complexity of their languages, literacies, and mobilities in the present. Again, the only literacies and mobilities of value in this system are the ones presented as credentials apparently predictive of future success. As David Blacker (2013) asserts, this de-tethering of a credential from actual practice is part of the commodification drive: "*the credential* is one's goal, and the classes, any incidental learning that might take place, etc., are so many streamlinable means to that end" (p. 244). Such mobility systems enhance motility for some, diminish it for others, and reduce everyone's needs and desires for reading and writing to individual and national economic concerns. Students' economic concerns are real, often pressing and certainly worthy of our careful attention; however, I don't believe these concerns are always fully articulated, are trained on a stationary target, or can be isolated from other motivations and values. The assumption that students are singularly motivated by economic and social advancement reduces the multiple and often conflicting needs and desires formed and transformed in their movements within and across scenes of literacy (Lu and Horner 2009).

Educating for the Future

This reduction clearly informs the design of the Common Core Standards, which currently govern most literacy instruction in the U.S. In accordance with the Lumina Foundation's future-oriented education for national prosperity, the standards claim to reflect the "knowledge and skills that our young people need for success in college and careers. With American students *fully prepared for the future*, our communities will be best positioned to *compete successfully in the global economy*" (National Governors Association n.d.).

To explore possible ways in which students' understandings of language and literacy are shaped by the relentless future orientation of mainstream literacy education, I'd like to consider how the Common Core Standards circulate along and help constitute an educational scale that might enhance and/or diminish the linguistic, literate, material, representational, and embodied motilities of Nadif, James, and Katherine. To investigate how the standards influence potential for and recognition of mobile practice in the work of these students, I position a reading of essays composed by each student according to Common Core criteria alongside readings of these essays informed by the mobilities frame outlined in the previous chapters. Each of the following essays was composed to accommodate the anchor standards for one of three text types designated as "college level" by the Common Core: Argumentative, Explanatory/Informative and Narrative.[5]

Rather than presenting these passages as complete units of discourse that might be subjected to CCS assessment or as representative of the complex bodies of academic writing composed by these students over the courses of their high school careers, I'm using the following passages to investigate how certain literacy moves might be evaluated according to the CCS. Moreover, I'm choosing the Common Core as a representation of containment because it is currently the most influential model of literacy education in the U.S. I believe similar readings could be performed with most measures of literacy learning in the era of standardization.

I'll begin with an excerpt from an essay Nadif composed to meet the Common Core Standards for writing arguments. These standards are presented in abbreviated form in Table 3.1.

The excerpt below is from the final draft of a literary analysis written in response to Nadif's final assignment in senior AP English. In this text, he traces out relations among themes in three different works by Nigerian author Chinua Achebe: the role of women in African society, colonial education, and religious indoctrination. Here, Nadif is addressing the theme of colonial education in Achebe's (1996) *Things Fall Apart*:

> Achebe emphasis in his book "things fall apart" the British style of educating the elites of the region in order to backlash the expectation of the Igbo elders. The missionaries' message of new religion was not a goal they meant, but it was a plan to change divide among the people and get the attention of the young ones whom can easily be assimilated by educating them. Such lead to isolation of a father and a son "you all have seen the great abomination of your brother. Now he is no longer my son your brother. I will only have a son who is a man, who will hold his head up among my people," (Achebe 172). The Europeans had such a strong plan, which could lead them easily to divide the people against their wills and give them supporters by educating the young ones, though their goal was to colonize and start slavery across region. Using religion, as a tool to achieve your goal is what led the British to take over the Igbo people, thus Achebe in his novel "things fall apart" proves this claim is what made easy for the Europeans to divide the continent of Africa.[6]

TABLE 3.1 Common Core Standards, Writing Arguments (Grades 11 and 12)

Introduces claims and seeks to support these with the texts

Develops claims or counterclaims thoroughly with evidence

Connects sections of the essays in a coherent whole

Establishes a formal and objective tone and attends to the norms and conventions of literary criticism

Provides a concluding statement that follows the argument

Source: Adapted from National Governors Association Center for Best Practices, & Council of Chief State School Officers. *Common Core State Standards*. Common Core Standards Initiative. Retrieved from www.corestandards.org/

According to the standards, Nadif begins with the introduction of a clear claim; that is, Achebe depicts the ways in which British colonists used education and religion as tools for dividing and conquering the people of Nigeria. And the standards would lead us to note that he seeks to develop this claim with a quote that provides evidence for the success of this strategy in a father's denial of his son (Okonkwo's denial of Nwoye). Most of Nadif's attempts to connect claims in this passage and to connect sections throughout the essay result in restatements of the original claim. He also attempts to establish a formal and objective tone and accommodate the conventions of literary criticism, but I suspect most readers familiar with these conventions would suggest Nadif falls short of this accommodation. For instance, he uses quotation marks instead of italics for the title of a major work, his phrasings and terminology are slightly askew, he uses punctuation before parenthetical documentation, etc. Finally, a conclusion is present, but since it is essentially a restatement of the original claim, it would be a stretch to suggest that it follows from the argument, as the final standard for this text type stipulates.

So in response to Nadif's argument, and across text types, the Standards value the following: the presence of key content such as claims and counterclaims, evidence and conclusions; conformity to predetermined discursive and linguistic norms such as objective tone, standardized English, domain-specific vocabulary, correct usage and mechanics, and so on.[7] The Standards also value the clear and coherent transmission of ideas through appropriate language and transitions, connections, and cause–effect relations; appeals to authoritative sources of knowledge such as literary and informational texts and personal and sensory details in the case of narratives; and conformity to a pre-established process of writing—read, gather thoughts, write, revise, publish. With this final valuation, the Standards reduce process theories of writing to yet another series of steps on course to a predetermined target, a decontextualized product. In the same way that neoliberal reform seeks to streamline students' life courses, it attempts to streamline writing processes to ensure products worthy of the future.

In their exclusive focus on his preparedness for the future, the Standards neglect past and present mobilities shaping and shaped by Nadif's literacy practices and texts across multiple and intersecting educational scales (Nespor 2004). Among other things, the Standards are not concerned with: Nadif's daily commute to school; the desires, motivations, needs, allegiances, habits, and skills that make up his historical body; the multiple and often conflicting histories of participation in curricular and extracurricular contexts shaping and shaped by his practices; his perception of himself as a writer and of his own literacies and languages; his active constructions of meaning and transformations of convention; the people, objects, ideas, and information assembled in his processes of composing; and material resources available to him, including time, space, quiet, access to computers, internet, library, etc.

To attend to the concerns that closed mobility systems such as the CCS commonly neglect, a mobilities frame begins from a sociocultural perspective that takes literacies to be distributed across persons, objects, and contexts (Leander et al. 2010). Because scenes and scales of literacy are constantly being configured and reconfigured by circulations of people, objects, ideas, and information and because students are constantly on the move within and across such scenes and scales, I believe an examination of Nadif's literacy practices should involve an expanded series of questions concerning place and movement. For example, to attend to the mobile practices constituting his essay, I'm interested in asking the following questions: how does Nadif traverse or otherwise connect this particular scene of literacy with others in his everyday life; how might the literate and linguistic opportunities or motilities in this essay be expanded through trajectories connecting multiple scenes of literacy; how are the moving elements—people, needs, motivations, objects, literacies, languages, texts, ideas, and information— of the scenes of literacy in which he participates, including this one, configured and reconfigured across space and time; and how might engaging in reflective negotiations of these elements help him realize his own enactments of agency as he works to reproduce and transform conventions of discourse, genre, and discipline with his language and literacy resources.

If we return to Nadif's text with these considerations in mind, we're compelled to attend to ways in which it is shaped by material, representational, and embodied mobilities; the linguistic repertoire (Blommaert 2010) he's developed through these mobilities; and his perceptions of literacy and mobility and of himself. As I noted in the previous chapter, Nadif is a first generation Somali immigrant who moved to the U.S. from the world's largest refugee camp in Dadaab, Kenya. After attending primary school in the camp, he purchased forged Kenyan identification papers with the help of his family and caught a bus from Dadaab to Nairobi to attend secondary school as a Kenyan citizen. To "pass" in this system, Nadif had to learn to navigate the linguistic and cultural flows that circulated in the school. Language flows included various Englishes (including the British English of official school discourse), Kiswahili (the national language), and other ethnic languages (Somali, Kikuyu, Luo, and others). By the time he was granted a visa and entered Louisville's public school system as a junior at the age of 17, he was well practiced in negotiating the language demands of multiple contexts. While he was initially tracked into developmental English courses as an English language learner, by the beginning of his senior year, he had worked his way into advanced-level courses, Advanced Placement and a few Dual Enrollment courses, including Introduction to Pan African Studies, which he was taking onsite at the University of Louisville.

So while he was drafting his essay on Achebe for AP English, he was also studying the colonization of Africa in the context of this college course. Not only that, but he frequently engaged in virtual chats with friends and family in Kenya and other countries from his seats in both of these classes, and was adapting ACT test-prep worksheets into ESL teaching materials for his volunteer work at the Somali Community Center in Louisville. When we consider all of the mobile practices through which Nadif is constituting and connecting scenes of literacy across space-time, it becomes very difficult to approach this essay as an isolated, static, and individually authored text produced in a self-contained context.

It is also difficult to read his writing as an attempted (and failed) effort to compose in standard written English (SWE). In fact, we have no reason to assume that Nadif is trying to approximate the standardized English promoted by the Common Core.[8] Why would he when his ability to navigate linguistic mobilities has served, perhaps, as his greatest resource for both accommodating and transforming the demands of various institutional contexts? Nadif's negotiation of languages in this essay includes engaging and incorporating Achebe's English; demonstrating enough knowledge of the conventions of standardized English grammar and usage to appease institutional demands; meeting the idiosyncratic language preferences of his AP English teacher and the expectations of his classmates; and finally drawing on an expansive linguistic repertoire to find forms that can help him construct his own meanings and pursue his own purposes for writing.

For example, an assessment that assumes a target of SWE or academic discourse would most likely mark Nadif's verbal construction "change divide" as an error, characteristic of English language learners: "The missionaries' message of new religion was not a goal they meant, but it was a plan to *change divide* among the people and get the attention of the young ones whom can easily be assimilated by educating them." However, Nadif is emphasizing the British Empire's simultaneous and mutually reinforcing efforts of conversion and division, and he may feel that the insertion of a conjunction here would signal a causal relationship between these two verbs. In fact, when his teacher suggested he add a conjunction ("and"), he chose to ignore the comment in this final draft of the essay. He explained to me that "he liked it much better without." And we can find more evidence that this construction is a deliberate choice in the quote that follows it: "Such lead to isolation of a father and a son 'you all have seen the great abomination of your brother. Now he is no longer my son your brother. I will only have a son who is a man, who will hold his head up among my people.'" Achebe's construction, "my son your brother," emphasizes the totalizing affect of Okonkwo's denial of Nwoye's subjectivities, and, of course, we have no problem recognizing this construction as purposeful on the part of Achebe.

By reserving the possibility of writer error as an interpretation of last resort, a mobilities approach to Nadif's essay is in line with the translingual paradigm outlined by Bruce Horner, Min-Zhan Lu, Jacqueline Jones Royster, and John Trimbur (2011). A focus on linguistic motility—or possibilities for movement, fluidity, and flux that inhere in linguistic systems—enables us to consider how Nadif makes particular linguistic choices to negotiate the demands of concurrent scenes of literacy, investments, allegiances, and ideologies. Such choices contribute to the (re)assemblage of apparently static language standards, as he employs a diversity of representational means in the co-creation of this particular scene of literacy and consequent reconfiguration of the CCS. Horner et al. (2011) assert that "by addressing how language norms are actually heterogeneous, fluid, and negotiable, a translingual approach directly counters demands that writers must conform to fixed, uniform standards." Moreover, this approach "recognizes that, to survive and thrive as active writers, students must understand how such demands are contingent and negotiable" (p. 305).

Perhaps because of his experience moving within and across systems governed by diverse language and literacy standards, Nadif does understand and approach language demands as negotiable, and this approach enables him to play off of frictions and realize agencies in his movement among scenes of literacy in high school and college. This is not to say that Nadif is more mobile, linguistically versatile, or innovative than other students, only that he is accustomed to finding the exploit in seemingly fixed mobility systems. In the same way that he was able to use a fake ID to create an opening for himself in a Kenyan educational system to which he had no claim as a Somali refugee, Nadif utilized available mobilities and literacies to *make a place* for himself at Hughes and later at the University of Louisville. According to Kaufmann's (2002) definition of motility cited above, Nadif is particularly adept at putting the potentialities of mobility in various systems to use for his own activities (p. 37).

However, his is not a tale of individual achievement. Nadif's ability to find and act upon exploits in these systems depends, in large part, on the participation of a host of other human and nonhuman actors—an uncle who taught him English in Dadaab, a cousin who obtained forged identification papers, an affordable internet provider in Kenya, an American teacher who recommended he be placed into AP courses, a Somali diaspora in Louisville accustomed to sharing resources and protecting its youth, a cultural tradition that favors the first-born males of a family, a U.S. public school system that tends to be more accepting of the language and cultural differences of "immigrant minorities" than the differences of "involuntary or castelike minorities," and so on (Ogbu 1990, p. 46). In other words, Nadif's motility is contingent upon assemblages creating and delimiting his opportunities for particular types of movements within and among these systems.

The other students presented in this chapter operate with(in) collectives composed of actors working on and against their mobilities in much different ways. While James and Katherine also demonstrate a great deal of linguistic and literate versatility through their mobile practices in high school and beyond, their stories reveal a number of material, social, and psychological barriers to understanding standards and the mobility systems and scales they structure as contingent and negotiable. This next excerpt from James's urban school survival guide, *From the Hood to the Halls*, speaks to such barriers. The assignment that prompted this text was designed to meet Common Core Standards for writing explanatory/informative essays in a regular (read developmental) English class. Once again, here (Table 3.2) is an abbreviated version of the anchor standards for this text type:

TABLE 3.2 Common Core Anchor Standards, Writing Explanatory/Informative Essays (Grades 11 and 12)

Introduces a number of topics and relates these to each other in content and form
Develops these topics thoroughly with facts, definitions, details, quotations, etc.
Links major sections of the text with transitions
Uses precise language, domain-specific vocabulary and techniques
Maintains a formal style and objective tone. Attends to generic norms and conventions
Provides a concluding statement that follows from and supports previous material

Source: Adapted from National Governors Association Center for Best Practices, & Council of Chief State School Officers. *Common Core State Standards*. Common Core Standards Initiative. Retrieved from www.corestandards.org/

In his contributions to this collaborative text, James cautions against common pitfalls in high school education, social life, family life, and work. He concludes his guide by asking:

> What will happen? What about these educational issues? Will they get worse or better? Will homelessness, drug use, and despair become huge problems? I believe that these issues are more likely to increase. It's a commonly shared theory that these issues are based off of the economy and society itself. As the world seems to grow darker and become filled with more hatred, people act out as there's no hope. It's Tragic but very true. I can say that societal issues in the U.S. are increasing quickly when we look at how many people use drugs now. We will need to change this, because if we continue this what will the consequences be? These societal issues will affect the behavior of the population that habits our country and will become a big problem in the U.S.[9]

In this passage and throughout his portions of the text, James introduces homelessness, drug use, and despair as interrelated educational issues, and thereby meets the first criterion on the CCS list. While this excerpt only provides a glimpse of the text's adherence to the second standard in its brief reference to economic and social theories, in the complete work James offers a good number of facts, details, definitions, and quotations to make a case for the pervasiveness of these issues. Here and elsewhere, the primary transitional device is the rhetorical question, which James uses somewhat effectively to link major sections of the work. Moreover, he makes attempts, mostly successful, to use precise language and employ domain-specific vocabulary and techniques—using terms like "societal" and phrases such as "It's a commonly shared theory." While the style is formal, his use of the first person may call his objectivity into question, and in much the same way as Nadif's essay, James's text approximates, but doesn't always successfully attend to generic norms and conventions. Finally, he does meet the final criterion on the CCS list by concluding the piece with an answer to his own rhetorical questions.

But here again, by focusing on the writing skills James apparently needs for scenes of literacy in the future, the standards train us to gloss over the past and present mobilities that shape his text. Moreover, even as the standards claim to be rhetorical, they encourage James to take an a-rhetorical approach to this scene of literacy, as he attempts to employ academic discourse to convince a generic audience to avoid the pitfalls of an urban high school. And, perhaps most importantly, I believe the standards condition students like James to approach school-based languages and literacies as tools of accommodation and conformity rather than as ways of making meanings, identities, and the relationships that constitute and connect scenes of literacy. Once again, to better understand the literacy opportunities or motilities in this particular essay and in the scene from which it emerges, we must reflect on the relations among the mobilities coursing through and constituting the scene and James's historical body.

James and Nadif rode the same bus to school from an economically depressed neighborhood in South Louisville, but James's experience of the area was and still is much different than Nadif's. While Nadif benefited from the support and protection of the Somali community in this neighborhood, James and his siblings were relatively unsheltered from the poverty, drugs, and violence of the area. When I began working with James, his father was in prison for drug sales and his mother was in and out of recovery from drug addiction. This put James in the position of serving as a primary caretaker, along with his grandmother, of two younger siblings while attending school and working approximately 20 hours a week as a grocery store clerk. He remained in developmental courses throughout his high school career despite making As and Bs in these courses with relative ease. In the face of the material demands competing for his time and energy, James consistently attended class and performed well in his courses. He approached his education as not only a possible way out of his circumstance, but also as an opportunity to draw attention to, critique, and transform the social structures that produce and maintain the conditions in which he and his family live. These pursuits are evident in James's urban survival guide, but they read as platitudes unless you know something about his historical body.

However, James isn't making this body explicit in his text. And, of course, this is his prerogative. As a teacher, I would not force him in this direction. However, as a researcher I was interested in the extent to which James recognized the inclusion of his own experiences in the text as an option in the first place. When I asked if he thought it would work to include accounts from his life or resources from the predominant languages and literacies of his home and neighborhood in his guide, he suggested it would "work for me but not for my grade."

The longer James and I worked together, the more we both came to understand that after 12 years in the public school system, he had become particularly adept at accommodating the demands of what was presented as academic discourse in the performance of his school identity and in his literacy practices. It is perhaps this habit of accommodation that leads him to distance himself from the concerns he presents in this text and to project them into the future: "Will homelessness, drug use, and despair become huge problems?"

James encounters these problems in the present on a daily basis in very tangible ways. But he approaches this text as if his own life experiences have nothing to contribute to an academic investigation of the issues. Moreover, while he does draw upon a range of literacies in a blending of multiple media—print and hand-drawn text, graffiti, sketches, and photographs—his written text is seemingly void of the language varieties circulating in an "urban" school, including the variations of black English he speaks in the hallways, at home, and in his neighborhood.[10] Ultimately, James does not conceive of his literacies and languages as mobile practices that might enable him to act on opportunities for mobility in this text, scenes of literacy in his English class, or across interconnected scales of education. And he has good reason to maintain this conception.

James's partitioning of language varieties in his writing and in his classroom speech is, in many ways, an act of self-preservation. W. E. B. DuBois famously describes this partitioning as double consciousness, and Vershawn Ashanti Young (2009) asserts that it "shows up in one of its most pronounced and pernicious forms in both the theory and practice of teaching oral and written communication to black students, where code switching is offered as the best strategy" (p. 52). By his senior year of high school, James could not remember receiving explicit instruction in switching between black and standardized English, but his ability to do so effortlessly demonstrated his habituation of this distinction. When I asked him to describe his relationship to standardized English, he didn't hesitate in asserting that "It is the language used in college and in good jobs. So I'll need it to get by in those places." In other words, for James, standardized English is the language of upward mobility, and its mythically monolithic nature is maintained, in part, by discourses of readiness circulating in our school systems.

However, accommodating the demands of fixed linguistic, discursive, and generic standards was not enough in the case of James's survival guide and those of his predominantly black and Mexican-American classmates. Even though his guide conforms, for the most part, to the standards listed above, the school's response to his blending of media through the inclusion of "urban" images was enough to confirm his need to maintain clear distinctions between his performances of self in and outside of school. James's English teacher, who did encourage her students to experiment with varieties of language and literacy in this and other assignments, designed these projects to be published and circulated for other students at Hughes, particularly first- and second-year students at the school. To help present and future students avoid the pitfalls and confront the realities of life at Hughes, James's class distributed their guides throughout the school. They placed copies in the school library, delivered them to ninth and tenth grade English classes, and handed them out in the halls.

At first, the project seemed to me to be a clear depiction of possibilities for teacher and student agency in the face of increased regulation of classroom activities and performances. The student-authors of the guides seemed genuinely excited to share their work with the school and were optimistic about the impact this work might have on the experiences and trajectories of new and future students. Moreover, the teacher of the class had designed an assignment rooted in critical pedagogy that also encouraged students to meet the demands of the CCS. But the project's triumph was short lived. When the survival guides made it into the offices of Hughes's administrators, the copies already circulating in the school were promptly confiscated and additional copies were banned from further distribution. Not only that, the principal suspended the teacher of the course, removing her from the class in the middle of term. While individual students were not punished for their texts, these disciplinary actions sent a clear message that their work was not only inappropriate but was also harmful to the audience it was intended to serve.

The realities confronted in the guides were not officially recognized by the school's "culture of high expectations," so like the whitewashed walls of the hallways, these perceived deviations from sanctioned pathways were erased or, at the very least, suppressed. The administration justified these acts of suppression by appealing to the inclusion of themes and images of drug use, poverty, and violence. So, in effect, the daily realities James and his family struggled against in and outside of school were denied a place in official school discourse. As long as the urban (or what one teacher termed "ghetto") discourses of James and his classmates remained within sealed (developmental) tracks of study, the school could maintain an illusion of purity and order; however, when these students' racialized and classed differences seeped out into public spaces, the institution launched immediate strategies of containment, discipline, and punishment. In fact, the mechanisms of control exerted to curtail the circulation of these survival guides were paralleled by methods used to control the circulation of student bodies between classes. Called to action by the school bell, police officers, coaches, and administrators armed with two-way radios assumed strategic positions along major corridors to disperse congregating students and to usher them as quickly as possible from one class to the next. Students caught making inappropriate gestures, wearing inappropriate attire (jeans, hoodies, T-shirts, etc.), or wearing sanctioned attire in inappropriate ways, were punished with more solitary methods of confinement such as in-school suspension.[11]

Henry Giroux (2010) attributes such conditions to the strategies of containment increasingly shaping public schooling. He asserts that contemporary educational reform in collusion with the growing corporatization and militarizing of public schools encourages "the increased use of harsh disciplinary modes of punishment, surveillance, control, and containment, especially in schools inhabited largely by

FIGURE 3.3 Scan of Urban Survival Guide
Used with permission.

poor minorities" (p. 368). As the suppression of their survival guides and the control of their movements demonstrates, efforts to curtail James's and his predominantly poor minority classmates' texts, ideas, languages, and bodies were heightened when they threatened to permeate the boundaries of their designated tracks. The survival guide incident was not the first and would not be the last time James's material and representational mobilities would be restricted by institutional forces despite his attempts to conform to the standards of the system. But before I present

Drugs

Realities
The realities, drugs are taking over.
Drugs are everywhere in school,outside of school,in your neighborhood....etc
Individuals who take drugs have different reasons for doing so. Here are some of the reasons we can come up with:

Pitfalls
The pitfall of having drugs are that you could get robbed by a junkie or robbed by another person that wants your drugs so they can make money. And when buying drugs your taking the risk of getting robbed or better yet arrested handcuffed and taking down.

Personality changes: When doing drugs especially hardcore ones like (cocaine, heroin, Ecstasy, PCP...
etc) you become a cluck and are more intone to were your going to find your next high then you are about not having a home.
Friend changes: If your lucky enough to have friends that are not on that mess and you are, your friends wont want to hang with you. "Nobody wants to be around a crackhead."

Habit changes: You can't go without the drug. Your body is so used to the drug being their all the time it doesn't know how to function without the drug in your body. So all of the habits and things that you liked to do aren't going to amuse you as the once did.

Addictive changes: You will fill the addiction start to take over your body and mind their will be sudden urges that you may not be able to control.

Models
There are lots of societal models for us, as we think about how drugs affect our lives. Some positive models are: The teachers in your school, the adults of your household, and peers who got their shit together. Some negative models are: Drug addicts, Drug dealers, Most TV shows...etc

Vocabulary
Bar- either a fat king Kong blunt or usually xanax bars(yellow school buses)

Crack Cocaine- Chemically purified, very potent cocaine in pellet form that is smoked through a glass pipe and is considered highly and rapidly addictive.

Cluck- a person who does dumb shit when there high

Cigarelo- a big wrap to roll weed and other smoke onto a blunt.

Dank- very sticky weed that usually sticks to the bag.

Dro- a potent form of weed.

Extacy- a hardcore club drug.

Lick- An easy robbery.

Weed- A marijuana plant that can be cut up and rolled to smoke

Robitussin DM- a powerful cough syrup that is a dissociative hallucinogen and can be bought any where and is probably in your moms medicine cabinet (used to 'make lean)when this drug is consumed you feel slower and out .

Triple C's is a pill that you overdose on for you to get a "out of body high" , What gets you high is a ingredient called dextromethorphan .

Magic Mushrooms , ingested to get high contain psilocybin and create a similar psychedelic experience as taking LSD. They can be eaten raw or dried and made into a tea .

LSD , or recommended as Acid , can distort perceptions of reality and produce hallucinations; the effects can be frightening and cause panic. It is sold as tablets, capsules, liquid, or on absorbent paper. **19**

FIGURE 3.4 Scan of Urban Survival Guide

Used with permission.

more instances of blocked movement in James's mobility narrative, I'd like to explore how the pressure to conform to the demands of the future shapes Katherine's mobile practices as well.

This final excerpt is from a literacy narrative Katherine composed for a dual enrollment composition course to accommodate anchor standards for writing narratives.

In this essay, Katherine explores processes of translation among Spanish, English, and American Sign Language and discusses the influences of her multi-lingualism on her writing in standardized English.

> ASL has significantly affected my English and Spanish for that matter. ASL [American Sign Language] is a "choppy" version of English. All this means is that sentences in ASL are broken up from the normal structured sentences. (Ex. Hi, How are you? Would translate to How you?) I had to learn how to break up sentences in both English and Spanish because my deaf friends would stay at my house and my father spoke only Spanish. When they were there I was usually the "Google translator" as my dad had put it. I would have to convert what he was saying in Spanish to English to American Sign Language (ex. ¿Cómo te va en la escuela? To How are you doing in school? To How School?) I am so use to speaking in ASL and Spanish I have to always make corrections on papers for English class. I write them how I am use to speaking. My papers always turn out being written in Spanglish and to the point. I ended up ruling out detail because in ASL it is always to the point. Looking back now there has been more Language Arts involved in high school than I expected, especially because of the extra work I had to put into my writing pieces to make them sound "normal."[12]

In accordance with the first standard on the list (Table 3.3), Katherine begins this section with a problem of translating between ASL, Spanish, and spoken and written English. She employs dialogue, reflection, and humor as narrative techniques. The Standards would also have us recognize that the events that

TABLE 3.3 Common Core Anchor Standards, Narrative Essays (Grades 11 and 12)

Engages and orients the reader by setting out a problem, situation, etc.
Uses narrative techniques
Sequences events
Uses precise words and phrases, telling details, and sensory language
Provides a conclusion that follows from and reflects on what comes before

Source: Adapted from National Governors Association Center for Best Practices, & Council of Chief State School Officers. *Common Core State Standards*. Common Core Standards Initiative. Retrieved from www.corestandards.org/

comprise this essay are sequenced to portray occasions that give rise to her need to engage in such processes of translation. Katherine uses precise words in English and Spanish and provides details in the form of specific examples of translated phrases. Finally, her conclusion reflects both what comes before it in the passage and on a history of accommodating the norms of writing in standard English. But, once again, this sedentary lens misses much of the point of the narrative. Most significantly, this Common Core reading misses Katherine's need and desire to trace connections among scenes of literacy and to investigate relations among aspects of her own historical body.

Katherine is a partially deaf, second-generation Mexican-American. She's fluent in Spanish, English, and multiple varieties of sign language. She took honors and advanced placement courses in every subject throughout high school. And, as previously discussed, she volunteered regularly at a local hearing and language academy and worked approximately ten hours a week at a law firm. Katherine described her work at the law firm—translating conversational Spanish to standardized English for official correspondences between attorneys and clients—in much the same way that she described her reading and writing for school. As the above excerpt indicates, when she describes her movement among Spanish, ASL, and English in dialogue, Katherine uses terminology of translation: "I had to learn how to break up sentences in both English and Spanish because my deaf friends would stay at my house and my father spoke only Spanish. When they were there I was usually the 'Google translator' as my dad had put it. I would have to convert what he was saying in Spanish to English to American Sign Language." In contrast, when describing her work at the law firm and at school, Katherine adds the terminology of correction and accommodation to her description: "I am so use to speaking in ASL and Spanish I have to always make corrections on papers for English class. [. . .] there has been more Language Arts involved in high school than I expected, especially because of the extra work I had to put into my writing pieces to make them sound 'normal.'"

In our interviews, Katherine consistently associated her reading-writing at work with her reading-writing at school, presenting both as efforts of conforming her "natural" languages to the demands of fixed standards of English. During one conversation, she was on the verge of tears when she expressed her frustration with such processes: "I hate my writing. It always feels unnatural, like I'm writing for someone else in someone else's voice." It is perhaps this lack of ownership that caused Katherine, despite her proven record of success in school, to approach schoolwork with a great deal of anxiety, experiencing almost every assignment, test, and activity—especially those involving writing and speaking—as struggles. As the excerpt above demonstrates, she most often described this struggle in terms of language differences, focusing not only on phonetic, lexical, and structural differences between the Spanish spoken in her home and the English of school, but also on the modal differences between these languages and sign language.

Unlike her frequent associations between literacies of school and work at the law firm, Katherine did not see her practice with deaf students and their parents as contributing to her academic or workplace literacies, and she actively tried to keep these areas of her life separate in much the same way that James partitioned his languages and performances of self. The social and academic pressures that Katherine felt throughout high school prevented her from presenting as openly deaf to her teachers and classmates. In fact, Katherine's classmates learned of her deafness for the first time through this literacy narrative composed toward the end of her senior year.

In response to a question I asked in one of our interviews conducted via virtual chat about what it was like to keep this aspect of her identity hidden in school, Katherine wrote:

> I was ashamed because everyone around me was always immature and would attempt to impersonate my deaf friends by pretending to sign, which consisted of fingers crossing all sorts of ways, hand gestures, and the middle finger. This is where I had difficulties with my identity because I knew that if I revealed the fact that I was deaf the same thing would happen to me, so I would bicker back and forth in my head if that's what I wished for myself. Not being able to express myself with full honesty hurt me because I lost a part of myself that I loved not only because I was different but because it was a language that I had pride in.

Here, Katherine eloquently describes the internal struggle created by the social pressure to conform to certain expectations of (aural) ability, which she must demonstrate through adherence to the norms of standardized spoken English. Unlike the cases of Nadif and James, the language differences Katherine suppresses to accomplish this conformity are modal. Speaking with her hands could expose her to the sort of ridicule James might face if he were to incorporate black English into his survival guide. Moreover, the enforcers of the standards in Katherine's description are her peers rather than institutional authorities. In this way, her response reveals the ways in which the language demands of the institution are embodied and administered by all members of an institution.

Consequently, the mobility system enabling and managing Katherine's material, representational, and embodied mobilities is not merely instituted from the top down through scales of policy, curricula, and assessment; this system is also instituted laterally as students police each other's language and literacy practices and thereby diminish and/or enhance each other's motilities. Rather than drawing upon ASL as a linguistic resource in social and academic contexts, Katherine feels compelled to suppress her (dis)ability in school, which diminishes her opportunities for mobility in and, perhaps, beyond high school. But before moving on to discuss Katherine's post-high school trajectory, I'd like to consider how the Common Core and other official predictors of college and career readiness project these three students into the future.

According to the Common Core Writing and Language Standards, Nadif is the least prepared of the three for college. But, admittedly, any attempt to determine a student's attainment of certain skills and understandings based upon a single text, and, even more, a small portion of that text, is entirely artificial.[13] To expand the range of measures of readiness and to ensure students are meeting the standards comprising the Common Core, the Kentucky Department of Education administers a battery of ACT assessments as its statewide testing system. These tests, collectively called the Educational Planning and Assessment System (EPAS), include the ACT Explore for eighth-grade students, the ACT Plan for tenth-grade students, the traditional ACT for eleventh-grade students, ACT Quality Core end-of-course assessments administered in all grades, and the ACT Compass exam for students who do not meet ACT benchmark standards in math, English, or reading.[14]

Since the fall of 2012, all public postsecondary institutions in Kentucky have agreed to adopt the state's benchmark indicators of college readiness for the traditional ACT or the Compass. Students scoring at or above benchmark standards must be admitted into entry-level college courses and cannot be required to take non-credit-bearing developmental, supplemental, or transitional coursework. A score of 18 meets benchmark standards on the English/Writing portion of the ACT, and a score of 20 meets standards for Reading. For the Compass, the benchmarks are 74 for English/Writing and 85 for Reading. Table 3.4 shows Nadif's, James's and Katherine's scores on these portions of the exams.

Clearly, these measures only confirm Nadif's apparent unpreparedness for college. But as I've already suggested, Nadif was the only student to graduate from a four-year university course by the conclusion of this study. At the time of this writing, he has graduated from University of Louisville where he double majored in Political Science and Economics. He completed these degrees with a cumulative GPA of 3.85 and made the Dean's Honor Role in every semester of his college career. Moreover, he never scored lower than a B on an essay in college. In contrast, James's plans to attend a local community college after

TABLE 3.4 Nadif's, James's, and Katherine's Benchmark Scores

Student	ACT	COMPASS
Nadif	15 – English	68 – English
	15 – Reading	75 – Reading
James	17 – English	80 – English
	21 – Reading	N/A
Katherine	22 – English	N/A
	24 – Reading	N/A

graduation fell through when his high school guidance counselor failed to submit several scholarship and admission applications that James had completed over the course of his senior year. Discouraged by what he perceived to be an intentional institutional roadblock, James found an additional part-time job, and was working approximately 50 hours a week when we last spoke. And while Katherine's high school transcripts, grade point average, and test scores earned her admission into several research universities and one relatively selective private university, she decided to complete her general education coursework at a county community college in Louisville. After a difficult first year in which she struggled to find a place for herself in the college for many of the same reasons she struggled with her academic identity in high school, she decided to take a break from school to pursue a career as a hair stylist. And, when last we spoke, Katherine was pleased with this "alternative" trajectory.

Admittedly, I did not find these disconnects between Common Core and ACT predictions and students' post-high school trajectories surprising. As a literacy researcher and writing scholar, I would not have expected these standards and their attendant assessments to provide accurate measures of readiness for the future. How could they, given the unpredictability of the demands of the future and the needs of these individuals? However, by investigating the differences in the ways these and other students conceptualize the relations among literacy, language, identity, and mobility, our study may help to reveal attitudinal and metalinguistic indicators of college and career literacy and language readiness.

When I asked Nadif, James, and Katherine at the end of their high school careers for their general thoughts and feelings about literacy and language, here is how each student responded:

> James: Most of the time I hate writing. It's what they use to judge you.
> Katherine: Writing "is to help us get to college." Everyone assumes we're going to need it. In every job you have to know how to write a paragraph. It's not for anything else [pause] just getting ready for the future. We just do it 'cause it's there.
> Nadif: Learning to read, write, and speak in different languages has been a blessing. I feel as if there are no limits in my world, I could go to anywhere in the world today and be able to communicate and contribute there. Translating languages is a constant jogging, and that challenged me to think critically and grow my understanding of the human nature.

Of course, there are myriad influences shaping these students' different conceptions of literacies, languages, and mobilities and their own subjectivities in relation to these. I chose to engage in ethnography precisely to attend to the complexity of these influences. However, I do believe that the containerized presentations of literacy that accompany our relentlessly future oriented educational-occupational system have a tremendous influence on students' metalinguistic, sociolinguistic, and attitudinal preparedness for the demands of college and career. In other words, I suspect that Nadif's apparent preparedness for college and career can be attributed, in part, to his understanding of languages and literacies as practices enabling and resisting material, representational, and embodied mobilities: movements across national borders, academic tracks, educational institutions, and also across essay assignments, classrooms, and research interviews. By the time we met, Nadif had come to understand his movements across space-time as contingent upon literacies and his literacies as dependent on spatial and temporal mobilities. Contrastingly, authoritative sources of standardized English mark James's linguistic and discursive innovations as deficiencies that prevent him from progressing from one predetermined level of education to the next. And Katherine's relentless attempts to conform to perceived standards and conventions of "college-level" literacy belie the transformative aspects of her language practice.

James's and Katherine's mobilities are impeded (and overtly blocked in the case of James) by instrumental discrimination (measuring, tracking, and confining), relational discrimination (demanding acceptable identity and interpersonal performances), and symbolic discrimination (denigration of culture and language) (Ogbu and Simons 1998, p. 158). This record of discrimination is stored in historical bodies containing multigenerational accounts of systemic racism, classism, and ableism. Naturally, these embodied memories affect their perceptions of and responses to schooling. Unlike Nadif and other new Americans participating in this project, James and Katherine worked to remain within the boundaries of a fixed mobility system, trusting that it would transport them to the promised prosperity of the future.

While we cannot erase vast histories of discrimination or eradicate the social, economic, institutional, and cultural boundaries that work to keep students like James and Katherine in their places, by presenting scenes of literacy and scales of education as multiple, heterogeneous, and emergent rather than determined by the single scale of education that circulates preconceived standards and conventions, we might help these students recognize themselves as placemakers, actively making the environments in which they participate. If students can recognize and reflect upon the ways in which their literacies and mobilities both constitute and connect genres, discourses, places, scales, and social relations differently across space-time, they make use of agencies created by interplays of mobility and friction. Moreover, they may come to see themselves as agents continually making and remaking themselves and scenes of literacy through entangled mobilities.

In the next chapter, I seek to demonstrate the ways in which students take up such agencies through associations with and on mobile technologies—smartphones, search engines, and city buses. These technologies serve as mediators and aggregators of the people, objects, ideas, and information that constitute and connect scenes of literacy in high school, college, and work. Following participants and objects across classrooms, schools, the city, and digital networks helps us better understand how entangled mobilities constitute and connect places and scales.

Notes

1 It is perhaps this desire to develop and streamline a fully aligned educational-occupational system that has prompted Gates to contribute more money, personally and through his foundation, to the U.S. education system than any other person in history. By most accounts, Gates has contributed over US$5 billion to educational reform, including approximately US$300 million for the creation and implementation of the new Common Core State Standards (Osborne 2013).

2 I use the term *collapsing* here in reference to the Obama Administration's push for dual enrollment and accelerated courses and credits based on previous learning rather than "in seat" time (Fact Sheet 2013).

3 The official website of the CCS also emphasizes that "no set of grade-specific standards can fully reflect the great variety of abilities, needs, learning rates, and achievement levels of students in any given classroom" (corestandards.org). However, the standards themselves use grade-specific standards as the sole measure by which to describe achievement.

4 In an effort to maintain the anonymity of the school, I've changed the name of the school mascot in this quote.

5 In addition to reducing language and literacy practices and skills to modular entities that can simply be picked up from one situation and dropped down in another, the CCS reduce the complexity and fluidity of writing genres to three text types: Argumentative, Explanatory/Informative, and Narrative.

6 The full text of this essay is included in Appendix B.

7 The CCS's valuation of standard written English and linear writing processes are evident in the criteria that comprise the Language Standards and standards for the Production and Distribution of Writing.

8 CCS Language 11-12.1, Conventions of Standard English: "Demonstrate command of the conventions of standard English grammar and usage when writing or speaking." This standard applies to all students, including those labeled "limited English proficiency" like Nadif.

9 Portions of James's urban survival guide are included in Appendix C. I have only included portions of the text attributed to James. Because the entire guide was composed collaboratively, I am unable to include the full text.

10 The pages from James's survival guide reproduced in Appendix C demonstrate the ways in which he blends media in this text to communicate the daily reality of the issues he engages.

11 On his first day of high school in the U.S., Nadif was sent to in-school suspension for wearing a pair of white jeans. He was spotted in the hall after his first class and was directed immediately to what he described as a room full of other black men where he spent the remainder of the day engaged in activities entirely unrelated to his school work. Nadif had no knowledge of the school dress code prohibiting jeans before this incident.

12 The full text of Katherine's essay is included in Appendix D.

13 Of course, this doesn't prevent ACT, Inc. and the College Board from making and selling such determinations.

14 The state pays ACT, Inc. $9.2 million a year for this battery of exams (Spears 2014).

References

Achebe, C. (1996). *Things fall apart*. Portsmouth, NH: Heinemann.

Amin, S. (2011). The right to education. *Pambazuka News*, 557. Retrieved from http://pambazuka.org/en/category/features/77838. Accessed August 2013.

Bill and Melinda Gates Foundation. (2014). Educational pathways. Retrieved from www.gatesfoundation.org/What-We-Do/US-Program/Washington-State/Education-Pathways. Accessed March 2015.

Blacker, D. (2013). The illegitimacy of student debt. *Works and Days: Cultural Logic, 31*, 235–250.

Blommaert, J. (2010). *The sociolinguistics of globalization*. New York: Cambridge University Press.

Bourdieu, P., & Passeron, J. C. (1977). *Reproduction in education, society and culture*. London: Sage.

Conley, D. T., & Gaston, P. L. (2013). *A path to alignment: Connecting K-12 and higher education via the Common Core and the Degree Qualification Profile*. Indianapolis: Lumina Foundation.

Fact sheet on the president's plan to make college more affordable: A better bargain for the middle class. (2013, August 22). Retrieved September 1, 2016, from https://www.whitehouse.gov/the-press-office/2013/08/22/fact-sheet-president-s-plan-make-college-more-affordable-better-bargain-.

Foucault, M. (1977). *Discipline and punish: The birth of the prison*. New York: Vintage Books.

Gates, B. (2005). National Education Summit. Retrieved August 31, 2016, from www.gatesfoundation.org/media-center/speeches/2005/02/bill-gates-2005-national-education-summit.

Giroux, H. (2010). Dumbing down teachers: Rethinking the crisis of public education and the demise of the social state. *Review of Education, Pedagogy and Cultural Studies, 32*(4), 339–381.

Heath, S. B., & McLaughlin, M. (1994). Learning for anything everyday. *Journal of Curriculum Studies, 26*(5), 471–489.

Heidegger, M. (1977). *The question concerning technology: And other essays*. New York: Harper & Row.

Horner, B., Lu, M.-Z., Royster, J. J., & Trimbur, J. (2011). Opinon. Language difference in writing: Toward a translingual approach. *College English, 73*(3), 303–321.

Ingold, T. (2009). Against space: Place, movement, knowledge. In P. W. Kirby. *Boundless worlds: An anthropological approach to movement*. Oxford: Berghahn Books, 29–43.

James. Personal interview. September 13, 2011.

James. Personal interview. October 19, 2011.

James. Personal interview. May 5, 2012.

Julie. Personal interview. October 7, 2011.

Katherine. Personal interview. September 25, 2011.

Kaufmann, V. (2002). *Re-thinking mobility: Contemporary sociology*. Aldershot, UK: Ashgate.

Kentucky Department of Education. (2010). JCPS high school turnaround training. www.jefferson.kyschools.us/sites/default/files/HSTurnAroundTraining4122013.pdf. Accessed February 2012.

Kentucky Department of Education. (2013). Kentucky Core Academic Standards. education.ky.gov/districts/legal/Documents/Kentucky%20Core%20Academic%20Standards%20June%202013.pdf. Accessed June 2013.

Kim. Personal interview. October 21, 2011.

Leander, K. M., Phillips, N. C., & Taylor, K. H. (2010). The changing social spaces of learning: Mapping new mobilities. *Review of Research in Education, 34*(1), 329–394.

Lu, M.-Z., & Horner, B. (2009). Composing in a global-local context: Careers, mobility and skills. *College English, 72,* 113–133.

Michael. Personal interview. October 19, 2011.

Nadif. Personal interview. September 22, 2011.

Nadif. Personal interview. November 6, 2011.

National Governors Association Center for Best Practices, & Council of Chief State School Officers. (n.d.). *Common Core State Standards.* Common Core Standards Initiative. Retrieved from www.corestandards.org/. Accessed September 2011.

Nespor, J. (2004). Educational scale-making. *Pedagogy, Culture and Society, 12*(3), 309–326.

Obama, B. (2013). A transcript of President Obama's speech in Syracuse. Retrieved from www.syracuse.com/news/index.ssf/2013/08/a_transcript_of_president_obamas_speech_in_syracuse.html. Accessed July 2013.

Ogbu, J. (1990). Minority education in comparative perspective. *Journal of Negro Education, 59*(1), 45–57.

Ogbu, J., & Simmons, H. (1998). Voluntary and involuntary minorities: A cultural-ecological theory of school performance with some implications for education. *Anthropology and Education Quarterly, 29*(2), 155–188.

Osborne, E. (2013). Keep Fox News out of the classroom! Rupert Murdoch, Common Core and the dangerous rise of for-profit public education. *Salon.* Retrieved from www.salon.com/2013/12/16/keep_fox_news_out_of_the_classroom_rupert_murdoch_common_core_and_the_dangerous_rise_of_for_profit_public_education/. Accessed July 2013.

Ravitch, D. (2010). *The death and life of the great American school system: How testing and choice are undermining education.* New York: Basic Books.

Scollon, R., & Scollon, S. W. (2004). *Nexus analysis: Discourse and the emerging internet.* New York: Routledge.

Sommers, N., & Saltz, L. (2004). The novice as expert: Writing the freshman year. *College Composition and Communication, 56*(1), 124–149.

Spears, V. H. (2013). Kentucky students might have to use pencil, paper for ACT Inc. test. *Lexington Herald Leader.* Retrieved from www.kentucky.com/news/local/education/article44452467.html. Accessed August 2013.

United States Department of Education, Office of Career, Technical, and Adult Education. (2015). Advancing Career and Technical Education (CTE) in State and Local Career Pathways Project: Jobs for the Future. Washington, D.C.

Urry, J. (2007). *Mobilities.* Cambridge, MA: Polity Press.

Wheat, L. (2011). *Common Core Standards brief/Kentucky Core Academic Standards.* Frankfort, KY: Kentucky Department of Education.

Young, V. A. (2009). "Nah, we straight": An argument against code switching. *JAC, 29*(1–2), 49–77.

4
MOBILE COLLABORATIONS

> At the entire root of all [Hughes's] problems is lack of transportation.
>
> (Nadif 2013)

Appropriately enough, Nadif and I recorded our first official interview on a city bus in transit from Hughes to the University of Louisville. We had been working together for months in his AP English class—interpreting assignment prompts, reading essay drafts, and discussing course texts—and had been attempting for weeks to meet outside of class to share experiences and perceptions of academic literacies in high school and desires and expectations for college. But, as you can imagine, the schedules of high schoolers and academics seldom align. Between his school schedule and a host of extracurricular and social commitments and my teaching, administrative, research, and family responsibilities, we could not "find" overlapping and unreserved time and space to meet.

In fact, after months of attempting to listen to and record the thoughts of high school students, who seemed to operate in an even more accelerated state of hypermobility than myself, I had begun to recognize the futility of my search for unoccupied moments. So when Nadif suggested we talk during his bus ride to a Pan-African Studies course he was taking at the University of Louisville for dual enrollment credit, I seized the opportunity to go along. In the months leading up to Nadif's high school graduation, we rode and talked once a week from Hughes to the university through 79 potential stops about histories of participation in formal education, language learning, conceptions and experiences of literacy in and out of school, desires and expectations for the future, and much more.[1]

As I suggest in Chapter 2, it was only later that I learned that this method of moving with research participants was a well-established method in multi-sited ethnography and mobility studies (Elwood and Martin 2000, Kusenbach 2003, Lee and Ingold 2006, Jirón 2011). Unlike the single-sited *mise-en-scène* of traditional ethnographic research, multi-sited ethnography follows the movements of participants to attend to multiple forms of real and imagined presence accomplished through circulations of people, objects, ideas, and information across sites of study (Chayko 2002). Marcus (1989) asserts that this orientation assumes that places and scales are constituted "by multiple agents in varying contexts, or places, and that ethnography must be strategically conceived to represent this sort of multiplicity" (p. 52). So, rather than naming objects of study and locating subjects in fixed spaces where identities are made static, multi-sited ethnography seeks to attend to circulations that constitute systems and subjectivities. As I've asserted throughout this book, such attention reveals the scenes of literacy that students move within and among to be comprised of and connected to *meshworks* of dynamic relations rather than preexistent and fixed standards and conventions (Ingold 2009).

Moreover, this orientation complicates categories that tend to naturalize students in particular groups and communities (Keller 2004). And so in this project, I cannot position my participants at a common starting point for their post-high school trajectories; they do not operate within a shared paradigm; and they are not reducible to singular subjectivities—student, Black, Hispanic, African, poor, disabled, low-performing, and so on. Rather, they are multiply situated; they read, write, think, and live from a plurality of subject positions; and these positions are perpetually reconstituted by their material, representational, and embodied mobilities within and across places and scales.

Along with the precarity and indeterminacy of education revealed by the state-mandated "turnaround" at Hughes (Tsing 2015; see Chapter 2), this process of ethnographically tracing relations among scenes of literacy alongside Nadif and other participants and reflecting on our observations and experiences moving in and across scenes of literacy began to initiate an epistemological and methodological shift in the project. What I originally conceived as a traditional longitudinal study of "entering college" students' attempts to transfer academic literacies from one location (high school) to another (college) developed into a study of the constitution of places, scales, and identities through entangled literacies and mobilities. This transformation can be attributed, in part, to the ways my bus rides with Nadif oriented me to processes in which mobilities mediate the journeys of other mobilities (Adey 2009).

As any user of public transport can attest, the linear and relatively predictable routes of city buses belie the mobilities that circulate with, in, and around them. From the moment it begins its journey through the city, the bus becomes a mediator of countless other mobilities as passengers fill its carriage with contradictory and transformative movements. With newspapers and finance reports, smartphones and iPods, school work and Sudoku, and the occasional conversation, riders transform the path of the vehicle's movement through the city into a collective of overlapping and diverging mobilities, a collective reconfigured at every stop. Likewise, as I've argued in previous chapters, even the most conventional school-to-college-and/or-career trajectories are comprised of entangled mobilities that generate the constant and reiterate production of each by each. Like a bus route, the journey from high school to college and/or career comprises a complex meshwork of mobile people, objects, ideas, and information.

In the previous chapter, I sought to reveal the complexity of students' trajectories by demonstrating how the mobile practices of Nadif, James, and Katherine—spanning continents, countries, cultures, languages, neighborhoods, places, and scales of education—shape their academic literacies and expand possibilities for attending to and understanding their literacy practices and texts. In this chapter, I combine methods of following people and texts to investigate how these students partner with each other and objects to pluralize scenes of literacy in high school and college. In all of the scenes I observed over the course of this three-year project, students interacted with objects to alter the temporal and spatial arrangements of their material contexts. Like passengers on a city bus, students and teachers (and researchers) interact with objects—computers, books, smartphones, tablets, assignments, standards and assessments, and so on—to bring distant locations within the range of their senses and thus "violate the constraint that one can only be in one place at one time" (Moores 2012, p. 15).

Attention to these technologies of pluralization is especially fitting for a study of students' movements in space-time because, as Latour (1996) suggests, objects provide for and speak to connections beyond the present. They mediate our interactions with other places and times. Moreover, this orientation accounts for the materiality of literacy apparent in legible and durable objects (print, paper, hardware and software, etc.) and the ways in which these objects act within and across scenes of literacy and scales of education. As Deborah Brandt and Katie Clinton (2002) assert, the need to recognize that things are not just acted through or upon by readers and writers but are also actors in themselves is especially critical to investigations of the material dimensions of literacy. In this way, "Figuring out what things are doing with people in a setting becomes as important as figuring out what people are doing with things in a setting" (p. 348).

To investigate how students and objects interact with and on each other across scenes of literacy, this chapter attends to the ways human–object partnerships enable and constrain multiple and simultaneous forms of mobility. These mobilities *relocalize* students' literacies and languages to both accommodate and transform places and scales (Pennycook 2010, p. 48). In addition to attending to the material movements of people and objects that comprise scenes of literacy, I consider the imaginative, virtual, and communicative mobilities contributing to the constitution of these scenes. Urry (2007) differentiates among these mobilities by describing imaginative movement as facilitated by "the images of places and peoples appearing on and moving across multiple print and visual media"; virtual movement as occurring in real time and "thus transcending geographical and social distance"; and communicative movement as consisting of person-to-person communication "via messages, texts, letters, telegraph, telephone, fax and mobile" (p. 47). As a result of these mobilities, overlaps always exist among multiple material scenes of literacy and historical, imaginary, communicative, and virtual environments, and embodied experiences of these. Consequently, analyses of such scenes must be sensitive to the pluralizations of space-time these interactions produce.

Through complex assemblages of these various mobilities, students constitute and contingently maintain connections across varied and multiple locations and embodied and electronic realities. Because of this interplay of mobilities, students are not only located in networks of disciplinary power but also continuously relocate themselves and others within and thus actualize places and scales. As in de Certeau's (1984) account of "Walking in The City," these interdependent mobilities ensure that seemingly omnipotent mobility systems are always "prey to contradictory movements that counterbalance and combine themselves outside the reach of panoptic power" (p. 95).

To tease out the threads of such assemblages, this chapter is divided into sections investigating overlaps among forms of mobility. I begin with an exploration of embodied and imaginative mobilities accomplished through James's and Nadifs's interactions with and on school buses. By reading their perceptions of and experiences on buses in light of the history, politics, and logistics of school busing in Louisville, I consider how they work through this mobility system to help transform Hughes, located in a predominantly white middle-class neighborhood, into an "urban" school at the same time that the institution works through the busing system to inscribe white, middle-class values upon James, Nadif, their classmates, and their communities. Next, I explore how Nadif and Katherine imagine places of college and link domains of work, social life, and family to these places through material, imaginative, communicative, and virtual mobilities propelled by information and communication technologies. Through their partnerships with material and virtual objects—televisions, computers, smartphones, wifi hotspots, software applications, websites, and so on—Nadif and Katherine project themselves into geographies of the future, bringing real and imagined features of distant locations to bear in present scenes of literacy. Moreover, they pluralize scenes by augmenting face-to-face participation with multiple and simultaneous dialogues conducted via virtual chat, email, social networks, and text messages. In this way, the communicative mobilities afforded through partnerships between students and smartphones enable them to maintain and intermingle simultaneous co-presence and distant communications in courses across high school and college. Once again, by demonstrating how these students' entangled mobilities contribute to scenes of literacy as *processes of becoming*, I hope to reveal them as *makers* of dynamic and heterogeneous educational places and scales.

Follow that Bus

When anticipating the 21st century technologies sure to figure prominently in a study of student mobilities, I did not imagine a central role for the bus. Primed by scholarship on the influences of information and communication technologies and new media on educational mobilities (Gee 2004, Jenkins 2006, Ito et al. 2008, Williams 2009), I was prepared to keep pace with passages across virtual highways into worlds desynchronized from historical contexts. While this preparation did pay off, as my co-researchers proved to be more than proficient transmedia navigators and networkers, my preoccupation with newer forms of mediation—no doubt influenced by my own, now middle-class perspectives and assumptions—threatened to obscure the significance of older mobile technologies for students' travels among scenes of literacy at home, school, and work.

However, methods of shadowing people and texts quickly revealed the enduring relevance of such technologies, especially for students living in neighborhoods in south and west Louisville participating in the project. As James asserts, "My day starts and ends on a bus. I get to the stop at 6:50 to wait for the bus to Hughes, take the TARC [Transit Authority of River City] to work after school, take the TARC home after work—do it again tomorrow. I'm sick of buses, but I'm stuck without them." Or as Nadif describes in a proposal essay for AP English: "Most of our students live far away from school. . . . It usually takes 1 to 2 hours to reach home if the students take the TARC, however this issues made them not to staying for after school activities" (p. 2). Nadif goes on to consider how students' dependence on busing influences the positions they take up in relation to the institution, their teachers, and each other: "The problem to students at [Hughes] behavior . . . is lack of interaction with other students, and teachers beyond the class. This happened because students rush to the bus after the last bell and do not get a chance to interact with their teachers, and classmates" (p.3).[2]

These comments highlight issues of access and control underlying many of my participants' experiences with and perceptions of bus travel. They also demonstrate how buses consistently surfaced as "relevant propositions" in the scenes of literacy shaping and shaped by students' mobile practices (Latour 2004, p. 110). As I express in Chapter 2, I believe that to account for the complexity of students' movements within and among places, literacy researchers must seek to attend to the material, representational, and embodied mobilities constituting such scenes. And so in this section, I investigate the ways in which school bus travel occasions and shapes students' literacies and subjectivities.

Busing for (De)segregation

On the surface, bus riding seems an essentially passive activity. After the walk (or run) to the stop, the standing in wait, the spring into an unfolding doorway, and search for a seat, the slow lurch and tumbling acceleration of the vehicle coax passengers into relinquishing control of their trajectories through the city. Unlike the readily apparent embodied and sensuous natures of walking or driving, commonly associated with invention and a degree of free play in apparently rigid systems (de Certeau 1984, Katz 2000, Thrift 2004), riding seems distantiated, spectatorial, and even restrictive. The world passing behind the windows of the bus appears to be one over which passengers have very little control. This question of control is central to James's depiction below (Figures 4.1 and 4.2).

James sketched these images for a journal writing exercise in his senior English class in which he and his classmates were given 15 minutes to compose representations and projections of the relationship between their educations and their lives before and after high school.[3] As in all journaling exercises in the course, students were encouraged to respond to this prompt with whatever means of representation they felt would most effectively convey their ideas. Choosing his preferred medium (even while he regularly mocked his own ability to draw), James began working on this sketch with very little hesitation, as if these representations of mobility, symbols of the past and future, were already at the forefront of his mind.

When I asked about the meaning of the sketch, he suggested that after graduating high school he would be able to earn enough money to afford a car: "Right now, I make minimum wage and can only work like 20 hours a week, or something like that. I'm going to make more and work more after high school.

FIGURE 4.1 James's Education Sketch, Part 1

Used with permission.

FIGURE 4.2 James's Education Sketch, Part 2
Used with permission.

So I'm going to be done taking these buses to school and work and everywhere—going to get a car to go wherever I want." On the surface, James's explanation of his sketch accords with predominant assumptions of student motivation in education. According to widely circulated sources such as the Cooperative Institutional Research Program's annual "Freshman Survey," which consistently trumpets an increase in job- and salary-related motivations for pursuing college, students like James want, above all else, to be well-off financially (Egan et al. 2013). However, as I assert in Chapter 3, these assumptions often reduce the multiple and conflicting needs and desires informing students' educational practices, decisions, and aspirations. For instance, the second half of James's description conveys a desire for freedom over and possession of his own material movements through the city. While this desire is related to James's pursuit of goods (a car in this case), it cannot be reduced to this pursuit.

To represent his previous (and current) mobilities, James labels the bus in his sketch as Route 23, which runs back and forth from the Highlands, down Broadway Avenue through downtown Louisville, to Shawnee Park located on the far western boundary of the city (Figure 4.3).[4]

In this trip, the bus connects one of the most economically advantaged neighborhoods in the city (the Highlands) with one of the most disadvantaged (Shawnee). While James was not living on the west end of Louisville at the time of this study, he identified as a member of the "extremely segregated" African

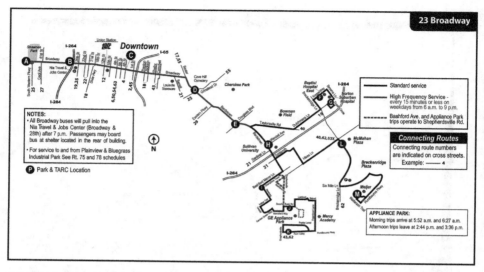

FIGURE 4.3 Transit Authority of the River City, Route 23

Source: Transit Authority of the River City. "Route 23, Broadway."
https://www.ridetarc.org/uploadedFiles/23.pdf

American community in the area, having lived in west-end neighborhoods until his final year of middle school (Fosl 2013, p. 8). When I asked why he chose TARC's Route 23 for this sketch, he suggested that he always thinks of it as the bus that takes him home: "I don't go out that way much anymore, but it's where I come from. It's where my people are." I also suspect that by selecting this route, James was seeking to maintain credibility with the majority of his classmates who were bused to Hughes from west-end neighborhoods.

James's decision to memorialize a bus route that he seldom traveled by the time of this study emphasizes the symbolic significance of the choice. In the context of a prompt about the future payoff of his education, this representation of his past as a bus linking west and east Louisville demonstrates the simultaneity and interdependency of his material, representational, and embodied mobilities. In this sketch, he seems to be mapping elements of his promised future—financial prosperity, freedom, control, etc.—onto the route of his historical and physical journeys to and within school. This imaginative travel is informed, in large part, by discourses of readiness discussed throughout this book, as representations of an eminent future inspire James's material movements within scenes of literacy, through the school building, and across the city. The future is made ever-present in the relationship between these representations and James's imagination.

Through grade school and middle school, James was bused from west to east according to his grandmother's wishes and the district's desegregation policy, requiring institutions to maintain African American student populations of between 15 and 50 percent in grade school and between 16 and 46 percent in middle school. For high school, James bused east to Hughes from his new neighborhood in south Louisville, again, in accordance with his grandmother's wishes and a revised assignment system designed to integrate schools by neighborhood clusters arranged according to census data on percentage minority residents, educational attainment of adults, and household income (Semuels 2015). And so for his entire primary and secondary school career, James traveled east for an education that was presented by both his family and his schools as a ticket into the middle class. Perhaps because Route 23 moves in the same direction as his physical journeys from home to school and back, James presents it as a symbol of the promise of education for his future: west to east, poverty to prosperity.

Of course, this symbol also carries an implicit threat: buses run both ways. While institutions located in predominantly white middle-class neighborhoods promised James financial stability and independence through a curricular stairway to prosperity, school buses, as agents of these institutions, delivered him, along with most of his classmates, back to largely segregated, economically depressed neighborhoods after school. In this way, the elliptical journey of the bus mirrors the ways in which the larger mobility system of public education tends to manage the movements of poor and working-class minorities (Guryan 2004, Alexander 2010, Rothstein 2013). As I showed in the previous chapter, by blocking his access to tertiary education, this system ultimately worked, like the bus, to return James to his neighborhood—to his place in society. In many ways, for James and most of his regular-track classmates, the district's busing system carries out a strategy of containment similar to those presented in the previous chapter in the forms of academic tracking, hall monitoring, and the attempted erasure of literate and linguistic diversity.

While it is true that students of diverse races, ethnicities, and socioeconomic statuses are bused in every direction to schools across the Jefferson County Public School District, since the implementation of mandatory busing for desegregation in Louisville in 1975 the burden of travel has been borne primarily by African Americans and other students of color.[5] As Tracy E. K'Meyer (2013a) asserts in *From Brown to Meredith: The Long Struggle for School Desegregation in Louisville, Kentucky, 1954–2007*, whites have traditionally "assumed that desegregated schools must be majority white," and "even the most ardent integrationists took for granted that black students would bear the burden of busing by being transported for more years than whites, and they rarely appreciated that something of value might be lost with the end of black-led institutions" (p. 183). Because a particular construction of white, middle-class America still exists as the default for school culture at Hughes and has become even more pronounced as a result of the school's rebranding efforts after a state audit, busing works in the service of a larger system designed to contain and manage cultural differences.

This is not to say that I disagree with the practice of busing for the pursuit of equality and diversity in schools. Alongside K'Meyer and others (Semuels 2015,

Orfield 2015), I applaud the efforts of Louisville's activists, parents, students, teachers, administrators, politicians, and voters to preserve this system in the face of sustained and sometimes violent opposition. According to K'Meyer (2013b), Louisville is one of the most desegregated public school systems in the country, which reflects a history of support for integration and considerable community defense of busing as a means to achieve it. For instance, in 1983 when the superintendent of schools proposed changes to the city's desegregation plan that would shift the burden of travel almost exclusively onto black students while undermining the quality of schools in their neighborhoods, integration advocates decried the plan as "one-way busing" and organized to stop it. K'Meyer quotes African American civil rights activist Mattie Jones describing the plan as Jim Crow racism alongside a white mother from a middle-class neighborhood on the eastern edge of the city, who asserted that "any plan that does not bring kids from the suburbs into the city is morally wrong" (2013b).

While I agree with K'Meyer and those she cites here, I would argue that as long as white middle-class values and assumptions, presented as racially neutral, continue to dominate the cultural and academic standards of schools like Hughes, busing will always be one-way regardless of the directions in which students are shuttled. While this mobility system does make Hughes a demographically diverse institution, with a total minority enrollment of 64 percent and an economically disadvantaged student population of 74 percent, the school, in accordance with district and state policy, delimits interactions across differences by dividing students into separate tracks of study, creating separate academies and programs within the school to contain certain student populations ("freshman," English language learners, special education), isolating a disproportionate number of black and Hispanic students in In-School Adjustment Programs and with suspensions (Skiba et al. 2002, Mendez and Knoff 2003), and failing to provide adequate transportation so that all students can participate in extracurricular activities (Jefferson County Public Schools n.d., *2012–2013 Data Books*).

Writing about his impression of the nature and effects of these mechanisms of partitioning and containment in a paper composed for his second-semester college composition course at the University of Louisville, Nadif asserts:

> To my observations the school [Hughes] is divided into two sections: a small group of AP and Honors students and the rest of the school, these students are totally separated academically and socially because of the fact that they don't have classes together and of course they don't hang out together. While I was part of the AP students it still seemed to me like a class warfare, where the rich and the poor don't even shop at the same store, except at [Hughes], it's educational warfare where the same students in the same building don't get the same level of education.
>
> (p. 3)[6]

Approximately one year before he composed this critique, Nadif highlighted the role of transportation in this process of resegregation in his previously mentioned proposal for AP English:

> Students don't get to know themselves, neither did they get the chance to see what activities Hughes offers. They don't care about the school while some will say "I don't go to school I go to Hughes." The only way to clean that from the students mind is offer transportation, so they get the chance to show their school spirit.
>
> (p. 4)

In these passages, Nadif associates students' shared sense of detachment from the school with a lack of collective participation due, in large part, to academic tracking and an inadequate system of transportation. Rather than feeling integrated, many students feel isolated from each other, their teachers, and from the activity of the school. Administrative efforts to combat this sense of isolation and fragmentation focus on celebrating academic and behavioral achievement, which, again, is measured according to a shared set of standards based on white middle-class norms and expectations.

As de facto means of resegregation, the policies and procedures Nadif addresses in these passages transfer responsibility for students' circumscribed or blocked mobilities onto the students themselves (Southworth and Mickelson 2007, O'Connor et al. 2011). As long as all students are measured according to the same standards, assessed by the same exams, and granted access to the same opportunities—at least on paper—the system can exonerate itself from the injustices of social reproduction. By providing James his choice of schools along with transportation to and from these schools, supplying TARC vouchers for extracurricular activities, maintaining an open enrollment policy for advanced placement, and so on, the school system can maintain its claim of providing students equal access to opportunities for mobility. When James chooses not to act on these opportunities, he is the one to blame for his own immobility. And yet, his school choices are largely contingent upon racially biased standardized tests scores (Kidder and Rosner 2002, Freedle 2003, Santelices and Wilson 2010), his academic track is essentially set in the third grade and maintained by his scores on periodic Cognitive Abilities Tests (also racially biased), and his participation in extracurricular activities is limited not only by his part-time job and family obligations but also by time and safety concerns associated with TARC travel.[7]

Ultimately, the school system's dual strategy of (1) partitioning according to academic achievement, which tends to separate poor, minority, and ESL students from their white middle-class peers (Garet and DeLany 1988, Mickelson 2001, Heilig and Holme 2013); and (2) promoting white middle-class literate, linguistic, and behavioral norms as racially neutral standards transforms a system of busing for integration into a system for resegregation, exclusion, and obstruction of student mobilities.[8] In this way, the operations of the system accord with a history of literacy education in the United States that has traditionally served as a means of demarcating, containing, and managing literacy and language differences. As Catherine Prendergast (2003) demonstrates in *Literacy and Racial Justice*, "In American history, literacy has been treated as White property, whereas the paths for groups of color to lay ownership to literacy have been more obstructed" (p. 166). As a consequence of resegregation or second-generation segregation, James experiences this obstruction in the form of institutional divides between being Black and being academically elite (O'Connor et al. 2011, p. 1249).

Riding in the City

It is, perhaps, this sense of obstruction that James is resisting by claiming what he perceives to be a more agentive form of mobility—the car—for his future. According to his representation, he is moving beyond the prescribed mobilities of formal education, which he associates with bus travel, to a future in which he is able to control his own comings and goings. In this way, James shares de Certeau's (1984) impression of public transportation, which the latter describes as a "travelling incarceration" in which human bodies are able to be ordered because, although the carriage is mobile, the passengers are immobile. Inside this "bubble of panoptic and classifying power . . . there is the immobility of an order. . . . Every being is placed there like a piece of printer's type on a page arranged in military order" (p. 111). For de Certeau, public transport holds passengers in a mechanism of objectification by pigeonholing and regulating them in the grid of the carriage. Within this closed and autonomous insularity, disciplinary power constitutes and arranges individuals as objects without discourse (de Certeau 1984, p. 112).

In light of de Certeau's commentary on public transit, James's depiction of his educational past as a city bus is an apt metaphor for common conceptualizations of public schooling. Like Sommers and Saltz's (2004) assumption of the mechanized and structurally determined nature of writing in high school, which forestalls students' "paradigm shifts" into college (p. 140), de Certeau's carriage conceals its essentially immobilizing operations with a promise of mobility. According to these representations, movements of passengers from one predetermined stop to another and students' movements between scenes and stages of education are predicated upon objectification and arrangement. Progress in a unified system appears to require a renunciation of wayfaring as a way of being and knowing (Ingold 2009).

And yet, also like a bus, this system is not as determinative of practices and subjectivities as these depictions suggest. In the same way that my rides with Nadif helped me to recognize the carriage and route of the city bus as a mediator of countless other mobilities, I believe that K-16 literacy pedagogies and curricula must help students like James recognize and make use of the possible mobilities that circulate with, in, and around their prescribed movements across scenes of literacy and educational scales. In other words, students must develop new and recognize existing *tactics* for exploiting openings in the apparently autonomous, containerized power structures of formal education. De Certeau (1984) describes a tactic as: "A mobility that must accept the chance offerings of the moment, and seize on the wing the possibilities that offer themselves at any given moment. It must vigilantly make use of the cracks that particular conjunctions open in the surveillance of proprietary powers" (p. 37). As I've attempted to help James identify and extend these potential tactics, he has revealed openings for new spaces of action through his mobile practices that I would have never recognized on my own.

In fact, James's co-creation of the *interplace* (Casey 1996) of bus travel was more tactical than de Certeau seems to have imagined possible. Far from a "bubble of panoptic and classifying power," the school bus James and his classmates rode for their daily 30- to 45-minute trip from south to east Louisville was exploited as a reoccurring crack in the surveillance of the school system's propriety power. Through the achievement of coordinated action around licit and illicit academic collaboration, students appropriated this vehicle and its mechanized route for the formation of collectives that worked across differences to create and share material and conceptual resources, challenge standards of individual effort and authorship, negotiate subjectivities, and make use of literacies and languages restricted within the confines of the school building. In other words, James and his classmates participated on and with the bus to open up a space-time of resistance against the pedagogies of containment described in the previous chapter (Giroux 2010).

I first learned about these bus collectives when I began asking students, including James, about what seemed to me to be unique associations across racial, ethnic, and linguistic differences in one of the regular English classes I observed. After several weeks of mapping James's and his texts' material mobilities in the class through methods described in Chapter 2, I began to notice patterns of exchange in which James, who almost exclusively socialized with his African American classmates from the west end, would travel to the other side of the classroom to partner with a group of Vietnamese, Burmese and African students for group activities such as peer reviews and shared reading response worksheets. Not only that, but I noticed that James regularly exchanged papers and text messages after and occasionally during class with his international classmates.

At first, I assumed James had been assigned to work with this group. He wasn't the only student crossing ethnic, linguistic, and neighborhood boundaries for these activities and he had established himself as one of the more confident writers in the class, so I assumed his teacher had assigned him and a few others to serve as peer tutors for English language learners. I operated under this assumption for several months before James let me know that I had him confused, assuring me there was no chance he would be asked, much less agree, to assume such a role:

"No, that's not me, man. Ms. X doesn't even like me, and I'm not really that kind of student." As we looked over a series of classroom time-space maps together, James explained the formation of his small group: "We're busmates, we ride the school bus together from Iroquois [neighborhood in south Louisville]."

> Brice: So, you became friends on the bus?
> James: No, we just help each other out in classes sometimes.
> Brice: You work together because you ride to school together?
> James: Well [long pause], we work together on the ride to school.
> Brice: I see, so you do your work together on the bus on the way to school.
> James: Right, like homework and papers and stuff. No big deal.

At this point in the conversation, I could sense that James was feeling uncomfortable with the direction we were taking, so I asked a few more clarifying questions and quickly moved on to another subject.

However, I did note a few details from this brief exchange in a "talkback sheet" that would inform subsequent conversations with James (Lillis 2001, p. 147). First, I was curious about his move to differentiate a school self from the sort of student who might be appointed as a peer tutor. Despite his model behavior in class and consistently strong academic performances, James did not seem to see and/or want to identify himself as a "good" student. Second, I was interested in the assertion of his strictly academic relationship with busmates, as he seemed to want to establish that their collaboration in class and on the bus was not socially motivated—they were not friends. Third, I noticed James's desire to downplay the significance of the work of these collaborations, suggesting that the assignments were of little concern—"no big deal." Finally, I noted his indication of plural "classes," implying that these collectives worked across the curriculum as well as the city. We would return to these points in later conversations, which I discuss below.

In the meantime, this initial exchange served as a healthy reminder that after months of participating in the activity of the course, I still had very little knowledge of the "underlife" of the class. Robert Brooke (1987) describes underlife as "the activities (or information games) individuals engage in to show that their identities are different from or more complex than the identities assigned them by organizational roles" (p. 142). Following Erving Goffman, he identifies two primary forms of underlife—*disruptive* and *contained*—and suggests that most activities correspond with the latter, as individuals and groups often work "around the institution" to assert differences from assigned roles, rather than present overt challenges and threats to the institution (p. 143). From his position of participant observer in a first-year college writing course, Brooke identifies four major types of student underlife activity: (1) Applying class materials and practices in ways unintended by the teacher; (2) Engaging in commentary on available and assumed roles in the course most often to exchange ideas about how to "get by" in the class; (3) Evaluating and critiquing the activity of the class; and (4) Dividing attention between class activities and concerns other than these activities.

Brooke asserts that students participate in this underlife to demonstrate that they are more than just students: "The point is not to disrupt the functioning of the classroom, but to provide the other participants in the classroom with a sense that one has other things to do, other interests, that one is a much richer personality than can be shown in this context" (p. 148). In other words, students engage in activities that might be perceived to be disruptive by a teacher to create space for their historical bodies in institutions that tend to neglect or reduce such bodies.[9]

While Brooke's presentation of underlife helps to explain James's resistance to the role of compliant student, his collaborations with Vietnamese, Burmese and African classmates, and his social distancing from these classmates, it doesn't speak to the ways in which a racially stratified system forces students like James to balance performances of identity and racial affiliation with demands and perceptions of academic achievement (O'Connor et al. 2011).

As demonstrated in the previous chapter, by this point in his educational career James had undergone 12 years of discipline and punishment to maintain the separation of his school self from his identities and affiliations outside of school. However, when he is confronted with a reading of his identity that implies the institution has successfully accomplished this separation, such as my suggestion that he might be a peer tutor, he defends the differences from this institutional role that he has worked to preserve. O'Connor et al. (2011) explain that racially stratified academic hierarchies, like the one operating at Hughes, in which non-Asian minorities are disproportionally tracked into lower level courses, "amplify and animate the individual peer group meanings Black students take to school to produce social and academic consequences" (p. 1252). According to this theory, for James and his classmates from the west side, to serve as a peer-tutor is to "act White," not because he sees his blackness as conflicting with academic excellence—again, James was by all measures an excellent student—but because in a resegregated system, positions of academic achievement are usually perceived as "White niches" (Carter 2006).

This perception might also help explain why James remained in regular-track English classes throughout his educational career despite his seemingly effortless success in these classes. The process of jumping tracks into AP English would have placed more strain on his affiliation with the west end, which he was already working hard to maintain because of his residency on the south side, and may have jeopardized the support and acceptance he felt from his Black peers. As Susan Yonezawa, Amy Stuart Wells, and Irene Serna (2002) assert, minority students are prone to "bypass more challenging classes because they hunger for 'places of respect'—classrooms where they were not racially isolated and their cultural backgrounds were valued" (p. 40). For James, staying connected with his Black classmates in a racially stratified system required remaining in regular courses.

To prevent being twice removed from his neighborhood—physically by the bus and socially by curricular segregation—James participates in the institution's restrictions on his academic mobilities. Foucault (1982) describes this participation as characteristic of power relations in liberal democracies. Defining government as a structuring of the possible fields of action of others, he suggests that coercion requires the complicity of the coerced (p. 790). In this sense, to govern is to affect the way in which individuals conduct themselves. The process of governing involves "a versatile equilibrium, with complementarity and conflicts between techniques which impose coercion and processes through which the self is constructed or modified by himself" (Foucault 1993, p. 203). In this way, James's distancing from proposed institutional roles and maintenance of subversive subjectivities keep him on this designated track of study.

However, by collaborating with his busmates across space-time and cultural, linguistic, and literate differences, James works to reconstitute or relocalize the scenes that comprise this track. This extension of underlife activities to "get by" in a system that consistently devalues students' ways of reading, writing, thinking, and living includes distributing the work of classes beyond the confines of these classes and among participants, exploiting blind spots in hierarchized surveillance, subverting strategies of atomization, and permeating the boundaries between designated tracks of education. In these ways, the bus collectives highlight the fragility of disciplinary power. As John Ransom (1997) asserts, "The fact that we are vehicles of disciplinary power reveals . . . not the omnipotence of power but its fragility. Such vehicles might go off the designated path in directions that frustrate the purpose for which they were originally developed" (p. 36). By co-opting the space-time of the school bus to pursue routeways otherwise blocked by the institution, James and many of his busmates are assuming agencies produced through mobilities and frictions among each other, the school bus, the school system, and a host of other actors. If James were to revise his journal entry sketch to account for this assumption of agency in his educational *present* (at the time of the study), he would need to acknowledge his adoption of both driver and passenger roles in the practice of his academic literacies. However, as I asserted in the previous chapter, the relentless future orientation of neoliberal education often prevents students from recognizing the innovation, power, and complexity of and agencies produced through their literacy practices in the present.

Mobile Collectives

Ransom's metaphor is particularly appropriate for a system of education predicated upon designated lines of transport, and over the course of this project I did often observe students (and teachers and administrators) venture off these paths in manners that frustrated the system. However, I observed few divergences that worked within and against this system as effectively as James's bus collectives. As we continued to develop our conversations about these collectives over time,

James, Nadif, and others who rode what students called the "international bus" from the south side began to provide more details about the ways in which the bus served to recruit and enroll students, objects, ideas, and information into "literacy networks" extending across and beyond localities at Hughes. I was able to trace out threads of these networks by shadowing students' bus travel from the south side to Hughes (Latour 1996, Leander and Lovvorn 2006).

By our third interview, James seemed to trust that I was not interested in subjecting him to more punitive surveillance and reporting; although we did discuss how research involves surveillance and interpretation of a different sort, with different risks and possible rewards. Starting with the talkback sheet described above, the topics of discussion in this third interview circulated around his English class/bus group's formation and operations. In this interview, James describes how he was initially hesitant to engage in conversation with his international busmates because he assumed their language differences would put too much strain on their exchanges: "I knew most of them [international students] from classes, but never really talked to them because I didn't think I could understand them. And I didn't think they could understand me either. . . . I was always tired on the bus, so I just rode and tried to sleep and didn't really talk to anybody at first."

When I asked how his attitude and practice on the bus began to change, he mentioned noticing how certain groups of students studied together and divided schoolwork among themselves. He also noticed how students formed these groups across ethnic and linguistic differences: "The students working together weren't just from one place. . . . different kinds were helping each other and other kids, and I saw them helping each other in classes too." By highlighting his recognition of this collaboration, James points to a change in his own under- standing of possibilities for accomplishing shared tasks by working across cultural and linguistic differences. This recognition is supported by speech accommodation theory, which shows how "speakers don't have to be experts in another variety of English in order to speak to other communities. They simply need the meta- linguistic, sociolinguistic, and attitudinal preparedness to negotiate differences even as they use their own dialects" (Canagarajah 2006, p. 593). And so, through his observations of and eventual participation in this multilingual bus collaborative, James began to develop metalinguistic, sociolinguistic, and attitudinal skills often neglected by the boundary-based standards and assessments that dominated his formal literacy instruction.

James admitted that at first he would ask busmates to share their homework, specifically reading-review and math worksheets from which he could easily copy answers: "Sometimes I didn't get schoolwork done because of work or something else, so I would ask these guys who I knew were good at math and stuff to see their homework." However, over a period of time, he began to recognize reciprocation as a shared expectation of this collaborative and, consequently, started helping his busmates meet the demands of the standardized English required in their papers. As demonstrated in the previous chapter, James was adept at accommodating the standards of academic discourse presented in his classes, and this ability quickly made him a valuable member of bus collectives comprised primarily of English language learners.

On the trips I observed, James could hardly keep up with the demand for his feedback. Completed and partial worksheets, essay drafts, and word puzzles circulated over vinyl seats to James's spot, and one student after another slid in beside him to consult and then slide back out. I remember being surprised by the quietness of this collaboration in the dim light of early morning. No doubt, my presence contributed to the muffled and quick conversations. Nonetheless, students did not attempt to conceal their collaboration. Exchanges clearly picked up where they left off the day or night before, and students were attentive to each other's work in ways I seldom observed in school settings.

While it would be easy to dismiss these mobile collaborations as common instances of cheating, the development of students' roles in the relationships and the shared efforts of this group signals a much more complex and pedagogically valuable scene of literacy. This pedagogical value is especially pronounced in James's collaborations with Nadif, who had come to rely on James's feedback on

An appeal to the people.

In an advertisement shown on TV, a boy is loaded with rifle, pistol, and multiple grenades. The advertisement has been aired from a TV show in America, to convince the American people give their support to Israel. A country that is in desperate for help with a fight against Palestine. This is what puts one into a hopeless condition. The ad targets an audience who finds child soldier as an offensive. The ad urges people to consider child soldier as foolish act. It appeals to ethos, logos, pathos, and kairos to convince the crowd in different ways. The designer made his message clear at the way he loaded the young boy with weapons. Looking into the eyes of the boy in the picture, you feel and passionate he is about his job. This ad exposes the dangers of a pro-Israel stance that supports children as victims and participants of a war.

It seems that children are already been convinced to consider going to war as an option. "What kind of society raises six-year old on dream of suicide, homicide, and hatred? A society that targets Israel." the children of Israel has an enemy that has exists, and the

FIGURE 4.4 James and Nadif Peer Review, Part 1

Used with permission.

almost all his writing for school. Figure 4.4 shows a section of a draft composed by Nadif for AP English and marked by James on the bus ride to Hughes.

As evidenced in this text, James's review of Nadif's work goes beyond surface-level corrections to include the sort of formative commentary we might associate with genuine investment in the meaning-making processes of Nadif's composition. In this way, the collaboration involves the pedagogical value of genuine peer review often promoted and pursued in literacy classes.[10] However, this review could not have occurred within the confines of the institution because Nadif and James were separated into different tracks of study.[11] Moreover, some of the marks James makes on Nadif's paper, such as replacing and correcting terms, might be seen as pushing the boundaries of collaboration, presenting a challenge to demands of individual authorship. When I asked Nadif if he would ever consider telling his English teacher about James's role in his process of composing, he responded by suggesting that she may get the wrong idea: "She may believe he does work for me. I would not want to risk of telling her."

Nadif's comment here represents a perspective that frequently emerged among students participating in this research. In both high school and college, students seemed to embrace ideas and practices of collaborating around academic literacy practices outside classes, but most often avoided showing signs of collaboration within official scenes of school. While Nadif was frequently encouraged and even required to engage in peer review activities in high school and college English classes—activities that resembled his reviews with James in almost every way—he was hesitant to admit to engaging in these activities outside institutionally sanctioned scenes of literacy. This tendency to conceal collaboration was especially pronounced in the student-led writing collectives I observed after following Nadif and others to college. Like the high school bus collectives, these groups formed around shared places rather than shared tasks.

For instance, Nadif's Muslim Student Association at the university often operated as a cross-curricular, interdisciplinary study group, as students working on assignments and projects for different classes in different disciplines congregated in library study rooms, dormitory lobbies, and dining halls to share material, discursive, and conceptual resources in their work together toward different objectives. Most often students participating in such collectives were reluctant to admit their influences on each other's work. They seemed to conceive of their activities as anti- or, at least, counter-institutional. And in secondary and tertiary institutions that tend to privilege the apparently original productions of independent actors through individual assessments, plagiarism threats and detection strategies and software, physical and virtual surveillance, and so on, these students' suspicions and anxieties are often well-founded (Williams 2009, p. 65).

In this way, according to the perceptions of most participating students (and observant teachers), collectives like those formed on the "international bus" to Hughes and among ethnic and/or affinity groups in college, engage in forms of underlife that circulate around classroom activities. The students comprising these collectives make use of their daily patterns of material mobility, often coordinated via virtual and communicative mobilities, to participate in underlife activities that enable them to not only maintain the complexity of their identities, but also to share tasks and resources across places, bodies, texts, and objects. Of course, this division and redistribution of labor has significant impacts on the practices and performances that constitute the institutionally sanctioned scenes of literacy and scales across which these collectives circulate.

Consequently, these underlife activities are not merely *contained* or even *disruptive* forms of resistance that work around or against institutions, as Brooke and Goffman assert; they are *constitutive* forms of resistance that (re)shape scenes of literacy and, thus, scales of education by pluralizing the space-time of these scenes. As demonstrated in James's movement across the space of his English class to resume work with busmates that began and would continue on their daily commutes to school or in text trajectories (Kell 2013) that include impromptu peer reviews on Nadif's academic essays, the mobilities that configure students' practices and realities outside scenes of literacy reconfigure the space-time of these scenes and visa versa.

Up to this point in the chapter, I've focused primarily on how such pluarlizations are accomplished through student collaborations on and with school and city buses. But multiple objects are always involved in producing heterogeneous space-time (Leander and Lovvorn 2006, p. 293). As Latour (1996) asserts: "Any time an interaction has temporal and spatial extension, it is because one has shared it with non-humans" (p. 239). In the next section, I continue to investigate constitutive underlife activities by attending to the ways in which Nadif and Katherine interweave face-to-face interactions with academic texts and information and communication technologies (ICTs) to extend the space-times of scenes of literacy in high school and college.

ICTravel

Nadif's process of imagining the University of Louisville and himself within it began in a cybercafé in Nairobi. Because he spent his early childhood in Dadaab living with his grandmother, his United Nations identification number matched her household's rather than his immediate family's. And so when his father, mother, and two younger siblings received U.S. visas, they were forced to leave Nadif behind in Nairobi, where he was attending secondary school. As he explains, when UN officials select you for resettlement, "You don't want to lose the opportunity. If you're standing in front of somebody [offering you passage to the U.S.] and you delay, you will not get another offer. That's the one time you'll get it." And so, rather than risk forfeiting the passages of four people to retrieve one, his parents seized their opportunities for relocation and trusted Nadif's would come later. Over the course of the year it took to obtain appropriate identification, undergo security interviews, and receive his own visa, Nadif was resigned to navigating his future home on a rented computer, network connection, and search engine in the Burger Dome Cybercafé located a few blocks from his school.

When he learned his family had settled in an apartment complex eight miles from the University of Louisville, he began to regularly browse the school's website. Speaking of his initial impressions of the university, he laughingly suggested that "First, all I know about the college was a sports stadium. Every time I went to the website, I saw a picture on the front page. I showed my friends how big it was and got excited and proud to go to school at this place." Eventually he began investigating the website of the university's Department of Political Science with aspirations of studying a subject that would enable him to serve his home country: "I was interested in politics because I understood that in order to be a good peacemaker, who could help solve Somalia's problems and educate others, I needed to have good understanding of politics." He studied the program's requirements, course offerings and descriptions, location on campus and images of the building, faculty photos and areas of expertise, internship opportunities, and so on. By the time he left Kenya, Nadif had already spent hours experiencing and anticipating the "atmosphere of the place"—representations of the department's materiality, values, expectations, and discourses—through virtual and imaginative mobilities (Halgreen 2004).

After months of this virtual and imaginative travel, Nadif received word from friends in Dabaab that UN officials were looking for him in the camp. He was in the process of taking an end-of-term chemistry test when he checked his cell phone and noticed 15 missed calls in a period of 20 minutes from the three people designated to watch the wall where all official communications were posted at the camp and notify him if his name appeared. Nadif describes his reaction to these missed calls: "As soon as I saw these calls, I knew something was up. So I just went to the restroom. That's the only way you can use your phone in the school. So I made a phone call and found out that my name is on the wall and I am needed, like, today." Upon receiving this news, Nadif immediately left school, called his parents to wire money for travel, packed his belongings, and contacted a transportation service to drive him the 500 kilometers from Nairobi to Dadaab. He did not make it back to the camp until early the next morning, but after pleading with UN officials, he was allowed to take his place among a group of newly approved U.S. immigrants en route to New York City.

This brief sequence of Nadif's mobility narrative demonstrates the complexity of inter-relational dynamics among material, representational, and embodied mobilities and their imaginative, virtual, and communicative dimensions. While it is clear that his material trajectory to the U.S. required coordinated movements of people, objects, ideas, and information across both distant and proximate spaces and times—movements of information through various bureaucracies, movements of messages across cellular networks, movements of money across wire transfer systems, movements of bodies via ground and air transportation, and so on—of particular significance to this exploration of educational mobilities are the ways in which the virtual, communicative, and imaginative travel made possible by Nadif's partnership with information and communication technologies (ICTs) informed his perceptions of and practices in the scenes of literacy in which he participated at Hughes and the University of Louisville. Like the intertwining of mobilities shaping his experiences with and on buses, Nadif's engagements with the internet and mobile phones blend physical, virtual, communicative, and imaginative mobilities to project and transform scenes of literacy in high school and college.

Colleges of Collage

By now, it is a commonplace that the proliferation of objects supporting virtual and communicative travel—mobile phones, personal computers, tablets, email, chat, text messages, search engines, etc.—have contributed to a complex and rapidly changing technoscape (Castells 1996, Urry 2007, Thrift 2004). As Ilana Snyder (2002) asserts, a "new communication order, centred around information technologies, is part of the technological revolution that is reshaping the material bases of society. New technologies have made massive incursions into all facets of life, albeit unevenly in different parts of the world" (p. 4). Despite the uneven distribution of such technologies, elements of Nadif's mobility narrative demonstrate how ICTs create possibilities for relatively seamless multimodal, sensory, and affective connections across space-time in even the most under-resourced environments.

In the case recounted above, Nadif's family's physical travel to Louisville initiated a pattern of imaginative, virtual, and communicative mobilities through which he not only collected information about the city and the university but also reassembled this information to produce unique representations of these localities along with new ways of conceiving of the possible subjectivities he might take up in relation to them. In this way, Nadif's partnerships with rented computers, internet connections, websites, and so on contribute to more than space-time compressions (Massey 1994, Harvey 1990, Soja 1989) or a utopian global community commonly associated with the proliferation of ICTs (Fox 2001). These partnerships contribute to virtual and material *becomings of place* by altering the ways in which Nadif represents these places to himself and others.

Nicholas Burbules (2002) describes the navigational and semiotic elements of such becomings of place in his proposal of the internet as a rhetorical *place*.

> Calling the Web a rhetorical space captures the idea of movement within it, the possibility of discovering meaningful connections between elements found there; but it does not capture the distinctive way in which users try to make the Web familiar, to make it *their* space—to make it a *place*. Individual users do this by selecting a homepage for their browser, by

bookmarking sites, by visiting the same familiar sites frequently, and by making their own webpages.

(p. 78, author's emphasis)

So as Nadif chats with relocated family and friends in Louisville, follows the university's Twitter feed, browses the city's official website, and participates in conversations on the wall of the Young Somalis for Louisville Facebook page, all from a cybercafé in Nairobi, he is not merely bringing distant locations within the range of his senses or producing an "illusion of closeness," as Nedra Reynolds (2004) suggests (p. 18). He is developing idiosyncratically meaningful ways of relating linked sites in the co-creation of a virtual geography that comes to represent his future destination city and university. By establishing a pattern of web browsing and communication that connects frequently visited sites of institutions, affinity groups, and friends and family, Nadif is identifying and charting movements among key points in fields of future participation. In this way, he creates a virtual map—selecting, simplifying and schematizing representative aspects of the city and university and, thereby, developing concepts of the places he will eventually inhabit and transform.

After discovering that Nadif spent the year leading up to his resettlement engaged in such extensive virtual travel, I designed a memory activity for one of our bus rides from Hughes to the university to retrace and materialize a portion of the virtual map Nadif charted from Nairobi. My hope was that this process of remapping would provide an occasion for reflecting on his expectations for participation in college. The activity essentially consisted of working in reverse from his perceptions of college to locate them in particular sites of information. Of course, as in any attempt at remembering, the past is transformed in the process of retrieving and recounting it. Nonetheless, by the end of our ride, Nadif and I were able to reconstruct an interesting string of connections in his virtual map of the university and to consider its influences on his present practice and future expectations.

When I asked Nadif why he decided to attend UofL, I was surprised by his response: "Because the school and I both care about Africa. [. . .] People there will help me accomplish my goal to help and bring peace to Somalia." In addition to the suggestion of linguistic mobility and attitudinal preparedness presented in the previous chapter, the alignment Nadif perceives between his own interests and goals and those of the university provides another possible explanation for his success in college. Figure 4.5 offers a representation of the map Nadif and I sketched to retrace one route by which he came to an understanding of this alignment.

Nadif's map begins with the names of two professors in the political science department: "I found out these two teachers: [Professor 1], who studies Islam, and [Professor 2], who does politics of Africa." While Nadif had not met either of these professors at the time of this interview, he knew their areas of expertise from searching the department's website. He remembered finding Professor 1's

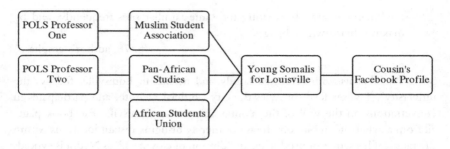

FIGURE 4.5 Map of Nadif's Internet Searches

Used with permission.

name in an event description posted on the webpage of the university's Muslim Student Association (MSA), and he found Professor 2's name listed for a Pan-African Studies (PAS) course on religion and politics. He had learned of the school's MSA and PAS programs, along with the African Students Union, through the Young Somalis for Louisville group page, which he had discovered on Facebook through a cousin's personal profile. This cousin had immigrated to Louisville two years before Nadif's parents' arrival in the city. While this visual traces the initial chronological formation of this chain of associations, in practice, Nadif would have revised this chain with every browsing session—altering the order and frequency of circulation, adding and removing sites from this progression, following different links to and from these sites and so on.

While it would be interesting to observe how Nadif's process of rhetorical placemaking on and with the internet changes over time and according to context, the key point here is that by Nadif's account, on this particular occasion the virtual map contributing to his conception of the university as an institution that shares his concern for Africa was developed through patterns of movement among sites of information in a meshwork he created before emigrating to the U.S. This conceptualization not only informed his choice to attend the university, but also influenced many of his decisions while still in high school.

As previously mentioned, we sketched the above map en route to the university, where Nadif was already taking an Introduction to Pan-African Studies course for dual enrollment credit. Moreover, his topic selection for papers in high school was often motivated by his desire to prepare for future studies. Across his senior classes, Nadif wrote about the consequences of the colonization of Africa represented in the work of Achebe and about the possibility of a representative World Court. He wrote case briefs on several major U.S. Supreme Court decisions and researched NATO's invasion of Libya and the U.S. intervention in Somalia. He declared on multiple occasions that he chose to write about these issues because he knew he would need to understand them for his political science program.

It is interesting to note that Katherine engages in similar processes of mapping future geographies of tertiary education with representations assembled from television shows depicting college life. In an interview we conducted during her senior year of high school, Katherine responds without hesitation to a question about where most of her impressions of college come from:

> TV [. . .] I watch *Gilmore Girls* a lot, and she [Rory Gilmore] goes to Yale, so, like, I have that impression of college. And there's another show; it's called *Best Years of Our Lives* or something. And it's based in college, and it's more focused on social life. And then I watch *Greek*, and it's more about fraternities and sororities, which I know I won't really be a part of, but it does seem fun.

Like Nadif's processes of imagining and charting the terrain of his future geographies, Katherine deliberately and inadvertently samples fictional scenes and experiences from these shows to piece together a *collage of college*. While there is very little novelty in the assertion that students develop their own gestalts of college from information and impressions provided by and circulating through various sources, including family members and friends, Katherine's assertion that popular culture sources are more prevalent in her gestalt than relational and academic sources is relevant to the discussion of rhetorics of college and career readiness presented in the previous chapter. While neoliberal reform efforts work to define and project college as a spatially and temporally fixed target with predictable and uniform standards and expectations, popular culture provides a range of alternative representations, which may be more compelling and, thereby, more influential to students' perceptions of and practices in college. And although these representations reduce the dynamic and heterogeneous spaces of college in many of the same ways as rhetorics of readiness, students' participation in popular culture might enable them to sample from a greater diversity of sources to create more complex projections of their lives in college.

Discussing online composing practices, Bronwyn Williams (2009) asserts that "popular culture provides the largest, most varied, and most accessible assortment of images, video, and sound for people to sample as they compose" (p. 66). Drawing, in part, from de Certeau's concept of poaching to describe a process by which individuals appropriate pieces of text to assemble new creations that serve their own interests and experiences, Williams proposes that in their interactions with new media technologies, students are "like nomadic poachers roaming across texts hunting not just for meanings but for pieces they can incorporate and reuse in their everyday lives" (p. 80). While Nadif and Katherine are not composing digital texts in these particular instances (though they are engaged in creating such texts elsewhere), the idea of poaching from popular culture for conceptualizations of college does accord with the accounts of many students participating in this project.

Processes of poaching from mass media representations and the experiences of fictional characters contribute to the development of ersatz memories— nostalgia without lived experience—that inform students' expectations, decisions, and practices in college. For instance, when I asked Katherine why she made the decision to stop attending community college, she stated: "Because it didn't feel like college, [long pause] like what college is supposed to be." As we continued to unpack the specific elements of her community college experience that she felt conflicted with her preconceptions, we came to the conclusion that her experiences were different in most every way from those of the characters on her favorite television shows. Among other differences, the actual work of college is seldom depicted in these shows; characters are seemingly completely consumed with social life; their off-campus work is rarely displayed; and material needs are met behind the scenes. Ultimately, Katherine's experience of community college was nothing like Rory Gilmore's experience of Yale, which likely has very little in common with the experiences of students at the actual institution.

Here, it is important to note that the virtual and imaginative mobilities made possible by Nadif's and Katherine's partnerships with networked computers, search engines, personalized web browsers, and television are not limitless. Like students' material movements on school and city buses, through the halls of Hughes and across college campuses, Nadif's and Katherine's virtual and imaginative mobilities are shaped and constrained by strategies directing and channeling navigation. Strategies employed to control portals, filter information, direct lines of inquiry, spread ideologies, divert attention, and attract viewers have a significant impact upon the content and contours of Nadif's and Katherine's virtual and imaginary maps. Additionally, "accidental" diversions, such as outdated information, broken hyperlinks, slow processing speeds, cancelled shows, and alternative programming, delimit and prevent meanings they might otherwise make of their investigations. While there seems to be a high degree of choice in how and where users move within the space-time of the internet and mass media, barriers to virtual and imaginary mobilities, along with the pragmatics of limited material resources, can constrain possible meanings users and viewers derive from their investigations. As Burbules (2002) suggests, "Semantic possibilities relate to, and can be constrained by, navigational possibilities" (p. 78).

Of course, the virtual maps and imagined localities formed by these possibilities and constraints eventually influence Nadif's and Katherine's patterns of mobility within and among geographies of tertiary education, as the values, desires, expectations, and perceptions they develop through this process of virtual co-creation and navigation transform the college scenes of literacy in which they participate. Of particular interest to this discussion are the ways in which Nadif and Katherine maintain connections across space-time by pluralizing present scenes of literacy through their partnerships with ICTs. As I've argued throughout this book, scenes of literacy are always already pluralized through interaction of participants' historical bodies; however, in the contemporary classroom these interactions are almost always augmented by mobile communications.

Classrooms of Co-presence

To bring Goffman's concept of underlife—along with Brooke's adaptation of it for literacy studies—into the technoscape of the contemporary classroom, we must consider the ways in which a proliferation of mobile technologies affords new forms of student resistance, co-presence, collaboration, play, and innovation. Regardless of level or location, most teachers recognize the prevalence of mobile devices as one of the most transformative features of education in the 21st century. As Katherine's dual enrollment English teacher asserts:

> I'm lucky if I look out at the class and make eye contact with a single student. Everyone's looking down at their laps, as if I don't know what they're up to. . . . I've tried everything to get them off their phones. I've tried collecting them at the door, confiscating them when I see them out, sending students to the office, using them in class activities. By now, I've pretty much given up. Why try to stem the tide?

I can sympathize with this expression of frustration and futility. I've attempted to implement some of these same measures, and to the same effects. But as the portion of Nadif's mobility narrative recounted above demonstrates, even in schools with stringently enforced restrictions on cell phone usage, students (and teachers, staff, and administrators) will find ways to maintain connectivity to and through them—if only from bathroom stalls. This is largely because many individuals experience their devices as extensions of themselves. As Larsen et al. (2006) demonstrate in their research of mobile phone usage on public transit, "many young adults describe their mobile phones as prosthetic, as physically coterminous with their bodies. Mobile phones allow them to be 'proper' social beings. Without them, they are 'lost' being dependent upon such systems" (p. 113).

An increasing number of teachers, programs, and institutions are making use of the connectivity afforded by mobile devices to extend opportunities for teaching and learning (Cortesi et al. 2014). While tensions among institutionally sanctioned and restricted uses of these devices represent an important site of ongoing and future study (Motiwalla 2007), in the final section of this chapter I am most interested in investigating the ways in which students partner with mobile ICTs to exploit cracks in systems of institutional surveillance, increase linguistic and literate possibilities, connect scenes of literacy across space-time and, thereby, make and remake places. Like James's and his busmates' transformations of the space-time of their school bus to extend and connect academic scenes of literacy, students' partnerships with mobile devices create possibilities for forms of underlife that draw upon otherwise marginalized aspects of historical bodies and thereby reconstitute historical localities.

As previously suggested, students are not merely engaging in forms of underlife to resist the available activities and identities of school scenes of literacy. Rather, through partnerships with mobile technologies, they are actively reconstituting these scenes through a multiplication of spaces, times, and subjectivities. Following Casey (1996), Urry (2007) describes this process of multiplication as a creation of "interspaces," "where different 'fields' or 'domains' of activity overlap" (p. 176). He asserts that "this merging and overlapping of fields engenders simultaneity rather than linearity," which "means that identities may well be less place-based and more engendered through relations made and sustained on the move, in liminal 'interspaces'" (p. 177). In this way, students' *face-to-face-to-interface* forms of underlife enable them to maintain the complexity of their identities in classrooms through communicative mobilities across multiple institutional, academic, social, cultural, and home/life interspaces.

The portion of Katherine's text message conversation reproduced in Figure 4.6 demonstrates the "simultaneous multiplicity of spaces" and subjectivities accomplished through such constitutive forms of underlife (Massey 2005, p. 3).[12] Katherine engages in this conversation in her intermediate-level composition class at the community college. As she participates in face-to-face peer review with a partner in class, who is also texting from her smartphone, Katherine is simultaneously engaged in the exchange excerpted here and is contributing to a Facebook group chat excerpted below.

In this portion of a conversation that spans approximately 20 minutes of a 50-minute course and includes over a hundred individual messages, Katherine is fielding school-related questions from a friend and classmate. Up to this point, the exchange has covered a wide range of topics from weekend plans to South Korean pop music and, finally, to schoolwork. The friend, represented in light gray text bubbles, is expressing her anxiety about end-of-term deadlines. In the screenshot on the left, Katherine is attempting to assuage her friend's anxiety by reassuring her of the time she has to finish assignments and by offering to help her with work she is unable to complete because she lacks internet access at home.

In the screenshot on the right, Katherine is providing an overview of an essay assignment for a shared introductory psychology course and is teasingly fending off requests to offer more information about the essay. After sending the basics of the assignment, her friend asks her to continue: "siguele mija siguele [*go on, girlfriend, go on*]." To which Katherine responds: "y te lo mande [*I already sent it to you*]. K mas kieres [*what more do you want?*]. K lo haga x ti [*What? Do you want me to do it for you too?*]."[13] Discussing the language of this exchange and explaining her need to translate, Katherine asserts:

> Just like in English there is text language, this is the same in Spanish. To be specific, this conversation is in Spanglish, so it has its own slang.

FIGURE 4.6 Screen shot of Katherine's Text Messages
Used with permission.

The *K* stands for *Que* because my friend and me know English and Spanish—the sound is the same. *X* in Spanish is times, which is *por.* For example *one times one* would be *uno por uno.* The sentence correctly is supposed to be *Que lo haga por it,* and it is said sarcastic.

In many ways, this translingual exchange works like the mobile collectives James, Nadif, and their classmates co-create with and on the school bus. Through a similar process of negotiation around licit and illicit forms of collaboration, Katherine and her friend partner with their devices to share resources—information and interpretations—and school work across space-time.

Similarly, Nadif responds to prompts from his smartphone (the prod of a glowing screen and gentle buzz) to co-create a work collective from his second-semester composition class at UofL:[14]

Nick: Did you work 1st or 2nd half?
Nadif: I work 2nd half.

Nick: Nice. Will you and/or Ryan make sure that time sheets make it to Pinkie? Brian is supposed to pick them up, but if he hasn't by early afternoon, make sure they get to pinkie by 5! Thanks [Nadif]! $$$

Nadif: I can take of that. Take care.

Nick: Thank you [Nadif]. I'm Michael and you are Dwight. Thanks #2:)Haha.

Nadif: Haha! Yes were Dwight and Jim? So who signs the DA time sheets? But you aren't as funny as Jim, maybe you could be Michael. Lol.[15]

Like Katherine's appropriations of popular culture sources for her projections of college, Nick and Nadif appeal to characters from the U.S. version of the popular television show *The Office* to define and negotiate their roles within this collective. Moreover, both Katherine's and Nadif's communicative mobilities occasion material mobilities, as they serve to coordinate co-present collaborations. Katherine: "Ill show you the video manana. We can do it together before class." Nick: "Brian is supposed to pick them up, but if he hasn't by early afternoon, make sure they get to pinkie by 5!" Unlike the timetabled, rational, and linear organization of traditional places of school and hourly labor, the places created and coordinated through these communicative mobilities are fluid and negotiated. As Urry (2007) suggests, "Mobile phonespaces afford fluid and instantaneous meeting cultures where venue, time, group, and agenda can be negotiated with the next call or text" (p. 174). In this way, the flexibility and continuity of the mobile collectives Katherine and Nadif form through partnerships with ICTs reconstitute the clock-times and bounded spaces of school and work localities.

Moreover, the languages and discourses of these exchanges contribute to performances of identities distinct from those Katherine and Nadif take up in their respective classes and in additional virtual exchanges. Participants in the following group chat conducted on Facebook are responding to an image of Katherine and her older sister, Abby, recently posted on the latter's profile page. Katherine pivots from her more continuous text and face-to-face peer review conversations to periodically review and respond to comments on the photo.

Irene: OH MY GOD i didn't know you all were sisters!! I feel so dumb right now . . . but so happy i know both of you!!

Katherine: Yeah the other day I told her that you sang in my high school and she was like oh yeah I know Irene. I was like no way!

Irene: what a small world!

Katherine: Thts exactly what I was thinking!:D

Meagan: Aww que linda!

Abby: Ya lo se Meagan Hope you have fun in Nashville Stay safe!

Meagan: Thanks girl! I saw mi hermanita today too so I feel great!

Abby: Que bueno, me da gusto Te cuidas y que te diviertas

Meagan: Muchísimas gracias! Por fin me siento llena jeje . . . que the diviertas también;)

Katherine: Haaaaa k lindas yo kiero una mija haci . . . Gracias x su amistad a las dos son muy lindas y tiernas k Dios las siga bendiciendo.

In this portion of a longer exchange, Katherine moves among languages associated with different audiences and domains. Rather than blending Spanglish text and English text in single responses as she does in her text message conversation, she responds to Irene, a monolingual English-speaking friend from high school, in English text, and reserves Spanglish text for her older sister, Abby, and her sister's Mexican-American friend, Meagan. Moreover, unlike the sarcasm with which she concludes her text conversation, her final contribution to this chat is quite sentimental: "Haaaaa k lindas yo kiero una amiga haci [*How sweet, I want a friend like that*] . . . Gracias x su amistad a las dos son muy lindas y tiernas k Dios las siga bendiciendo [*Thank you for your friendship; you both are very kind and sweet. God bless you.*][16]

Moved by this image of and support for sisterly affection, Katherine assumes the role of gracious and devout younger sibling by praising her sister's friendship and offering a more formal blessing. When I asked how she would describe the linguistic and discursive differences among her responses, Katherine stated: "My sister and her friends are more, like, [pause] traditional. I guess I was more serious in this last response because I'm more used to talking like this around my family." In this group chat and simultaneous text message exchange, Katherine is drawing upon a range of literacies and langauges to create and maintain connections across and position herself within various places and scales in and out of school. In Ingold's (2009) terms, she's partnering with her smartphone to create a meshwork in the overlap among paths of participation. This partnership enables her to maintain the complexity of her identities in the school space-time of her writing class.

Mapping and Translating Mobile Practice

Perhaps most interestingly, these communicative mobilities reorganize the space-times of Katherine's and Nadif's embodied presences, as their interactions in scenes of literacy are mediated by and connected to a host of other meetings. Through their communicative mobilities, their material localities are pluralized by "the absent presence of others" (Callon and Law 2004, p. 6). Among other things, this co-presence creates possibilities for translingual and transmedia negotiations in scenes otherwise demarcated by institutionalized languages (i.e., standardized English) and literacies (academic and discipline-specific). And as I've asserted throughout this chapter and book, the metalinguistic, sociolinguistic, and attitudinal preparedness students develop in and through their mobilities across localities can, in many ways, be more valuable than the development of literate and linguistic competencies in apparently discrete disciplines promoted by containerized pedagogies and curricula (Leander et al. 2010).

The notion that literacy learning is always already distributed across space-time and among individuals and objects in localities that cross-cut, intersect, and align with one another or exist in relations of paradox or antagonism has transformative implications for literacy research and teaching. For ethnographies of literacy, a mobilities approach challenges the concept of a circumscribable "literacy event" (Heath 1983) and instead focuses on continuities and discontinuities among scenes of literacy, practices, resources, and social alignments. As Mary Hamilton (2000) asserts: "Visible literacy events are just the tip of an iceberg: literacy practices can only be inferred from observable evidence because they include invisible resources, such as knowledge and feelings; they embody social purposes and values; and they are part of a constantly changing context, both spatial and temporal" (p. 18). As I suggest in the introduction to this chapter, attention to complexities of associations created and assembled by reading-writing practices requires the adoption of epistemologies grounded in the fluidities of space-time. Moreover, such attention requires the implementation and innovation of research methods that can follow and represent fleeting, distributed, multiple, non-causal, chaotic, and complex language and literacy practices and their sensory and affective dimensions.

A concerted examination of basic research methods for attending to mobile literacies has only emerged relatively recently in concert with a growing demand among researchers for analytical frames and methodological strategies that can account for the complexity of literacy practices across localities (Brandt and Clinton 2002, Lillis 2008, Ivanič et al. 2009, Perrin 2012, Brent 2012). This effort has generated a number of methods for mapping students' everyday literacy practices. Through time-space journaling (Leander 2003), video ethnography (Fraiberg 2010), photo elicitation (Hamilton 2000), annotative and iconographic mapping (Mannion and Ivanič 2007), rhizomatic analysis (Leander and Rowe 2006), and other methods, researchers seek to trace students' literacy networks across contexts, cultures, languages, media, tracks, and stages of education. I hope that my investigation of students' mobile practices contributes to these efforts and opens up possibilities for future study and methodological development.

By sketching partial and subjective maps of Nadif's, James's and Katherine's movements within and among scenes of literacy, I have attempted to demonstrate the difficulty of locating their literacy practices, languages, and identities in bounded sites of activity. While a great deal of meaning could be made from observing, interviewing, and analyzing texts produced by these students in single sites of activity, participating in their patterns of movement across im(material) pathways (Burnett et al. 2014) from high school to college and/or work, among institutions, and between classes reveals the meanings they make in perpetual motion. This focus demonstrates the ways in which students are involved in ongoing productions of places and scales. By tracing Nadif's projection of the

University of Louisville back to a cybercafé in Nairobi, following the writing collectives James forms in the space-time of bus rides between home and school, and mapping the intertwining threads of Katherine's multiple face-to-face-to-interface dialogues, this chapter has attempted to show how student–object collectives constitute, connect, and pluralize scenes of literacy across space and time.

Of course, this concept of mobile literacies has implications not only for new frameworks for understanding literacy but for the teaching of literacy as well. As students translate meanings across discourses, languages, media, and localities—often through their underlife activity—they are negotiating the demands of concurrent and conflicting contexts, investments, allegiances, and ideologies. Rather than prohibiting, discrediting, and marginalizing these mobilities, as is often the case in containerized systems, literacy pedagogies might make use of them by providing students opportunities to connect and reflect upon their processes of translation so that they come to see themselves as contributors to becomings of dynamic and heterogeneous scenes of literacy. As demonstrated in Katherine's, James's, and Nadif's contributions to this chapter and the larger project, when provided an occasion and conducive material conditions, students reflect on their mobilities in ways that often provide valuable insights into how meanings are made in and through convergences of material, representational, and embodied mobilities. In the next chapter, I consider affordances and limitations of metaphors of mapping and translating for designing literacy activities and larger projects that make use of a mobile literacies framework. I suggest that by creating opportunities for students to map their literacy practices within and across places in and out of school, and prompting them to reflect on translations across asymmetrical relations of power that attend these mobile practices, they might locate agencies, or ways to appropriate, resist, and transform dominant discourses, genres, ideologies, and disciplines.

Notes

1 See Appendix E for a map of our shared bus route.
2 See Appendix F for the full text of Nadif's proposal.
3 See Appendix G for several of James's classmates' responses to this exercise.
4 While Shawnee Park is now widely recognized as a gathering place for African American youth, it served as a whites-only park until 1957. In fact, African Americans had to walk south through the expansive and meticulously manicured park to reach the much smaller and more scantily resourced Chickasaw Park, which was open to Blacks.
5 According to the city's original desegregation plan implemented in 1975, black students were to be bused for up to 10 of their 12 years in school, while white students would be bused for 2 of their 12 years (*Courier Journal* 2005).
6 See Appendix H for the full text of this paper.
7 Describing the problems associated with offering TARC tickets as an alternative to providing transportation in an interview conducted via virtual chat, Nadif writes: "The school use to give us a free TARC ticket, but first you had to walk all the way to Shepardville road and wait for the bus, that usually took like an hour. And that bus

will drop you off at Downtown, then you have to take another bus to home, and then walk to home like a half a mile. It was rough."

8 During the 2011/12 school year, students at Hughes took 87 Advanced Placement exams; 19 of these exams were taken by African American students and two were taken by Hispanic students. These numbers are especially startling considering African Americans made up 47.3 percent and Hispanics made up 12.9 percent of the total student population during the same school year (Jefferson County Public Schools n.d., 2012–2013 Data Books).

9 Following postcolonial theory (Bhabha 1994) and postmodern cultural geography (Soja 1996), some literacy theorists (Gutiérrez et al. 1995, Moje et al. 2004) and compositionists (Reynolds 2004, Grego and Thompson 2008) make use of the classroom conflict Brooke describes for the creation of *third space*. This space is made possible through the disruption of the traditionally binary nature of student scripts and teacher scripts. While I think this concept of third space is a useful pedagogical tool, I find Brooke's concept of underlife more descriptive of the sorts of resistances I observed in high school and college classrooms because it emphasizes the persistently subversive nature of these activities, and their resistance to being appropriated for institutional use.

10 See Appendix I for the second half of Nadif's draft with James's comments.

11 James and Nadif were first acquainted in regular-track courses during their junior years. They maintained a tenuous friendship despite cultural, linguistic, and social differences. In fact, I suspect it was Nadif who convinced James to participate in this project despite his initial skepticism.

12 I have erased Katherine's name in the banner of this image to preserve her anonymity.

13 Katherine translated these texts during an interview focusing on these and other examples of text message conversations she engaged in while in class.

14 All names in these exchanges have been changed to maintain participants' anonymity.

15 Nadif transcribed this conversation into a Word document to share with me rather than saving it in a screenshot.

16 Again, Katherine is translating her own correspondences as we talk through together.

References

Adey, P. (2009). *Mobility*. New York: Routledge.

Alexander, M. (2010) *The new Jim Crow: Mass incarceration in the age of colorblindness.* New York: New Press.

Bhabha, H. K. (1994). *The location of culture*. New York: Routledge.

Brandt, D., & Clinton, K. (2002). Limits of the local: Expanding perspectives on literacy as a social practice. *Journal of Literacy Research, 34*(3), 337–356.

Brent, D. (2012). Crossing boundaries: Co-op students relearning to write. *College Composition and Communication, 63*(4), 558–592.

Brooke, R. (1987). Underlife and writing instruction. *College Composition and Communication, 38*(2), 141–153.

Burbules, N. C. (2002). The web as a rhetorical place. In I. Snyder (Ed.). *Silicon literacies: Communication, innovation and education in the electronic age*. New York: Routledge.

Burnett, C., Merchant, G., Pahl, K., & Rowsell, J. (2014). The (im)materiality of literacy: The significance of subjectivity to new literacies research. *Discourse: Studies in the Cultural Politics of Education, 35*(1), 90–103.

Callon, M., & Law, J. (2004). Introduction: Absence–presence, circulation, and encountering in complex space. *Environment and Planning D: Society and Space, 22*(1), 3–11.

Canagarajah, A. S. (2006). The place of world Englishes in composition: Pluralization continued. *College Composition and Communication, 57*, 586–619.

Carter, P. L. (2006). Straddling boundaries: Identity, culture, and school. *Sociology of Education, 79*(4), 304–328.

Casey, E. (1996). How to get from space to place in a fairly short stretch of time: Phenomenological prolegomena. In S. Feld, & K. H. Basso (Eds.). *Senses of place.* Santa Fe, NM: School of American Research Press.

Castells, M. (1996). *The rise of the network society.* Malden, MA: Blackwell.

Certeau, M. de (1984). *The practice of everyday life.* Berkeley: University of California Press.

Chayko, M. (2002). *Connecting: How we form social bonds and communities in the Internet age.* New York: State University of New York Press.

Cortesi, S., Haduong, P., Gasser, U., Aricak, O. T., Saldaña, M., & Lerner, Z. (2014). Youth perspectives on tech in schools: From mobile devices to restrictions and monitoring. Social Science Research Network. Berkman Center Research Publication no. 2014-3. Rochester, NY. Retrieved from http://papers.ssrn.com/abstract=2378590. Accessed September 2015.

Courier-Journal (2005). Timeline: Desegregation in Jefferson County public schools. Retrieved March 23, 2014 from www.courier-journal.com/apps/pbcs.dll/article?AID=2005509040428&nclick_check=1.

Egan, K., Lozano, J. B., Hurtado, S., & Case, M. H. (2013). *The American freshman: National norms.* Los Angeles, CA: Higher Education Research Institute.

Elwood, S. A., & Martin, D. G. (2000). "Placing" interviews: Location and scales of power in qualitative research. *The Professional Geographer, 52*(4), 649–657.

Fosl, C. (2013). *Making Louisville home for us all: A 20-year action plan for fair housing.* Louisville, KY: University of Louisville Anne Braden Institute for Social Justice Research.

Foucault, M. (1982). The subject and power. *Critical Inquiry, 8*(4), 777–795.

Foucault, M. (1993). About the beginning of the hermeneutics of the self: Two lectures at Dartmouth. *Political Theory, 21*(2), 198–227.

Fox, K. (2001). *Evolution, alienation and gossip: The role of mobile telecommunications in the 21st century.* Oxford: Social Issues Research Centre.

Fraiberg, S. (2010). Military mashups: Remixing literacy practices. *Kairos, 14*(3), Web. April 6, 2014. http://kairos.technorhetoric.net/14.3/topoi/fraiberg/.

Freedle, R. (2003). Correcting the SAT's ethnic and social-class bias: A method for reestimating SAT scores. *Harvard Educational Review, 73*(1), 1–43.

Garet, M., & DeLany, B. (1988). Students, courses, and stratification. *Sociology of Education, 61*, 61–77.

Gee, J. P. (2004). *Situated language and learning: A critique of traditional schooling.* New York: Routledge.

Giroux, H. (2010). Dumbing down teachers: Rethinking the crisis of public education and the demise of the social state. *Review of Education, Pedagogy and Cultural Studies, 32*(4), 339–381.

Grego, R. C., & Thompson, N. S. (2008). *Teaching/writing in third spaces: The studio approach.* Carbondale: Southern Illinois University Press.

Guryan, J. (2004). Desegregation and black dropout rates. *American Economic Review, 94*(4), 919–943.

Gutiérrez, K., Rymes, B., & Larson, J. (1995). Script, counterscript, and underlife in the classroom: James Brown versus *Brown v. Board of Education. Harvard Educational Review, 65*(3), 445–471.

Halgreen, T. (2004). Tourists in the concrete desert. In M. Sheller, & J. Urry (Eds.). *Tourism mobilities: Places to play, places in play*. New York: Routledge.

Hamilton, M. (2000). Expanding the new literacy studies: Using photographs to explore literacy as social practice. In D. Barton, M. Hamilton, & R. Ivanič (Eds.). *Situated literacies: Reading and writing in context* (pp. 35–54). New York: Routledge.

Harvey, D. (1990). *The condition of postmodernity: An enquiry into the origin of social change.* Oxford: Blackwell.

Heath, S. B. (1983). *Ways with words: Language, life, and work in communities and classrooms.* New York: Cambridge University Press.

Heilig, J. V., & Holme, J. J. (2013). Nearly 50 years post-Jim Crow: Persisting and expansive school segregation for African American, Latina/o, and ELL students in Texas. *Education and Urban Society, 45*(5), 609–632.

Ingold, T. (2009). Against space: Place, movement, knowledge. In P. W. Kirby. *Boundless worlds: An anthropological approach to movement*. Oxford: Berghahn Books, 29–43.

Ito, M., Horst, H., Bittanti, M., boyd, d., Herr-Stephenson, B., Lange, P. G., . . . Robinson, L. (2008). *Living and learning with new media: Summary of findings from the digital youth project*. Cambridge, MA: MIT Press.

Ivanič, R., Edwards, R., Barton, D., Martin-Jones, M., Fowler, Z., Hughes, B., . . . Smith, J. (2009). *Improving learning in college: Rethinking literacies across the curriculum*. London: Routledge.

James. Personal interview. October 19, 2011.

James. Personal interview. April 14, 2012.

James. Personal interview. May 5, 2012.

Jefferson County Public Schools. (n.d.) *2012–2013 Data Books*. Division Data Management, Planning and Program Evaluation. Retrieved August 31, 2016, from http://assessment. jefferson.kyschools.us/DataBooks1213/High_Data_Book.html.

Jenkins, H. (2006). *Convergence culture: Where old and new media collide*. New York: New York University Press.

Jirón, P. (2011). On becoming the shadow. In M. Büscher, J. Urry, & K. Witchger (Eds.). *Mobile methods* (pp. 36–53). New York: Routledge.

Katherine. Virtual chat interview. March 7, 2012.

Katherine. Personal interview. April 14, 2012.

Katherine. Personal interview. September 9, 2013.

Katz, J. (2000). *How emotions work*. Chicago, IL: University of Chicago Press.

Kell, C. (2013). Ariadne's thread: Literacy, scale, and meaning-making across space and time. *Working Papers in Urban Language and Literacies, 118*, 1–24.

Keller, C. (2004). Unsituating the subject: "Locating" composition and ethnography in mobile worlds. In S. G. Brown, & S. I. Dobrin (Eds.). *Ethnography unbound: From theory shock to critical praxis*. Albany: State University of New York Press.

Kidder, W. C., & Rosner, J. (2002). How the SAT creates built-in headwinds: An educational and legal analysis of disparate impact. *Santa Clara Law Review, 43*(1), 131–212.

K'Meyer, T. E. (2013a). *From Brown to Meredith: The long struggle for school desegregation in Louisville, Kentucky 1954–2007*. Chapel Hill, NC: University of North Carolina Press.

K'Meyer, T. E. (2013b). Busing and the desegregation of Louisville schools. *University of North Carolina Press Blog*, August 12, 2013. Web. 23 April 2014. http://uncpressblog. com/2013/08/12/tracy-e-kmeyer-busing-and-the-desegregation-of-louisville-schools/

Kusenbach, M. (2003). Street phenomenology: The go-along as ethnographic research tool. *Ethnography, 4*(3), 455–485.

Larsen, J., Urry, J., & Axhausen, K. (2006). Geographies of social networks: Meetings, travel and communications. *Mobilities, 1*, 261–283.

Latour, B. (1996). On interobjectivity: Symposium on "The Lessons of Simian Society." *Mind, Culture, and Activity, 3*, 228–245.

Latour, B. (2004). *Politics of nature: How to bring the sciences into democracy.* Cambridge, MA: Harvard University Press.

Leander, K. M. (2003). Writing travelers' tales on new literacyscapes. *Reading Research Quarterly, 38*(3), 392–397.

Leander, K. M., & Lovvorn, J. F. (2006). Literacy networks: Following the circulation of texts, bodies, and objects in the schooling and online gaming of one youth. *Cognition and Instruction, 24*(3), 291–340.

Leander, K. M., & Rowe, D. W. (2006). Mapping literacy spaces in motion: A rhizomatic analysis of a classroom literacy performance. *Reading Research Quarterly, 41*, 428–460.

Leander, K. M., Phillips, N. C., & Taylor, K. H. (2010). The changing social spaces of learning: Mapping new mobilities. *Review of Research in Education, 34*(1), 329–394.

Lee, J., & Ingold, T. (2006). Fieldwork on foot: Perceiving, routing, socializing. In S. Coleman & P. Collins (Eds.). *Locating the field: Space, place and context in anthropology* (pp. 67–86). Palo Alto, CA: Ebrary.

Lillis, T. M. (2001). *Student writing: Access, regulation, desire.* New York: Routledge.

Lillis, T. (2008). Ethnography as method, methodology, and "deep theorizing": Closing the gap between text and context in academic writing research. *Written Communication, 25*(3), 353–388.

Mannion, G., & Ivanič, R. (2007). Mapping literacy practices: Theory, methodology, methods. *International Journal of Qualitative Studies in Education, 20*(1), 15–30.

Marcus, G. E. (1989). Imagining the whole: Ethnography's contemporary efforts to situate itself. *Critical Anthropology, 9*, 7–30.

Massey, D. B. (1994). *Space, place, and gender.* Minneapolis: University of Minnesota Press.

Massey, D. B. (2005). *For space.* London: Sage.

Mendez, L. M. R., & Knoff, H. M. (2003). Who gets suspended from school and why: A demographic analysis of schools and disciplinary infractions in a large school district. *Education and Treatment of Children, 26*(1), 30–51.

Mickelson, R. A. (2001). Subverting Swann: First- and second-generation segregation in the Charlotte-Mecklenburg schools. *American Educational Research Journal, 38*(2), 215–252.

Moje, E. B., Ciechanowski, K. M., Kramer, K., Ellis, L., Carrillo, R., & Collazo, T. (2004). Working toward third space in content area literacy: An examination of everyday funds of knowledge and discourse. *Reading Research Quarterly, 39*(1), 38–70.

Moores, S. (2012). *Media, place and mobility.* New York: Palgrave Macmillan.

Motiwalla, L. F. (2007). Mobile learning: A framework and evaluation. *Computers and Education, 49*, 581–596.

Nadif. Personal interview. September 22, 2011.

Nadif. Personal interview. April 5, 2012.

Nadif. Personal interview. October 20, 2012.

Nadif. Personal interview. February 8, 2013.

O'Connor, C., Mueller, J., Lewis, R. L., Rivas-Drake, D., & Rosenberg, S. (2011). "Being" black and strategizing for excellence in a racially stratified academic hierarchy. *American Educational Research Journal, 48*(6), 1232–1257.

Orfield, M. (2015). Milliken, Meredith, and metropolitan segregation. Retrieved from www.uclalawreview.org/milliken-meredith-and-metropolitan-segregation-2/. Accessed July 2016.

Pennycook, A. (2010). *Language as a local practice*. New York: Routledge.

Perrin, D. (2012). Coming to grips with complexity: Dynamic systems theory in the research of newswriting. In C. Bazerman, C. Dean, J. Early, K. Lunsford, S. Null . . . A. Stansell, *International advances in writing research: Cultures, places, and measures* (pp. 539–558). Fort Collins, CO: WAC Clearinghouse.

Prendergast, C. (2003). *Literacy and racial justice: The politics of learning after Brown v. Board of Education*. Carbondale: Southern Illinois University Press.

Ransom, J. S. (1997). *Foucault's discipline: The politics of subjectivity*. Durham, NC: Duke University Press.

Reynolds, N. (2004). *Geographies of writing: Inhabiting places and encountering difference*. Carbondale: Southern Illinois University Press.

Rothstein, R. (2013). *For public schools, segregation then, segregation since: Education and the unfinished march*. Washington, D.C.: Economic Policy Institute.

Santelices, M.V., & Wilson, M. (2010). Unfair treatment? The case of Freedle, the SAT, and the standardized approach to differential item functioning. *Harvard Educational Review*, *80*(1), 106–134.

Semuels, A. (2015). The city that believed in desegregation. *The Atlantic*. Retrieved from www.theatlantic.com/business/archive/2015/03/the-city-that-believed-in-desegregation/388532/. Accessed July 2016.

Skiba, R. J., Michael, R. S., Nardo A. C., & Peterson, R .L. (2002). The color of discipline: Sources of racial and gender disproportionality in school punishment. *Urban Review*, *34*, 317–342.

Snyder, I. (Ed.). (2002). *Silicon literacies: Communication, innovation and education in the electronic age*. New York: Routledge.

Soja, E. W. (1989). *Postmodern geographies: The reassertion of space in critical social theory*. London: Verso.

Soja, E. W. (1996). *Third space: Journeys to Los Angeles and other real-and-imagined places*. Malden, MA: Blackwell.

Sommers, N., & Saltz, L. (2004). The novice as expert: Writing the freshman year. *College Composition and Communication*, *56*(1), 124–149.

Southworth, S., & Mickelson, R. A. (2007). The interactive effects of race, gender and school composition on college track placement. *Social Forces*, *86*(2), 497–523.

Thrift, N. (2004). Driving in the city. *Theory, Culture and Society*, *21*(4–5), 41–59.

Tsing, A. L. (2015). *The mushroom at the end of the world: On the possibility of life in capitalist ruins*. Princeton, NJ: Princeton University Press.

Urry, J. (2007). *Mobilities*. Cambridge, MA: Polity Press.

Williams, B. T. (2009). *Shimmering literacies: Popular culture and reading & writing online*. New York: Peter Lang.

Yonezawa, S., Wells, A. S., & Serna, I. (2002). Choosing tracks: "Freedom of choice" in detracking schools. *American Educational Research Journal*, *39*(1), 37.

5

CONCLUSION
Pedagogy for the Present

> I am not proposing a return to the Stone Age. My intent is not reactionary, nor
> even conservative, but simply subversive. It seems that the utopian imagination
> is trapped, like capitalism and industrialism and the human population, in a one-
> way future consisting only of growth. All I'm trying to do is figure out how to
> put a pig on the tracks.
>
> (Le Guin 1989)

> The focus on activism draws attention to the point that this is not a question
> of . . . reveling in difference and the fascinations of cultural incommensurability;
> rather; this is a question of unsettling common relations, not only of entering
> traffic but of disrupting the traffic.
>
> (Pennycook 2008)

Our work as educators is governed by *geographies of the future*. Built from stores
of measured and makeshift materials, from experiences, memories, rumors,
assumptions, outcomes, standards, and metrics, these geographies locate our
students and ourselves on trajectories of unified progress-time (Tsing 2015). They
challenge us to keep immediate and distant horizons always in mind, building
paths and charting growth in increments. Accordingly, our studies and assignments
anticipate and our assessments measure readiness for the next unit, grade level,
the first year of college, an academic discipline, a global marketplace. By focusing
on how to best prepare for these presumably self-evident futures, we often forget
to consider the ways in which students' and our own projections and histories
shape current needs, desires, perceptions, and practices. By considering students'
movements predominantly in reference to progress, development, transition, and
transfer, we often fail to see education as a process of *placemaking* in the present.

The photo below (Figure 5.1) demonstrates the ubiquity of forces pulling us and our students toward "one-way futures" (Le Guin 1989). In it, Katherine's school bag spills open on the floor of her high school English classroom to reveal an ACT college-prep brochure sandwiched between a handbook of writing standards and other texts and materials. The brochure exhorts Katherine to "Gear Up for Life," as if she's spent her previous 18 years doing something other than living. The familiarity of this sentiment belies its widespread acceptance and disguises its damaging effects. Among these are an invalidation of Katherine's past and present experiences, skills, and knowledges and a separation of academic literacies from habits of thinking and living. Rather than shaping and being shaped by a historical body in the present, the message implies that her literacies and mobilities have, up to this point, only been preparing or failing to prepare her for the future.

I see the juxtaposition of this brochure alongside a writing handbook purporting to contain the rules and guidelines Katherine will need to master for college, as a symbol of my own participation in the development and maintenance of this relentless future orientation. As I argued in Chapter 2, our tendency to position students on trajectories from fixed points of departure to fixed points of arrival works to preserve the academic capital of such handbooks. If students are not moving in a straight line toward fixed and stable targets of "college-level" literacies, it becomes more difficult to sell such guides and, more importantly, to maintain institutional positions at corridors between students' literacy histories and futures. I've asserted throughout this book that such messages reduce the

FIGURE 5.1 Photo of Katherine's School Bag
Used with permission.

value and complexity of students' literacies, mobilities, and identities and delimit what we as teachers and researchers can accomplish alongside them in the places we co-create and maintain. By designing studies, outcomes, curricula, and pedagogies to, above all else, accommodate the apparent needs and demands of the future, we miss opportunities to attend to creations and transformations of places in the present.

The tradition of place-conscious education confronts this relentless future orientation (Gruenewald 2003a, 2003b, Gruenewald and Smith 2008, Brooke 2003, 2015, Dobrin and Keller 2005, Robbins and Dyer 2005, Ball and Lai 2006, Somerville 2010, Mannion and Adey 2011). By centering curricula in deep under-standings of local place, place-conscious educators seek to engage students in "schoolwork that *matters* to them and to the communities around them" (Brooke 2015, p. 2). The tradition gathers insights from phenomenology, critical geog-raphy, bioregionalism, ecofeminism, and indigenous studies to develop pedagogies and curricula for broadening perception and experience, examining relations between cultures and places, reflecting on ideologies and power dynamics shaping and shaped by spatial forms, appreciating cultural and biological diversity, and encouraging stewardship of the nonhuman world (Gruenewald 2003a, p. 646).

According to these objectives, models of experiential learning, natural history, cultural journalism, action research, service learning, community literacy, and ecocomposition have claimed and have been claimed under the banner of place-conscious education. Such approaches share a commitment to engagement with local settings often framed in terms of a "connection between teachers, learners, and 'real life' outside schools" (Gruenewald 2003a, p. 646). As David Gruenewald (2003a) asserts, "Place-conscious education . . . aims to work against the isolation of schooling's discourses and practices from the living world outside the increasingly placeless institution of schooling. Furthermore, it aims to enlist teachers and students in the firsthand experience of local life and in the political process of understanding and shaping what happens there" (p. 620).

In ways I've been advocating for throughout this book, place-conscious traditions conceptualize teaching and learning as placemaking and students and teachers as placemakers. And yet, in a manner similar to the ACT brochure encouraging Katherine to "Gear Up for Life," such approaches also tend to disassociate schooling from living: "real life" and the real, "living world" exist beyond the confines of "placeless" schools (Gruenewald 2003a, p. 620). In this way, place-conscious approaches tend to accept and perpetuate a *logic of inversion* (Ingold 2009), converting the pathways of people, objects, ideas, and energies that constitute classrooms and schools into boundaries within which activity is contained. According to such approaches, to participate in placemaking and realize themselves as placemakers, students and teachers must escape containers of modern education.

But as I've attempted to show through research represented in previous chapters, despite ostensibly enclosed systems, students and teachers constitute and connect places and scales in and out of school and across time through perpetual and entangled material, representational, and embodied mobilities. Regardless of what is supposed to happen in standards-based, assessment-driven, and accountability-focused systems of education, *wayfaring* (Ingold 2009) is still always our most fundamental mode of being in the worlds we bring forth with others (Maturana and Varela 1992). Such worlds don't begin and end at imaginary thresholds between schools and communities, high schools and colleges, or colleges and careers. This means that "the first (and last) problem of 'place' in learning," as Leander et al. (2010) assert, is "how to think about place as a multiplicity, a product of interrelations, and thus, as constantly opened up to interactions with other places" (p. 336).

Through a discussion and depiction of mobile theory and methodology, I've asserted that attention to becomings of place in literacy research requires participation in material mobilities in addition to analyses of discursive representations of movement. I've attempted to show how multi-sited, mobile ethnography can provide orientations and methods for working at interfaces between mobile bodies and texts, literacy practices, and representations of literacy and mobility. By following students, objects, texts, and ideas across classrooms, schools, roadways, educational mobility systems, and digital networks, I've tried to account for embodied experiences of movement, including my own, and for knowledges coproduced through shared movements. And through representations of entangled mobilities and literacies, I've presented a necessarily incomplete and uneven mosaic of students' and texts' temporal rhythms and spatial arcs (Tsing 2015, p. 20). My empirical argument throughout the book has been that in addition to discursive representations of mobility, literacy ethnography requires attention to mutually constitutive historical bodies, literacies, and more-than-representational doings of mobility.

In these ways, I have attempted to offer glimpses of scenes of literacy in and out of school as emergent, heterogeneous, and multiple (Massey 2005) and to work through implications of a mobilities frame for literacy research. I'd now like to conclude by imagining how we might attend to entangled literacies, mobilities, and places in contexts of teaching and learning across high school and college literacy courses. We can borrow a question from Sheller and Urry (2006) to launch this pursuit: "What if we were to open up all sites, places, and materialities to the mobilities that are always already coursing through them?" (p. 209). Or, more specifically, we can ask as I did in Chapter 1: What kinds of practices, relationships, and knowledges are possible when we approach schools, classrooms, students, and ourselves as "complexes of mobility"? (Lefebvre 1991). When our pedagogies account not just for circulations of texts, but also of bodies, practices, materials, ideas, and information across classes and schools to other places-in-the-making?

While I believe a complete pedagogy of mobile literacies could be sketched out in accordance with the observations and arguments presented in this book and with those made in scholarship on mobilities from a range of disciplines, here I only touch on possibilities for mobile literacy projects or assignments that could work in the context of more traditional approaches to teaching academic literacies. To frame these possibilities, I consider some of the affordances and limitations of metaphors and methods of mapping and translation, often used to research and theorize spatiotemporal dimensions of literacy practice. I return to examples of Nadif's, James's, and Katherine's mobile practices from previous chapters to demonstrate how these metaphors and methods can be applied to literacy pedagogies. And I assert that by approaching these practices as not only productive sites of research but also as opportunities for critical reflection, negotiation, and agency, we may expand possibilities for the teaching and learning of literacy in high school and college.

Mapping Mobile Literacies

Through activities that attend to the ways individuals and collectives traverse and connect scenes of literacy in their everyday lives, students and teachers might pursue two key objectives of critical pedagogy or the pedagogical activism Pennycook (2008) promotes in the epigraph above. First, we can seek better understandings of how mobile literacies produce, maintain, and transform material places and social relations across lines of race, gender, class, language, ethnicity, nationality, and more. Second, such reflections may help us locate agencies, or ways to appropriate, resist, and alter dominant discourses, genres, and ideologies through literacy and language practice. By tracing and reflecting on mobile literacies, students can come to see how their own practices both accommodate and resist dominant forms. To design and describe such tracings and represent literacies as interrelated, many researchers and teachers employ metaphors and methods of mapping (Clarke 2002, Reynolds 2004, Leander and Rowe 2006, Mannion et al. 2007, Ivanič et al. 2009, Arnold et al. 2015).

As Greg Mannion, Roz Ivanič, and the Literacies for Learning in Further Education Research Group (2007) assert, whether in reference to material or conceptual terrain, mapping involves boundary making—ordering, categorizing and flattening—often with far-reaching political, social, cultural, and economic effects. While maps always provide a subjective view of reality, they often pretend to be objective and final (Mannion et al. 2007, p. 18). In this way, assumptions of scientific exactitude and objectivity can serve as constraints when using metaphors of mapping in research or teaching. However, when conceiving of place as continually produced through practices creating, altering, and cutting off relations to other places, multiple and layered mapping practices can provide different interpretations, and therefore different maps, of the terrains under investigation. In this way, mapping affords not only a method for representing connections across space-time and practice but also for composing representations of literacy and mobility that can be read alongside and against representations offered by other maps. Through processes of composing, sharing, and revising maps, students and teachers can attend to how and why they and others construct meanings and realities through processes of map-making. As Richard Edwards and Robin Usher (2000) assert, "meaning is made through mapping rather than found" (p. 138).

Paul Prior's (1998) concept of "chronotopic lamination" provides a good starting point for imagining how literacy and text trajectories (Kell 2009) can be mapped by teachers and students. Extending Bakhtin's (Bakhtin and Holquist 1981) notion of the chronotope (time-place) as a tool for literary analysis, Prior poses chronotopic lamination as an optic for attending to "the dispersed and fluid chains of places, times, people, and artifacts that come to be tied together in trajectories of literacy" (Prior and Shipka 2003, p. 181). To recall and represent such trajectories, Prior and Shipka (2003) ask undergraduate and graduate research participants to draw scenes of writing a specific text—the place(s) where they wrote, resources they used, the people involved, activities that accompanied the writing, and their feelings during this process. In a follow-up drawing, participants re-scale their depictions to include a web of practices, feelings, and associations extending beyond the initially depicted act of writing. These broader maps trace the origins of a project; people, texts, and experiences that have shaped the project over time; a history of drafts, responses, and revisions; and accounts of shifting feelings about and evaluations of the project (p. 182). Through these mapping exercises and attendant interviews, Prior and Shipka's participants reflect on their struggles to communicate ideas, the motivational and affective forces influencing their decisions, the intricate coordination of schedules and activities for writing, and the ways in which they tune into and (re)structure their writing environments. While Prior and Shipka are primarily concerned with the value of these reflections for research in writing studies and activity theory, their methodology for mapping literacy trajectories has a clear import for literacy pedagogies, an import both scholars discuss in subsequent publications, though not in terms of mobility (Bazerman and Prior 2004, Shipka 2005, 2011).

For teaching and learning mobile literacies, making use of chronotopic lamination as a theory and methodology could involve prompting students to map interconnected literacy practices and places and then read their maps alongside and against other individual and institutional representations of the same or similar practices and places. Students' maps might include literacy artifacts that serve as guideposts—student, teacher, and institutional texts; images; video; audio; graffiti; posters; social media; text messages; etc.—with reflective commentary or annotation connecting one guidepost to another and, thus, "illuminating" the map. To move beyond retrospective accounts of literacy trajectories, students could document in situ practices with time-space journals, mobile observations apps, photos, audio, and video.[1]

Annotated maps could be composed, shared, and revised on interactive platforms such as blogs, digital archives, or increasingly available and often open-source mapping software. The project *Cleveland Historical*, developed by the Center for Public History + Digital Humanities at Cleveland State University, offers a robust model for imagining how students might represent literacy or text trajectories; attach literacy artifacts and representations of practice to particular geospatial points or routes; and layer or "rectify" multiple maps to investigate overlaps and divergences. The project attaches multimedia stories of historically significant places, people, and events to particular location markers on a digital street- or terrain-view map of Cleveland, Ohio and surrounding areas.

These stories are comprised of text-based narratives, past and present photos, oral histories, and short videos that offer multiple and often conflicting perspectives of an occurrence or locale. Stories are thematically linked by tours (designated by black and white markers in Figure 5.2) that users can access with the project's mobile app. For example, users can take a walking tour on the theme of "conflict" that spans from the 1919 Mayday riots starting in Cleveland's Public Square to debates in the 1960s over proposed freeway construction in the Shaker Lakes and Cleveland Heights neighborhoods. In this way, stories of formative conflicts are interrelated and attached to physical locations and routes and are activated or retold through mobile locative media as participants move through and dwell in the city.

The potential of such interactive maps for a pedagogy of mobile literacies is obvious. By mapping interconnected literacy practices onto representations of physical places (city maps, bus routes, school blueprints, campus maps, and so on) and attaching multimedia literacy narratives to markers of these locations,

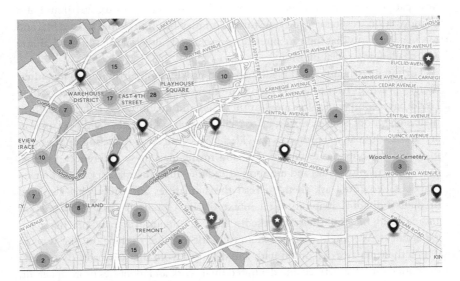

FIGURE 5.2 Screen shot of Cleveland Historical

Source: Cleveland Historical. (n.d.). Retrieved August 30, 2016, from http://clevelandhistorical.org/

students might better understand and communicate the ways in which places in and out of school shape and are shaped by the trajectories coursing through them. As Nedra Reynolds (2004) suggests, such a project might encourage students to "engage more fully with the geographical construction of difference—especially as it influences texts and discourses—and begin to consider teaching and learning, reading and writing, from the standpoint of moving through the world: through forms of walking, mapping, and dwelling" (p. 138). Relations among geographical and discursive constructions of difference can be further explored as students and teachers read their literacy maps in light of institutional representations of literacy development.

After rereading and revising maps of their literacy trajectories in light of each other's maps, students and teachers might focus on the ways in which their practices are located by various mechanisms—standards and assessments, program outcomes, evaluations, curricula, degree plans, etc.—on larger institutional maps designed to orient and make sense of these practices. On both secondary and tertiary levels, this process of reading individual maps alongside and against institutional charts of progress, such as the Common Core Standards, can reveal patterns of inclusion and exclusion, access and denial, embraces and threats, and other means of creating and policing social and institutional boundaries.

In other words, by engaging in processes of collaborative map-making and reading, students and teachers might come to better understandings of how meanings are made through boundary making. By studying their own literacies across space-time in relation to standardized representations of these literacies, new patterns of containment, security, and conformity (Giroux 2010) and also of innovation, resistance, and transformation may become visible to students and teachers, patterns that indicate literacy's present and potential roles in maintaining and challenging social divisions.

For instance, if James and Nadif had been provided opportunities to map their literacy practices over time and then share their maps across academic tracks, they could have compared differences in the types and quantities of tasks assigned in their high school courses, texts used to facilitate such tasks, teacher and peer support and feedback, material resources provided, and so on. After reflecting on the ways in which the boundaries that created and maintained these differences assigned them particular identities and interpreted and measured their language and literacy practices, we could ask them to read the similarities and differences depicted in their individual maps in the context of the Common Core Standards, as an idealized map of their supposedly shared academic literacy practices and experiences. We might then ask them to work together to trace out the ways in which their practices accorded with and diverged from the standards. By making the boundaries that defined and delimited their work and identities more apparent, James and Nadif could have joined their critical perspectives to reflect on and critique their own geographic and institutional situatedness and, subsequently, to develop additional tactics that responded to this situatedness by exploiting and expanding possibilities for movement within apparently closed systems.

Of course, the institutional boundaries that separated James and Nadif according to perceived academic ability would have made it very difficult for them to collaborate in this way in the context of their high school literacy classes. And this concern points to a limitation, or perhaps more accurately, a missed opportunity in the design of my own research. Rather than approaching James, Nadif, Katherine, and the other students participating in this project as a research team, I treated them primarily as individual participants. Apart from the time I spent as a participant-observer in their high school writing classes, we essentially worked together in dyads, meeting individually to share and interpret data. While it would have been risky or even impossible for James's and Nadif's high school English teachers to create occasions for their students to collaborate across academic tracks, as a researcher committed to interventionist practice and as an institutional outsider, I was in a better position to build occasions for this sort of collaboration into my research design. By conducting group interviews in which participants could have shared artifacts and asked questions of each other concerning their literacy practices, I might have facilitated the kinds of collaborative mapping proposed above. While the privacy and intimacy of individual interactions afforded opportunities that group interviews would have likely limited, some combination of individual and collective interviewing could have encouraged students to share critical perspectives on the boundarying activities that occasioned and constrained their literacies and identities. This is one potential way in which my pedagogy could have informed my methodology.

Translating Mobile Practice

By mapping (tracing and annotating) literacy practices across space-time and rereading and rewriting their maps in the context of other individual and "official" maps, students and teachers create opportunities to reflect upon and make sense of the ways in which literacies, languages, and meanings are ordered and re-ordered, networked and translated across locations and identities and to consider the ways in which people, objects, ideas, and information interact in these processes of translation. Along with metaphors of mapping, metaphors of translation for the teaching of literacy have proliferated in an age of globalization. As translation theorist Susan Bassnett (2014) proclaims, "The twenty-first century is the great age of translation" (p. 1). And in accordance with the mobilities paradigm informing this book, perpetual mobilities necessitate perpetual translations. These translations involve not only linguistic transactions but also social, economic, geopolitical, and cultural transactions across asymmetrical relations of power. As Lu and Horner (2013) assert, "In such transactions, meaning is necessarily and always the product of translation across differences, even in ostensibly monolingual settings" (pp. 27–28). In this way, meaning is made, exchanged, and transformed in and through motion.

For Claire Kramsch (2006) this "traffic in meaning" is precisely what language teaching should consist of, so that language competence is measured not as the capacity to perform in one language in a specific domain, but rather as "the ability to translate, transpose and critically reflect on social, cultural and historical meanings conveyed by the grammar and lexicon" (p. 103). From this perspective, the role of the language teacher is "to diversify meanings, point to the meanings not chosen, and bring to light other possible meanings that have been forgotten by history or covered up by politics" (p. 103). In this way, language and literacy teaching is indelibly tied to translation and a diversity of meanings (Pennycook 2008, p. 34).

As I've asserted throughout this book, I believe the pedagogical value of a mobile literacies approach can be located primarily in its potential to develop metalinguistic and sociolinguistic skills and dispositions open to negotiations across differences by challenging students to recognize and reflect upon the ways in which their mobile practices require them to translate meanings across identities, languages, texts, cultures, discourses, media, and localities. This approach moves beyond identifications and accommodations of communities of practice, discourse communities, or rhetorical situations to focus on the ways in which participation in rhetorical circulations (Edbauer 2005, Chaput 2005) requires literate and linguistic facility within and across diverse languages, markets, discourses, and texts.

One potential limitation of the metaphor of translation for literacy pedagogy is its association with conversions of seemingly discrete and unified languages into other languages. Like assumptions of objectivity and exactitude that may attend students' and teachers' perceptions of mapping, for many, the notion of translation signals one-to-one correspondence between language and meaning. Katherine demonstrates this assumption in the paper cited at length in Chapter 3 in which she describes herself as a "Google translator": "I would have to convert what he [my father] was saying in Spanish to English to American Sign Language." Again, aligning with and expanding a translingual literacy approach (Horner et al. 2011), a pedagogy of mobile literacies might ask Katherine to consider how and why this process of moving across languages, modalities, and audiences and also material places and scales requires translations of meanings as well as translations of lexicons and grammars.

Pennycook's (2008) concept of "translingual activism," which seeks to "grapple with the tensions around the politics of translations across spaces, times, ideologies and cultures," productively frames this expanded notion of translation for mobile literacies (p. 34). His approach attends to the multiplicity of available meanings within language as much as, if not more than, the multiplicity of seemingly discrete languages (p. 42). Unlike other approaches to linguistic diversity, which tend to focus on forms rather than meanings in the face of globalization, translingual activism centralizes a heteroglossic condition, which necessitates the translation of meanings within and among languages. In this way, the translation of meanings from one language to another becomes a "central aspect of social and global life that challenges the very notion of languages and their discrete operation." In line with a mobilities frame, this transgressive activity seeks to enable individuals and collectives to identify and contest processes of institutional boundarying and, consequently, "displace the hegemonic and subaltern locations of disciplinary knowledge" (Pennycook 2008, p. 41). While translations of meanings are always already reproducing and transforming scenes of literacy in and outside of school, literacy teachers could encourage students to actively participate in this traffic of meaning by making use of the mobilities circulating within their ostensibly bounded classrooms.

We can return to the *face-to-face-to-interface* mobilities Katherine practices in her community college writing class to demonstrate how this traffic in meaning might be illuminated and reflected upon in the literacy classroom. Again, this activity begins with mapping. Recognizing that students will likely not share all the mobilities that intersect with and diverge from their physical presences in class, nor should they be compelled to, they could be asked to map the literacies they engage in (and feel comfortable sharing) over the course of a single class period along with the places-in-progress these practices contribute to. Ongoing exchanges serve as the guideposts for these maps, as students trace out the identities, places, activities, histories, and discourses evoked in these mobilities.

Figure 5.3 is my own attempt to map Katherine's literacy scene as discussed in the previous chapter. In this map, simultaneous exchanges—peer review, essay, text message conversation, and Facebook chat—serve as primary nodes. Branching off from these guideposts are localities and texts evoked and identities and languages performed in each exchange. Of course, these branches are not comprehensive; they represent a small number of associations Katherine may or may not trace out in such an activity.[2]

The map reveals Katherine's peer review session as mediated by a number of texts—written and spoken feedback, her own and her partner's essays, and the text messages interrupting and augmenting their face-to-face interactions. The identity she performs in this exchange is different from those she takes up in other exchanges; while she is friendly and compliant, Katherine also communicates verbally and physically that she is only marginally invested in the activity, a level of investment that seems to match her partner's. The language she and her partner use to discuss their essays approximates the slightly elevated conversational English used by the teacher of the course, and the only locality referenced in this particular exchange is the classroom itself.

As this map demonstrates, the possible influences shaping and shaped by Katherine's contributions to this peer review activity and the larger scene of literacy are relatively easy to trace out. A more difficult, but perhaps more productive, task is creating opportunities for her to reflect on and make new meanings from transactions and translations within and across exchanges. In other words, after mapping associations that comprise these primary exchanges, Katherine and her

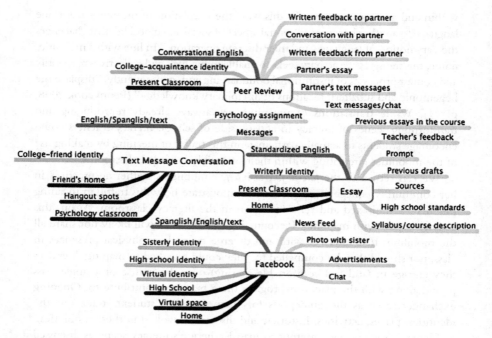

FIGURE 5.3 Map of Katherine's Discursive Associations

classmates should be prompted to consider how one seemingly discrete exchange shapes and is shaped by another. For instance, Katherine could consider how her text message conversation, which spans the duration of the peer review, influences the oral and written feedback she provides her partner and the identities or languages she performs in the session. Reading her text messages alongside her written review might help Katherine recognize similarities and differences in the ways she positions herself, frames her commentary, draws upon diverse language resources, and so on.

After considering the relations among these similarities and differences and notions of audience, purpose, genre, exigency, medium, context, and so on, we could ask Katherine to attempt to translate meanings across exchanges by investigating the ways in which meanings are lost, changed, and gained in translations of her peer review comments into the Spanglish of her text messages or by considering how the content and tone of her text conversation would change if it were conducted face-to-face in the context of her writing classroom. This practice of translating across differences might highlight the influences enabling and constraining her identities, languages, and literacies. And through this process of identifying affordances and constraints, she could locate possible agencies or ways to exploit and create openings for new mobilities and, thus, new processes of meaning-making within and across mobility systems.

To add a final dimension to this traffic in meaning, Katherine and her peer review partner could exchange maps to consider similarities and differences in the meanings and realities they construct through processes of map-making. Again, this process of comparative mapping might allow students to share critical perspectives and develop tactics for contesting institutional constraints and expanding and creating possibilities for movement. Of course, these activities could also fall flat. While it's useful to think through how Katherine and her classmates might take up such assignments, the chance of such processes unfolding in the ways I've outlined here is slim. Katherine could find more interesting ways to participate in such practices, or she could decide to reject these practices outright. Mobilities and, thus, teaching and learning are unpredictable.

Regardless of how they play out, pedagogies that attend to students' mobile literacies focus on how to best enable them to negotiate the demands of intersecting and often conflicting places-in-progress, challenging them to identify, reflect upon, and employ language and literacy choices to achieve personal, civic, educational, and professional objectives across scenes of literacy. Grounded in the epistemological and ontological orientations informing this book, such pedagogies approach students not as novices faced with tasks of conforming to the demands of specific scenes of literacy, but rather as placemakers continually reproducing and remaking themselves, the scenes, and the discourses they co-create through entangled literacies and mobilities. To help them realize the agencies that emerge from their language and literacy practices, such pedagogies seek to create opportunities for students to recognize and reflect upon the ways in which their mobile literacies both accommodate and transform conventions of discourse, genre, and discipline as well as social relations within and across places.

While I believe place-conscious education should begin in the classroom, I also believe that we must simultaneously work across levels of education, disciplines, programs, institutions, and places to form strategic alliances that can mobilize people, resources, information, and ideas to challenge and ultimately transform neoliberal systems of education and society. As I've demonstrated throughout this book, the structures that comprise these larger systems reduce the value and complexity of students' mobilities and literacies in the present. To reject such reductions and facilitate the systemic change called for in this text, the epistemologies, methodologies, and pedagogies of mobility informing our work as literacy teachers, researchers, and administrators must also transform the practices of policy makers, community leaders, parents and, most importantly, of the students themselves. While global educational reform calls for large-scale and long-term political, social, and economic change, by recognizing the sophistication and innovation of their daily literacy practices, students and teachers might discover new ways of mobilizing these practices to challenge and transform systems incrementally and from within. By working within and against the system to privilege the value and complexity of their shared work in the present, students and teachers might recognize themselves and each other as makers of the becomings of dynamic and heterogeneous educational places and systems shaped in part by their historical bodies and mobile practices.

Notes

1   I've used a mobile observation app called Ethos (ethosapp.com) as a tool for creating mobile literacy journals in an upper-level course titled *Literacy Networks* at Syracuse University. In the course, students used the smartphone app to collect literacy artifacts with photos, text, audio, and video on the move and to analyze (map and translate) these artifacts in shared workspaces. Students in my class used the app to not only collaborate with each other, but also to work with students in an upper-level literacy course taught by a colleague and professor of English at California State University, Chico.
2   Moreover, the identities, languages, localities, and texts referenced here are not singular or static.

References

Arnold, L., NeCamp, S., & Sohan, V. K. (2015). Recognizing and disrupting immappancy in scholarship and pedagogy. *Pedagogy, 15*(2), 271–302.

Bakhtin, M. M., & Holquist, M. (1981). *The dialogic imagination: Four essays*. Austin: University of Texas Press.

Ball, E. L., & Lai, A. (2006). Place-based pedagogy for the arts and humanities. *Pedagogy, 6*(2), 261–287.

Bassnett, S. (2014). *Translation*. London: Routledge.

Bazerman, C., & Prior, P. A. (Eds.). (2004). *What writing does and how it does it: An introduction to analyzing texts and textual practices*. Mahwah, NJ: Lawrence Erlbaum Associates.

Brooke, R. (Ed.). (2003). *Rural voices: Place-conscious education and the teaching of writing*. New York: Teachers College Press.

Brooke, R. (Ed.). (2015). *Writing suburban citizenship: Place-conscious education and the conundrum of suburbia*. Syracuse, NY: Syracuse University Press.

Chaput, C. (2005). Rhetorical circulation in late capitalism: Neoliberalism and the overdetermination of affective energy. *Philosophy and Rhetoric, 43*(1), 1–25.

Clarke, J. (2002). A new kind of symmetry: Actor-network theories and the new literacy studies. *Studies in the Education of Adults, 34*(2), 107–122.

Cleveland Historical. (n.d.). Retrieved August 30, 2016, from http://cleveland historical.org/.

Dobrin, S. I., & Keller, C. J. (Eds.). (2005). *Writing environments*. Albany: State University of New York Press.

Edbauer, J. (2005). Unframing models of public distribution: From rhetorical situation to rhetorical ecologies. *Rhetoric Society Quarterly, 35*(4), 5–24.

Edwards, R., & Usher, R. (2000). *Globalisation and pedagogy: Space, place and identity*. London: Routledge.

EthOS Ethnographic Observation System. (n.d.). Retrieved August 30, 2016, from https://www.ethosapp.com/.

Giroux, H. (2010). Dumbing down teachers: Rethinking the crisis of public education and the demise of the social state. *Review of Education, Pedagogy and Cultural Studies, 32*(4), 339–381.

Gruenewald, D. A. (2003a). Foundations of place: A multidisciplinary framework for place-conscious education. *American Educational Research Journal, 40*(3), 619–654.

Gruenewald, D. A. (2003b). The best of both worlds: A critical pedagogy of place. *Educational Researcher, 32*(4), 3–12.

Gruenewald, D. A., & Smith, G. A. (Eds.). (2008). *Place-based education in the global age: Local diversity*. New York: Lawrence Erlbaum Associates.

Horner, B., Lu, M.-Z., Royster, J. J., & Trimbur, J. (2011). Opinon: Language difference in writing: Toward a translingual approach. *College English, 73*(3), 303–321.

Ingold, T. (2009). Against space: Place, movement, knowledge. in P. W. Kirby. *Boundless worlds: An anthropological approach to movement*. Oxford: Berghahn Books.

Ivanič, R., Edwards, R., Barton, D., Martin-Jones, M., Fowler, Z., Hughes, B., . . . Smith, J. (2009). *Improving learning in college: Rethinking literacies across the curriculum*. London: Routledge.

Kell, C. (2009). Literacy practices, text/s and meaning making across time and space. In M. Prinsloo, & M. Baynham. *The future of literacy studies* (pp. 75–99). New York: Palgrave.

Kramsch, C. (2006). The traffic in meaning. *Asian Pacific Journal of Education, 26*(1), 99–104.

Leander, K. M., & Rowe, D. W. (2006). Mapping literacy spaces in motion: A rhizomatic analysis of a classroom literacy performance. *Reading Research Quarterly, 41*, 428–460.

Leander, K. M., Phillips, N. C., & Taylor, K. H. (2010). The changing social spaces of learning: Mapping new mobilities. *Review of Research in Education, 34*(1), 329–394.

Lefebvre, H. (1991). *The production of space*. Cambridge, MA: Blackwell.

Le Guin, U. K. (1989). *Dancing at the edge of the world: Thoughts on words, women, places*. New York: Grove Press.

Lu, M.-Z., & Horner, B. (2013). Translingual literacy, language difference, and matters of agency. *College English, 75*(6), 582–607.

Mannion, G., Ivanič, R., & the Literacies for Learning in Further Education Research Group (2007). Mapping literacy practices: Theory, methodology, methods. *International Journal of Qualitative Studies in Education, 20*(1), 15–30.

Mannion, G., & Adey, C. (2011). Place-based education is an intergenerational practice. *Children, Youth and Environments, 21*(1), 35–58.

Massey, D. B. (2005). *For space*. London: Sage.

Maturana, H. R., & Varela, F. J. (1992). *The tree of knowledge: The biological roots of human understanding*. Boston, MA: Shambhala.

Pennycook, A. (2008). English as a language always in translation. *European Journal of English Studies, 12*(1), 33–47.

Prior, P. A. (1998). *Writing/disciplinarity: A sociohistoric account of literate activity in the academy*. Mahwah, NJ: Lawrence Erlbaum Associates.

Prior, P. A., & Shipka, J. (2003). Chronotopic lamination: Tracing the contours of literate activity. In C. Bazerman, & D. Russell (Eds.). *Writing selves, writing societies: Research from activity perspectives*. Fort Collins, CO: WAC Clearinghouse, 180–238.

Reynolds, N. (2004). *Geographies of writing: Inhabiting places and encountering difference*. Carbondale: Southern Illinois University Press.

Robbins, S., & Dyer, M. (Eds.). (2005). *Writing America: Classroom literacy and public engagement*. New York: Teachers College Press.

Sheller, M., & Urry, J. (2006). The new mobilities paradigm. *Environment and Planning A, 38*(2), 207–226.

Shipka, J. (2005). A multimodal task-based framework for composing. *College Composition and Communication, 57*(2), 277–306.

Shipka, J. (2011). *Toward a composition made whole*. Pittsburgh, PA: University of Pittsburgh Press.

Somerville, M. J. (2010). A place pedagogy for "global contemporaneity." *Educational Philosophy and Theory, 42*(3), 326–344.

Tsing, A. L. (2015). *The mushroom at the end of the world: On the possibility of life in capitalist ruins*. Princeton, NJ: Princeton University Press.

APPENDIX A

Overview of Student Participants

TABLE AA.1 Overview of Student Participants

Student*	ENG section	Gender	Race/ ethnicity	Languages	Class	Post-H.S.
Yo Shu	Regular	Male	Burmese	Kayah English	2012	Two-year college
James	Regular	Male	African American	English	2012	Full-time employment
Jonathan	Regular	Male	Liberian	English Liberian-Creole Bassa	2012	Full-time employment
Julie	Dual enrollment	Female	White	English	2011	Two-year college
Katherine	Dual enrollment Advanced placement	Female	Mexican American	Spanish English	2012	Two-year college
Kim	Regular	Female	African American	English	2011	Full-time employment
Michael	Advanced placement	Male	White	English	2011	Four-year university
Nadif	Advanced placement	Male	Somali	Somali Kiswahili Arabic English	2012	Four-year university
Muhammad	Regular	Male	Somali	Somali Arabic English	2012	Two-year college
Sean	Advanced placement	Male	White	English	2011	Four-year university
Ling	Dual enrollment	Female	Chinese American	Mandarin English	2012	Four-year university

Note: *All names are pseudonyms.

APPENDIX B

Nadif's Literary Analysis (Argument) for AP English

Note: Used with permission

Africa through the eyes of Achebe

Chinua Achebe is one of Africa's greatest and recent writers. His books are mostly written for African readers who are mainly familiar with his point of views; however, over the last years Achebe's works have been translated into many languages. All his books talk about impact of colonialism and African cultures.

Achebe was born in Ogidi, Eastern Nigeria in 1930, having born to Isaiah Okafo, a Christian churchman and Janet N. He was the fifth of six children having been brought up under the new religion of Christianity. He belonged to the Igbo tribe, which one of the largest and prominent tribes in Nigeria. Most of the Igbo tribe members also speak English due to British colonialism (Metzger 3). Achebe who is now 81 years old lives in the United States due to health issue after a car accident left him paralyzed in Nigeria.

Achebe is naturally talented person and always excelled best in education. After sitting for the final high school test Achebe achieved great scores where he was admitted to the Government College of Umuahia in Nigeria, an institution established by the British colonizers, in order to educated future elites of Nigeria, especially boys only. He later attended University College, Ibadan in order to learn medicine, but later switched his career to English, History, and theology. He then on received a B.A in broadcasting at British Broadcasting Corp in London University (Metzger 3).

The theme of Achebe's books focus on the impact of British colonialism such as conversion to Christianity in which the British was trying to destroy the old ways and traditions of African countries. When British rulers imposed new cultures the African people thought civilization was coming, but Achebe believes it is far different. They later started practicing inhumanity and brutality across the region. Chinua Achebe seeks to show the effect of post-colonial tribalism and Igbo culture, role of women, and education in his books "things fall apart," his first novel, "Girls at war and other short stories," and "the education of a British protected child," in order to give readers knowledge of Achebe's on the Igbo culture and the continent of Africa at large.

Things fall apart

I. Woman in Society

Achebe's book "things fall apart" focuses the likeness of women being weak while strength in linked to men. Although people across the globe share many things, the only think many African countries are different than the rest of the world is the role woman play. Character Okonkwa once finds out that his daughter Enzima is growing to be strong a person, Oknokwo wishes that "she should have been a boy," (Achebe 64). It is such believe that makes woman in Africa to be considered much weaker while they are again highly needed in their communities. Through the eyes of Achebe woman in the Igbo culture are not considered to be humans, but instead as laborers, property and child producers. Achebe offers such a depiction in order to educate people about the Igbo culture and the continent of Africa.

In addition, the term woman is used an insult over the Igbo culture and continent of Africa. Okonkwo calls his father woman because of his laziness and his lack of title in his tribe, and his borrowing habit which led him to higher dept. Even Okonwko asks himself this question which is the worst insult to him "when did you become a shivering old woman," (Achebe 65), after killing a young man and became agitated. Women in Africa live in a very difficult life even after the colonial period, where they are not well represented in public offices and always have no value at all in their communities. Achebe shows what it means to be a woman over the Igbo culture and the continent of Africa as a whole.

Even though women were considered a very lower class people children knew that their mother was more important to them than anybody else. Okonkwo's son kenw that his mother had a lot better story than Oknowks, "So Okonkwa encouraged the boys to sit with him in his obi, and he told them stories of the land—masculine stories of violence and bloodshed. Nwoyes knew that it was right to be masculine and to be violent, but somehow he still preferred the stories that his mother used to tell him,"(Jeyifo 1). Okonkwo feminist beliefs will always leave a hate for woman because of his ways of threatening his wife, which even lead to his son Nwoye follow the ways of the British which taught him love for everybody.

II. Cultural change

In the novel "things fall apart," the Igbo culture is facing a dramatic influence enforced by powerful forces. The British colonizers are placing such an effect in order to change the gender roles, family structure, trade, and etc. Okonkwo a hero and a title holder realizes the presence of the white men is leading to division among the region, "he has put a knife on the things that held us together and we have fallen apart,". The arrival of the white men is a loss to the Igbo culture leading them to live their ancestor's cultures behind. Such impacts will positively affect woman leading them to have a voice in the presence of the white men who viewed woman were equal and had equal voices. Although it is rather a stressful situation to a man like Oknowkwo who enjoyed beating his wife even during the week peace in which according to the Umuofia tribe no evil things were allowed to happen. Achebe is placing this in order to show how the British dramatically changed the ways of the Igbo culture and the continent of Africa.

Furthermore, the people of Igbo belief sacrificing for specific days and specific people is the way of the land and who ever violates will receive the goddess punishment. Such a belief places the Igbo's to an extent in which they believe in order to be successful you will need to fulfill the needs of the goddess.

Okonkwo who is such an extreme believer of the Umuofia culture says "before I put any crop in the earth, I sacrifice a cock to Ani, the owner of all land. It is the law of our fathers," (Achebe 17). Believe of how fathers use to do is a strong believe to many African cultures, they believe in such a way that it is their obligation to practice what their fathers used to do. Okonkwo is in a position of fulfilling rituals to a goddess that has no control over him, while the presence of the western cultures is falsifying that there should be no small gods to belief other than the greater God. Achebe is showing how such an impact will change the ways of the Igbo culture.

III. Education

Achebe emphasis in his book "things fall apart" the British style of educating the elites of the region in order to backlash the expectation of the Igbo elders. The missionaries' message of new religion was not a goal they meant, but it was a plan to change divide among the people and get the attention of the young ones whom can easily be assimilated by educating them. Such lead to isolation of a father and a son "you all have seen the great abomination of your brother. Now he is no longer my son or your brother. I will only have a son who is a man, who will hold his head up among my people," (Achebe 172). The Europeans had such a strong plan, which could lead them easily to divide the people against their wills and give them supporters by educating the young ones, though their goal was to colonize and start slavery across region. Using religion, as a tool to achieve your goal is what led the British to take over the Igbo people, thus Achebe in his novel "things fall apart" proves this claim is what made easy for the Europeans to divide the continent of Africa.

Furthermore, use of good language and proverbs to communicate was a tool men used to show how strong and skilled they are. According to Merriam Webster dictionary education is defined as the knowledge and development resulting from an educational process, however in Igbo culture people get educated according to their ages, meaning the older you grow the more educated you become. That nation gave many African cultures that the more proverbs and saying you use from the past to get your point done, the more respect you get. Okonkwo one of the greatest people in the tribe and a member of the tribes head is among those who never had some form of education. Again smart and wise one in his tribe by praising himself from quoting from the past, "The lizard that jumped from the high iroko tree to the ground said he would praise himself if no one else did," (Achebe 21). It is these rather form that many African's use in order to explain their capacity of thinking and handwork. Achebe places this to share the meaning of education to the Igbo region and the continent of Africa at large.

Girls at war and other short stories

I. Woman's role

In his book "Girls at war and other short stories," Achebe now focuses on what role do women play in marriage even after the impact of the western cultures. Achebe wrote these book years after Nigeria underwent a whole revolution period where cities have been created, education started and women were now being some howl accepted by their communities. The acceptance of woman to the developing Nigeria only came from men who have been open to the western culture, but not the elders who lived over the doctrine of women being property and laborers. Character Nnaemeka who is a young man plans to marry a girl he meet with while in the city, he unveils the plan to his father who reacts due to his sons betrayal of marrying a woman teacher, "Teacher, did you say? If you consider that, a qualification for a good wife I should like to point out to you, Emeka, that no Christian woman should teach. St. Paul in his letter to the Corinthians says that women should keep silence," (Achebe 25 G.W). African elders still stick to the barbaric doctrine that woman must remain valueless in their community. No religion has ever allowed separating people according to their gender or what so ever, however the questions still remains, where did the African cultures inherited such fundamentalism believes of considering woman as valueless people, while they are mothers, sister, and grandmothers? Achebe puts this forward in order to show the movement woman made over the time.

In addition, according to Achebe's book "Girls at war and other short stories," show how the view of Marriage changed for the new generations. The Igbo elders stick to the uncivilized cultures, which determined woman less value than men, but still use values which many men all over in the world today might use to find a wife, "what one looks for in a wife are good character and a Christian background,"(Achebe 24). These values are not only used by the men, but women as well to find men of their choice, however the Igbo's interpreted in a way that defined Christian woman should not go to school neither work. Such rootless beliefs that left woman in the Igbo culture and the continent of Africa to be considered less human. Achebe brings ups such an issue in his books in order to show how such a baseless ideological beliefs dominated women in Africa.

II. Culture

In his short story book "Girls at war and other short stories," Achebe teaches Igbo's belief of goddess instead of the greater God. It is a belief of idols (goddess) that led to the traditions such as burying twins. The Igbo's belief magicians and medicine men can bring dead people alive "take a matchete and cut away the strangling climber. The spirits which have bound your sister will then release her,". Although it is believed that humans originated from Africa around 250,000 years ago, there is a myth that says early hunting men had small gods, however it is the possibility that many African cultures inherited the belief of goddess from their ancestors. Even though humans it is possible people to inherit certain things from their cultures, it is shame to have the Igbo's burry their twins alive. This is ugly and inhuman practices Africans believed until the arrival of the European missionaries. Achebe placed such stories in order to give people hint of knowledge of the Igbo culture.

In addition Achebe takes his heritage more superior to him than anything else, he proves this by writing about his traditions in his books. in his "Girls at war and other short stories" there is a story named "the madman" in that story, characrater Nwibe, an enterprising and eminent middle-aged man is about to take the Ozo title, one of the most prestigious awards his community,(Ogede 2). According to the Igbo beliefs titles are not achieved based on your level of education, but are achieved on your strength in terms of war, talk, and age as well. These are the principles that defined for a man to be an Igbo leader, however; title holders in the region were men who glued their brains the customs of the region such as burying twins alive, marrying more wives, and men whom their children followed the customs of the region. Such cultural beliefs were what made the young Igbo's who were growing up during the arrival of the missionaries to betray their fathers beliefs and follow the ways of the Europeans which were easy to follow, and learn more. Achebe displays his cultures in terms of writings in order to show what his people belief though he himself does not practice them.

III. Education

In his short stories book "Girls at war and other short stories," Achebe writes a short story named "The voter" in which he reveals the effects of the British education over the region. The continent of the Africa, as well as the Igbo region was ruled by tribe men who were elected by the elders of the region based on ages, warrior and experience from the past, however; after the arrival of the British things changed and leaders had to be elected. The new British system had both positive and negative impacts on the region, the negative impacts were, people who wanted to be elected started bribing for their vote, which lead to higher corruptions. Vote seekers made promises that never get fulfilled, leaders could only be seen when the election was coming nearer. While the positives were, people learnt a lot and the life style of people improved while urban life style started. The British brought some form of education that led to the deterioration of the Igbo culture. In Africa it is rare to believe the promises of a politician, and people always know few politicians seek the truth, "we believe every word you say to be true," (Achebe 16). He writes about these issues in order to share with the reader how the politics and cultures of African people moved from tribe decisions to real politics.

In addition, it is rare to find free education across Africa. This is because of lack of trusted leaders who can sacrifice their time and lives for their people. Leaders in Africa run for public offices in order to get rich and fame, which they do these by using the public funds. This is due to lack of transparency to know what the government does, and what happens behind the offices. The short story "Vengeful creditor" Achebe talks about a situation where the Nigerian government had proposed a free primary education. That was what free education had brought. It had brought even worse to the homes, Mrs. Emenike had lost three servants including her baby-nurse since the beginning of the school year, (65). This level of inhumanity and corruption can be traced back to the Europeans who divided the African people against their wishes, creating tribe and ethnicity divisions. That is why leaders in Africa do not feel helping their country, but only their tribe members. Achebe focuses on how the rich abuses the poor in the continent of Africa.

The Education of a British Protected Child

I. Woman

In his essay Book "The Education of a British Protected Child," Achebe talks about other difficulties women face than being vulnerable in their communities. Death related to childbirth is a very common and a disaster to the lives of many African mothers, "my father. He was an orphan child: his mother, had died in her second child birth, (35), Achebe tells his own family history. Death related to childbirth literally comes from lack of health care or unaffordable care, which is an issue in the African regions. This really threatens and discourages women to think of marriage, although many African cultures consider marriage as a priority. It is lack of governmental support that leads to death of women in childbirth, which should not happen; however, in many situations women are not given the chance to have other options such as birth control, or family plan if she knows she will not afford to afford to seek good health care. Achebe, his own personal story tells the difficulties women in Africa face.

II. Culture

Achebe's essay book "The Education of a British Protected Child," reveals how his father's acceptance into the missionary religion of Christianity changed their lives. Achebe who belongs to the Igbo people believed strong traditional customs which sometimes inhuman; however after the spread of Christianity his father followed the new religion. Although Achebe's parents died and he grew up as an orphan, these might be an issue that led him to follow the ways of the Missionaries. My father had a lot of praise for the missionaries and their message, and so have I (37). Achebe himself unveils how thankful he and his father are of the changes brought by the missionaries, however, he is not happy with the slavery secret that was brought by the missionaries who use the bible as a tool to divide the people of Africa. This method of using religion as a tool to achieve ones goal is highly affecting the 21st century we live today, leading to divisions among nations. Achebe is here thankful on one side while on the other his heart is broken by the ways the British used. Achebe teaches his readers how bad and the good side of the arrival of the missionaries in Africa.

III. Education

Achebe overall appreciates the arrival of the Europeans because of exposing dominated Africa to the rest of the world. Achebe himself is an educated African who lived during the colonial period and underwent the British method of Education, as well as his father. Once explaining the great gifts from his father "his great gifts to me were his appreciation for education, and his recognition that whether we look at one human family or we look at human society in general, growth can come only incrementally," (37). This pretty explains how Achebe the senior appreciated the ways of education brought by the Europeans while letting the Igbo traditional ways cease. The Method of Education was a benefit to the African people in order to develop and change their ways, which gratefully led to the outcome of great men like Achebe himself. However, Africa did not benefit the education of wisdom of a man like Achebe; he always lived outside of the continent. If Achebe would have taken back his knowledge to the continent, Africa would have produced millions and millions of Achebe's who could in turn let the people forget the past and move on the present. Achebe in his book tells how they appreciated as a family the arrival of the missionaries.

In conclusion, Achebe's books definitely teach the ways in which African people used to live. The books set scene for someone who never hard to experience what the early Africa was like. The language used Achebe to write about the ways people do is something that is true about how the people speak. In his book

Character Okonkwo who rises from the bottom to the top while again dies in fear, this character reveals what many African heroes tried to accomplish, like Jomo Kenyatta of Kenya. His theme of the impact of British colonialism over the Igbo region can be experienced over his wirings. Achebe is such a strong writer who could teach his readers what I mean to be an Igbo or an Africa.

Work cited page

Achebe, Chinua. Things Fall Apart. New York: Doubleday, 1959. Print.

——. Girls at War and Other Short Stories. New York: Anchor Books, 1972. Print

——. The Education of a British Protected Child. New York: Alfred A. Knopf, 2009. Print.

Jeyifo, Biodun. "Okonwkwo and this mother: Things fall apart and issues of gender in the constitution of African Postcolonial discourse." Literature Resource Centre. Web. May 17 2012.

Ogede, Ode. "The Politics of Story Telling." Literature Resource Center. Web. May 17, 2012.

Metzger, Linda, et al. "Black Writers. Michigan" gale Research Inc, 1989. Print.

APPENDIX C

Scan of Sections of *From the Hood to the Halls: Urban Fiction Meets Hip Hop Literacies Survival Guide*

From the Hood to the Halls
Urban Fiction Meets Hip Hop Literacies Survival Guide

DEDICATION

We dedicate this book to all of you
who are trying to figure out how
to survive in an urban high school.
You show up every day, but then what?
As Sapphire says in her dedication in *Push*,
"Every blade of grass has its angel that bends over it and
whispers, '*GROW.*'"

Our hope is that you GROW strong and tall and confident and
that you survive . . . maybe even thrive in the halls of Waggener
and beyond!

FIGURES AC.1 TO AC.3 Scan of Sections of *From the Hood to the Halls: Urban Fiction Meets Hip Hop Literacies Survival Guide*

Used with permission.

FIGURE AC.2

Violence

Realities

Knives, shanks, needles, ice picks – are no joke. A relatively unskilled thug can cut you dozens of times before you ever have a chance to defend yourself. Awareness is the best way to avoid an attack. Violence is a reality that all of us have to understand. Even people who are not violent need to know about violence. Unfortunately, it is the way people assert power in our world. Hip Hop students have a different type of flavor then their teachers. Some of the younger teachers has the flavor of Hip Hop students. This flavor means that you

Another reality is that violence lots of people don't know any other options.

because they have nothing else to do and no positive men in their life nobody to show then the right way. It seems like the only men they know are famous people who show off their violent ways.

Violence is all around us --on television and in real life. Just think about fights at Waggener. All of us enjoy watching them. What is that about? People like to see other people fight. They think it's entertainment.

There is a big debate about whether violence creates more violence. If you get in a fight at school for the first time, are you more likely to do it again? Well, I think that there is something contagious about fighting, but it is the way urban high schools role. If you've got to stand up for yourself, you fight. It allows you to take a stand.

Vocabulary:

Fire - means good as hell,
Bar: means absolute no

On butt--basically means act a donkey
Piff--means you on fire in the dice game

Rolling ___ deep--means that you're walking with that number of people
To steal someone--means that you hit them in the jaw
To crack someone--to hit someone really hard
Swag--a person style of fashion
Beef--two people don't like each other
Crackin'--means a girl that's going around doing everybody
Shake--means I am about to leave
Square up--means let's fight

Models:

Lil Webbie, Lil Wayne, Yo gotti, the coldest rappers out there right now. You can't leave out Lil Boosie that nigga goes hard he's realistic and speaks the truth. Busta rhymes is cold too. He is a fast rapper, but if you listen closely you can understand what he is

saying it is some cold shit. What do these artist have to do with violence? lil boosie been locked up for having people murdered. Lil webbie been in jail for drugs. Yo Gotti and lil Wayne been in jail for drugs too.

What is the connection between drugs and violence? Here's the answer:

Do's and Don't's

Do what you need to do then you'll do what you wanna do, and your dont's will make you have a difficult time of what you did back then like I said Karma can be a

nice looking female.
Just don't treat her bad and watch what you do.
Do's. finish high school. My plan's to go to college so I can be successful.

22

FIGURE AC.3

APPENDIX D

Katherine's Autobiography for Dual Enrollment English

Note: Used with permission

"Because I am different and speak with my hands, not my mouth, does not determine who I am, it simply states I am capable of learning something new" – unknown. The quote shows that the way you speak, write, or communicate does not show your identity but it clarifies that no matter what language you speak it does not show who you are. I know this from personal experience because I am actually deaf in one ear. I do not wish pity, sympathy, nor special treatment just because I am partially deaf such as yelling at me. I have spent my whole life training myself to not reveal my secret but I was told that I needed to prove how this paper was related to identity and language. When I was first told that I was deaf in my left ear I realized that one day an accident could occur and I would not be able to hear completely. So, with much enthusiasm I voluntarily decided to learn American Sign Language (aka ASL). On November 22, 2007, I was a freshman, and in the ASL class. I can remember my teacher telling/asking me that she needed me to give a tour to a new student who will be arriving around lunch time. Little did I know that she was deaf, and would soon be my best friend. When I arrived I was told to sit in the back and wait patiently because the new students meeting had gone longer than they expected. So as I sat there I can recall thinking to myself "she prolly thinks Ima creeper" just because I was sitting there without her knowing why I was there. When it was time for me to give the tour my teacher told me "if you succeed you will make a great interpreter one day." I had no idea what she was trying to tell me because I was focused on not trying to be the creeper I thought I was being.

So, the tour started and as I was talking she stopped me and started to sign. My first reaction consisted of my mouth dropping and I instantly took my hand shaped it into a fist and in a circular motion waved it around my chest, this decelerated motion meant "SORRY" in Sign Language. I now understood exactly what my teacher was speaking of. So we restarted the tour but this time in ASL. As the day progressed we grew closer and closer and before we knew it, we became best friends by the end of the year. Sitting there and knowing that the stares all around and side conversations were about us, we decided to stop our own conversation and go home from where ever we were. In my town it wasn't everyday someone would see a deaf person holding a conversation and wondering what was being said.

I had many experiences such as this where we would be "speaking" but people would only notice and remember the fact that we did not "talk" back and forth but just signal. I had always been the girl to be around "different" people so I was use to the constant stares but unfortunately for my friend, she was not. She had come from a school where everyone spoke her language so there were no weird looks or constant asking of "What did she say?" I became immune to it all because I didn't want to show her that it bothered me as much as it did her. I felt as if I should have said something but I felt ashamed that I didn't. Eventually, I started to let people know that I was partially deaf because I have come to notice that I have trouble understanding what is going on within my surroundings. As a high school student the days are busy and I have many people trying to communicate with me at the same time which makes it difficult to capture everything that is being said.

This brings me to the point of how ASL affected my English and Spanish for that matter. ASL is a "choppy" version of English. All this means is that sentences in ASL are broken up from the normal structured sentences. (Ex. Hi, How are you? Would translate to How you?) I had to learn how to break up sentences in both English and Spanish because my friend would stay at my house and my father spoke only Spanish. When she was there I was usually the "Google translator" as my dad had put it. I would have to convert what he was saying in Spanish to English to American Sign Language (ex. ¿Cómotevaen la escuela? To How are you doing in school? To How School?) I got so use to verbally speaking and writing in ASL and Spanish I had to always make corrections on papers for English class. I would write them how I was use to speaking. My papers would always turn out being written in Spanglish and to the point (ex. Me remember la hombre that help translation I remembered the man that helped me). I wouldn't described what he helped me with and why. I ended up ruling out detail because in ASL it was always to the point there was no time to describe any details. Even song lyrics when interpreted were to the point (ex. "Jesus take the wheel" would translate to "God help me"). My teachers would have to work with me when it was time to submit a final draft because my papers all looked liked rough drafts before turning them in. They would also give me ideas on how I could use my "unique" writing techniques in my papers. Looking back now there was more Language Arts involved than I expexted especially because of the extra work I had to put into my writing pieces to make them sound "normal."

Although I have had to let others know that I am Partially deaf I feel more at ease with myself. I can be completely who I am suppose to be, not the person who has a medical condition, or the person who has a passion for communicating without verbal words but, ME!

APPENDIX E

Transit Authority of the River City, Route 29

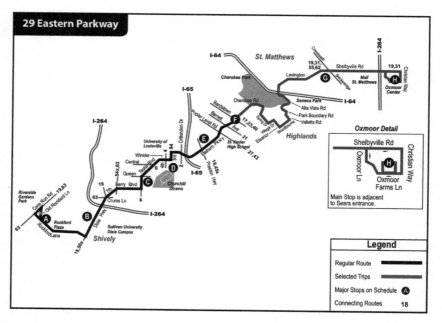

FIGURE AE.1 Transit Authority of the River City, Route 29.

Source: Transit Authority of the River City. "Route 29, Eastern Parkway."
https://www.ridetarc.org/uploadedFiles/29.pdf

APPENDIX F

Nadif's Proposal Essay for ENG 102, College Composition

Attached is a proposal that addresses [   ] need for after school activities transportation. The proposal gives the reasons why [   ] needs to provide transportation to students who stay for after school activity transportation. As a senior student who likes to see better [   ], I hope this remarks will help bringing back the school it's right position.

My proposal suggests that if after school transportation activities are offered, it will bring back life back to the dead school spirit. This process has been applied to many schools in different states, and helped improve students' academic performance, and behavior. The transportation can be provided by free or free reduced prices.

As a student who loves to see better [   ], I hereby forward my concern that will be of interest to future [   ] students, parents, and administrators who will love to see better students. We know that [   ] wants to have a diverse environment where students can shape their life. I believe my proposal helps you lean towards students needs where immediate improvements are hightly needed.

FIGURES AF.1 TO AF.5 Nadif's Proposal Essay for ENG 102, College Composition
Used with permission.

APPENDIX F

[____]2

Proposal summary.

This proposal argues that by not providing after school activities transpiration at [____],

school spirit will fade out and the expectation for doing better on the KCCT test, and ACT test will not

happen in which the state uses that scores to determine how the school is doing. I propose that

[____] to offer transportation to students who stay for after school activities to have a better school

that can produce the leaders of tomorrow.

Problem and Background

As known [____] is under state pressure after the students scored low on the state

monitored test (KCCT). The state uses the result of this test to determine how well the school is doing.

Due to a bill a passed by the state that gives, power the education board to regulate any school that

does not improve well. However, State audit has been sent by the education board to prove if the result

were true, and come to conclude with six defiance including "behavior plans," and replacement of the

school principal.

Most of our students live far away from the school, although the AP office couldn't figure out

the percentage, but approximately the majority live far away from school. It usually takes 1 to 2 hours to

reach home if the students take the TARC, however this issues made them not to staying for after school

activities.

The school has many activities and clubs like the National Honor Society, and the Green club

who do work after school. The National Honor society paints school doors, and poor attendance had

☐3.

been an issue, and no students could stay to help, since they all worry about who will pick them up. The

Green club works on planting, and usually stays Fridays after school, the same happens to the club. At

the entire root to all this problems lack of transportation.

Benefits

1-Improving student behavior

Student behavior is a big issue in schools, and ways of improving are always appreciated tried.

The problem to students at ☐ behavior in which that audit has seen it in two days is lack of

interaction with other students, and teachers beyond the class. This happened because students rush to

the buss after the last bell and do not get the chance to interact with their teachers, and classmates

while doing some fun activities.

2-Improving lower test scores.

The board of education is trying all the possible means to see better test scores here at

☐ but the one important thing to remember is letting students having fun by not worrying

about who will pick them up which helps them have more time at school. Alachua County Public Schools

in Florida provided after school activities transportation at school, and aimed in "improving the

academic performance and behavior of adolescents and pre-teens when school is not in session and

increase the overall engagement of students in school and in learning activities," (Guardian)

3- Student teacher relations

Students at ☐ don't get to see teachers after class, due to lack of chance. Students leave

the building as soon as classes finish while many have problems that they need help with.

☐4.

Students worry about who will pick them up, and how they might reach home. If this burden is taken

out students will probably stay and improve. Teachers usually stay after for some time, but fewer

students

meets with them. If after school, transportation is provided students will have the opportunity to meet

with teachers, and get one-on-one help.

4-School spirit.

☐ School spirit gets worse day after day due to lack of emphasis. Student don't get to

know themselves, neither did they get the chance to see what activities ☐ offers. They don't

care about the school while some will say "I don't go to school I go to ☐ ." The only way to clean

that from the students mind is offer transportation, so they get the chance to show their school spirit.

4

Below is pie chart that shows the view of 20 students

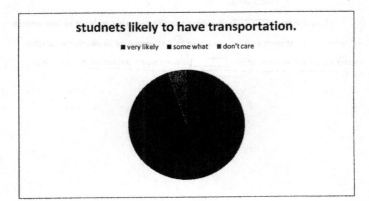

studnets likely to have transportation.

■ very likely　■ some what　■ don't care

Costs

The cost to such program will be cheap, compared to the needs of the student. It costs $150 per bus

each day. There are so many ways the school can get help with this money such as state funds, as well

using the school money. Having a better school where the student graduation rate is 100% is the

Kentucky education board first priority, and to have so such little money should be available.

5

Conclusion

It's my wish that if ▢ offers after school activities transportation, great improvements will be seen in both students behavior, and academics. Furthermore the introduction of such plan creates a legacy that will show the real ▢ and remove the bad name in the community.

APPENDIX G

Regular English Education Sketches

FIGURES AG.1 TO AG.3 Regular English Education Sketches

Used with permission.

APPENDIX H

Nadif's Research Essay for ENG 102, College Composition

Author's note: Rather than alter Nadif's text, I have blacked out names to preserve anonymity.

APPENDIX H
Nadif's essay for ENG 102
(Rather than alter Nadif's text, I have blacked out names to preserve anonymity)

Inside story of ███████ Traditional High School
███████ Traditional High School is located in the heart of Louisville's St. Matthews area, where Louisville's most middle and upper class people live. Looking at where the school is located, everyone will assume ███████ is a home to the middle class neighbors who live there, but the story is different. Despite the school being located at such a strategic place, most of its students come from Louisville's low-income neighborhoods, such as West Louisville and south Louisville while few live around the school's neighborhood. "Of the 790 students who attend ███████, 39.7% are white, 47.3% African American and 12.9% others" (Westerfield, Egan). According to the school principal, ███████ who just took over ███████ weeks before the end of 2010-2011 school year, the school is also famous for its diverse students body that comes from more than 30 countries. ███ took over ███████ after the school failed to perform well on the Kentucky Core Content Test (KCT), the state's benchmark measure for student's improvement. After the school failed the test, the state sent auditors who found that the school principal wasn't fit for the job, which later resulted in the departure of the school's long term principal. I remember attending the Jefferson County Public Schools (JCPS) board meeting months before my graduation as a reporter for the [...] student run newspaper. That night the board decided the fate of ███████, in which they said the principal will be replaced with a new principal who will then have the power to re-interview all the teachers and hire only the best. The new principal will be powerful, but she only has two years to turn around the school, otherwise she too will be fired. That's how ███████, a former deputy principal from ███ high school, came to ███████. ███, an enthusiastic and energetic principal took over promising new immediate improvements on students' performance in discipline and academics with the rule of an iron fist.

FIGURES AH.1 TO AH.3 Nadif's Research Essay for ENG 102, College Composition

Used with permission.

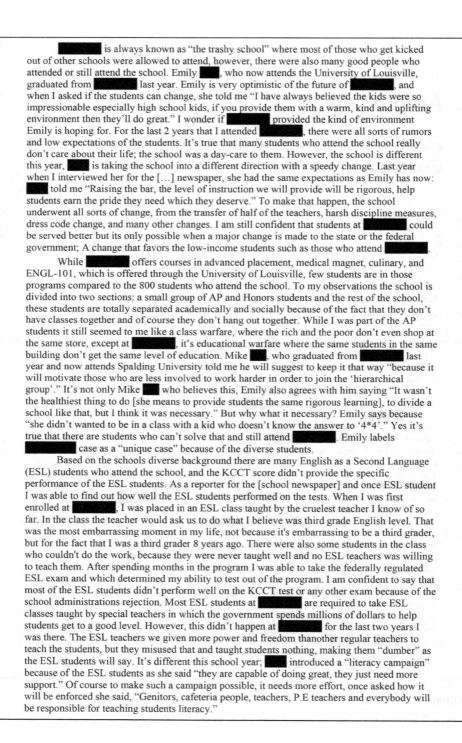

██████ is always known as "the trashy school" where most of those who get kicked out of other schools were allowed to attend, however, there were also many good people who attended or still attend the school. Emily ███, who now attends the University of Louisville, graduated from ████████ last year. Emily is very optimistic of the future of ████████, and when I asked if the students can change, she told me "I have always believed the kids were so impressionable especially high school kids, if you provide them with a warm, kind and uplifting environment then they'll do great." I wonder if ████████ provided the kind of environment Emily is hoping for. For the last 2 years that I attended ████████, there were all sorts of rumors and low expectations of the students. It's true that many students who attend the school really don't care about their life; the school was a day-care to them. However, the school is different this year, ████ is taking the school into a different direction with a speedy change. Last year when I interviewed her for the […] newspaper, she had the same expectations as Emily has now: ████ told me "Raising the bar, the level of instruction we will provide will be rigorous, help students earn the pride they need which they deserve." To make that happen, the school underwent all sorts of change, from the transfer of half of the teachers, harsh discipline measures, dress code change, and many other changes. I am still confident that students at ████████ could be served better but its only possible when a major change is made to the state or the federal government; A change that favors the low-income students such as those who attend ████████.

While ████████ offers courses in advanced placement, medical magnet, culinary, and ENGL-101, which is offered through the University of Louisville, few students are in those programs compared to the 800 students who attend the school. To my observations the school is divided into two sections: a small group of AP and Honors students and the rest of the school, these students are totally separated academically and socially because of the fact that they don't have classes together and of course they don't hang out together. While I was part of the AP students it still seemed to me like a class warfare, where the rich and the poor don't even shop at the same store, except at ████████, it's educational warfare where the same students in the same building don't get the same level of education. Mike ███, who graduated from ████████ last year and now attends Spalding University told me he will suggest to keep it that way "because it will motivate those who are less involved to work harder in order to join the 'hierarchical group'." It's not only Mike ███ who believes this, Emily also agrees with him saying "It wasn't the healthiest thing to do [she means to provide students the same rigorous learning], to divide a school like that, but I think it was necessary." But why what it necessary? Emily says because "she didn't wanted to be in a class with a kid who doesn't know the answer to '4*4'." Yes it's true that there are students who can't solve that and still attend ████████. Emily labels ████████ case as a "unique case" because of the diverse students.

Based on the schools diverse background there are many English as a Second Language (ESL) students who attend the school, and the KCCT score didn't provide the specific performance of the ESL students. As a reporter for the [school newspaper] and once ESL student I was able to find out how well the ESL students performed on the tests. When I was first enrolled at ████████, I was placed in an ESL class taught by the cruelest teacher I know of so far. In the class the teacher would ask us to do what I believe was third grade English level. That was the most embarrassing moment in my life, not because it's embarrassing to be a third grader, but for the fact that I was a third grader 8 years ago. There were also some students in the class who couldn't do the work, because they were never taught well and no ESL teachers was willing to teach them. After spending months in the program I was able to take the federally regulated ESL exam and which determined my ability to test out of the program. I am confident to say that most of the ESL students didn't perform well on the KCCT test or any other exam because of the school administrations rejection. Most ESL students at ████████ are required to take ESL classes taught by special teachers in which the government spends millions of dollars to help students get to a good level. However, this didn't happen at ████████ for the last two years I was there. The ESL teachers we given more power and freedom thanother regular teachers to teach the students, but they misused that and taught students nothing, making them "dumber" as the ESL students will say. It's different this school year; ████ introduced a "literacy campaign" because of the ESL students as she said "they are capable of doing great, they just need more support." Of course to make such a campaign possible, it needs more effort, once asked how it will be enforced she said, "Genitors, cafeteria people, teachers, P.E teachers and everybody will be responsible for teaching students literacy."

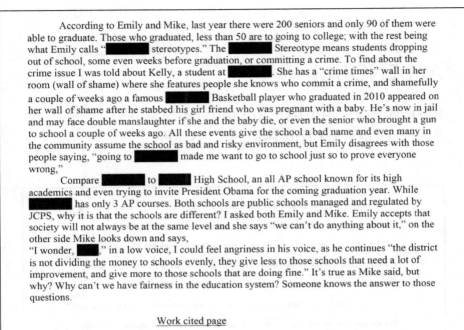

According to Emily and Mike, last year there were 200 seniors and only 90 of them were able to graduate. Those who graduated, less than 50 are to going to college; with the rest being what Emily calls "████████ stereotypes." The ████████ Stereotype means students dropping out of school, some even weeks before graduation, or committing a crime. To find about the crime issue I was told about Kelly, a student at ████████. She has a "crime times" wall in her room (wall of shame) where she features people she knows who commit a crime, and shamefully a couple of weeks ago a famous ████████ Basketball player who graduated in 2010 appeared on her wall of shame after he stabbed his girl friend who was pregnant with a baby. He's now in jail and may face double manslaughter if she and the baby die, or even the senior who brought a gun to school a couple of weeks ago. All these events give the school a bad name and even many in the community assume the school as bad and risky environment, but Emily disagrees with those people saying, "going to ████████ made me want to go to school just so to prove everyone wrong,"

Compare ████████ to ████████ High School, an all AP school known for its high academics and even trying to invite President Obama for the coming graduation year. While ████████ has only 3 AP courses. Both schools are public schools managed and regulated by JCPS, why it is that the schools are different? I asked both Emily and Mike. Emily accepts that society will not always be at the same level and she says "we can't do anything about it," on the other side Mike looks down and says,

"I wonder, ████," in a low voice, I could feel angriness in his voice, as he continues "the district is not dividing the money to schools evenly, they give less to those schools that need a lot of improvement, and give more to those schools that are doing fine." It's true as Mike said, but why? Why can't we have fairness in the education system? Someone knows the answer to those questions.

Work cited page

Westerfield, Jennifer and Egan, Susan. "2011-2012 school profiles." JCPS,
          November 2011.Web. 21 February. 2012.
████████ Personal interview. March 31, 2011.
████, Emily. Personal Interview. February 15, 2012.
████, Mike. Personal Interview. February 12, 2012.

APPENDIX I

Part Two of James's Review of Nadif's "An Appeal to the People Essay"

message has been passed to them by their parents. According to Israel, we know there is *has*
being a long existing problem between Israel and Palestine. This advertisement criticizes
those who use children soldiers to destroy nations. Linking America to Israel shows that
? Israel is going with the modern world, and letting its enemy know they moved as well
obeyed children's rights.

Although the text makes clear the logical argument that children should be innocent. *incomplete*
The ads appeals to ethos emphasize *ing* America's values of change "They target Israel because
Israel shares America's value-democracy, freedom of religion, women's' rights and a free
press." The ad makes clear that who *People* respect the ways of the modern world, and who too *also* follow
it. The ad appeals to its enemy by defining their expectations they can only move with
developing countries, not people who use children as a source to fight against nations. The
publishing of such an ad may change the opinions of some who supported child soldier. *No book supports this*

Though the ads child is innocent, the photo complicates the appeal to pathos. The picture
shows us how cruel and pathetic child soldiers are especially at a time when the world is talking
of freedom for women, press, and so on. "ISRAEL the front line of the free world," makes clear
that this message reaches the rivals in *the* picture or in words that is Israel is among the leading
nations of the free world. The designer also makes an appeal to kairos. *How?*

Finally the advertisement about the child soldier seem *s* to be persuasive and convincing
those who see Israel's link with America as a way to walk with the free line and America's value
?
of children. The persuasive ad influences each and everyone who reads and tells that innocent
children shouldn't be guarded with weapons. As well, the ads appeal to a time Israel is in need
given ?

FIGURE AI.1 Part Two of James's Review of Nadif's "An Appeal to the People Essay"
Used with permission.

INDEX